Dynamite!

Dynamite!

75 Years of
Vanderbilt Basketball

Roy M. Neel

Burr-Oak Publishers • Nashville

Library of Congress Cataloguing

Neel, Roy
    Dynamite! 24 Years of Vanderbilt Basketball
Nashville, Tenn.   Burr Oak Publishers
1975 Dec.

Card Number: 75-36690

Printed in the United States of America.

To Richard Baker

whose smile is like a 10-point lead with a minute to play.

Acknowledgements

The research, writing and production of this book would not have been possible without the generous assistance of many friends. Among these I would especially like to thank Lecia Brogdon for her tireless research efforts; Lou Harris and Randy Bibb of Vanderbilt's efficient sports information office for constant cooperation and tolerance of the writer's interference in their work routine; Vanderbilt Senior Vice-Chancellor Dr. Rob Roy Purdy, *Banner* sports writers Waxo Green, Edgar Allen, and Fred Russell for candid, invaluable background information; the Vanderbilt coaching staff and athletic department officials; Jo Ann and Deborah of Cumberland Graphics; and Henry, Carl, and Mike Zibart, for encouraging support when it counted most; Beth Tanner in the Vanderbilt Archives; and the many former players and coaches who sat through hours of interviews to bring back memories, both good and bad.

Most of all, loving gratitude to Suzanne Pickering Neel, who believed in this project and, in the end, transformed all the drivel into decent prose.

Contents

Introduction

My former associate, Roy Neel, has written an unusual history. Unusual, because Neel was, first of all, absolutely the worst manager in the history of Vanderbilt basketball, frequently contributing to the delinquency of several good athletes during the early Sixties. It's a wonder those teams were so good with him around to screw things up!

Secondly, the book is written not from the perspective of a "beat" reporter or an S.I.D. (sports information director at a school), but rather more from the player's viewpoint.

There are some stories here that have never been told in the daily sports pages, perhaps because we sportswriters have some sense of propriety and responsibility. With Neel nothing is sacred. In these pages he has poked fun at some of the over serious aspects of college sports, coaches, star players, university officials. Even the press come off a little more believable in this chronicle.

I have watched Vanderbilt basketball grow up. In the beginning, there was nothing. Then it was onward and upward with the coming of J. Robert Polk.

Of course, there were happenings in the early stages, such as championships in 1920 (Southern Intercollegiate Athletic Association) and in 1927 (Southern Conference); Josh Cody seeking a confrontation with official Frank Lane (later to become a prominent figure in major league baseball) after a game at the old Hippodrome; Jim Buford popping a fan in the Knoxville hotel after a Southeastern Conference tournament game.

But no mention of Vanderbilt basketball can be made without reference to Kentucky coach Adolph Rupp. It was Rupp who put Vanderbilt in the basketball business and led to Polk's appearance.

This was back in 1947 at the old Southeastern Conference tournament in the Louisville Armory, where Rupp handed the Commodores a 98-29 ignominious shellacking.

The late Red Sanders, Vanderbilt football coach and athletic director, was a spectator. It was fashionable then for athletic directors and football coaches to attend tournaments.

He suffered through this and retired to the hospitality room for a small libation. In Sanders' mind, the 98-29 humiliation marked the end of football assistants serving as basketball coaches at Vanderbilt.

"If we are going to lose basketball games, we are going to lose with a coach," was Sanders' closing remark.

With Polk's coming, there was the first basketball scholarship player: Billy Joe Adcock. Then came the "Traveling Bears" - Pete Robinson and George Kelley - and their theme song "Oh, What a Lovely Bunch of Coconuts!"

Dave Kardokus, Gene Southwood, Bob Dudley Smith, Jack Heldman and George McChesney - the first wholesale scholarship class—were the bunch that put Vanderbilt basketball on the map. Madison Square Garden was the Eden of collegiate basketball. It was there in New York that Bob Dudley Smith shot the basketball flat on his back.

It was the above group that beat Kentucky in the 1951 SEC tournament, 61-57, inspiring the late Walter Stewart, sports editor of the *Memphis Commercial Appeal,* to stun Rupp with, "Adolph, the calf killed the butcher."

The "friendly confines" (Memorial Gymnasium) were completed and proved a great backdrop for the likes of Dan Finch, Al Rochelle, Babe Taylor, Bobby Thym, John Russell, the late Bobby Bland, Jim Henry and Bill Depp.

A heart attack knocked Polk out of the box in 1958. He returned for the 1959-60 season, but the combination of basketball and athletic department wrangling forced his retirement.

Roy Skinner, Polk's assistant, was given the bouncing ball. He produced two Southeastern Conference championships, NCAA competition, an authentic All-American in Clyde Lee, additional seating in Memorial Gymnasium, and the conference's first black player, Perry Wallace.

It *has* been "Dynamite!"

Dudley "Waxo" Green
November, 1975

12

. . . It's history now. In the books.
You were a rare and beautiful thing,
boys . . . a miracle to see people play
beautifully together . . .

— The Coach
from *That Championship Season*
a play by Jason Miller

Part One
The Beginning

1. 1893

From Ollamalitzli to Naismith to Nashville

It had to happen, this game basketball.

In its present form, we have to look back only to 1891 and James Naismith at the International YMCA Training School in Springfield, Massachusetts, for its origin.

It is unlikely that Naismith was aware of *Ollamalitzli*, a 16th century Aztec game involving a small rubber ball and a stone ring, played in a walled stadium with serious consequences: the captain of the losing team was usually beheaded.

More unlikely is that these sadistic Aztecs knew about *Pok-ta-Pok*, played by the Mayans two thousand years before. Although similar to its successor, this version was mostly a one-on-one arrangement without the frightening social significance of *Ollamalitzli*.

Unfortunately, there are no box scores remaining from those games.

Dr. Naismith had a single objective—to produce a winter activity that would provide excitement to the dull process of body-building and calisthenics.

To do this he drew upon his wide experiences with the athletic contests of his day—baseball, football, lacrosse, hockey and rugby. It should be a game in which bruising contact should be kept to a minimum, stressing quickness and agility.

Most of all, it should incorporate a ball of some sort and two goals.

Since it would be a winter game, played indoors, running would be limited and tackling should be prohibited. The ball would be taken from rugby, large and light so it could not be concealed but could be tossed easily into whatever goals were chosen.

Naismith sought a pair of boxes for these goals, but settled for peach baskets, which he nailed to the walls of the Springfield Armory.

Adding a few refinements, such as a center jump and a set of basic rules stressing non-violence, Naismith had invented a new game. Basket Ball.

That first game in December of 1891 was played with nine men to a team, a referee and an umpire. It was an instant success, soon drawing the interest of the town and its College.

One unknown player or student made his way back to Tennessee that Christmas and told friends about what he had seen in Springfield. The Nashville Athletic Club, eager to test the concept of Basket Ball, sought a copy of Naismith's Rules of the Game. With this document and a probable eyewitness account from the North, the N.A.C. introduced the game to the city.

Out West End Avenue, however, the serious business of football, baseball and track kept the officials and athletes of Vanderbilt University occupied year-round. And this carpet-bagging foolishness basket ball was, after all, in conflict with gymnastics as an off season conditioning sport.

Dr. William Dudley, Professor of Chemistry and President of the University Athletic Association and its foremost supporter of "great outdoor games," read his copy of the Dec. 21, 1893 *Hustler* with great pride. The student newspaper included a glowing account of the recently-completed gridiron season, then another about the prospects for upcoming success in baseball and track.

On page four Dr. Dudley found the following two columns:

BASKET   BALL.

The Rules of the Game—A Team to
Be Organized.

It is now time for training in basket ball to begin, and for the benefit of lovers of this indoor sport we print below the rules for playing. It is hoped that more interest will be aroused among the students this year by the formation of a Basket Ball League, composed of teams from Vanderbilt, the Normal College, and the Nashville Athletic Club. Quite a number of games will be played, and a lively contest is expected for the championship of the league.

GOALS

The goals are a couple of baskets or boxes about fifteen inches in diameter across the opening and about fifteen inches deep. If the field of play is large the baskets may be large, so as to allow of more goals being made. When the field is 150 feet long the baskets may be thirty inches in diameter. These are to be suspended, one at each end of the grounds, about ten feet from the floor.

The object of the game is to put the ball into your opponents' goal. This may be done by throwing the ball from any part of the grounds, with one or both hands, under the following conditions and rules:—

The ball to be an ordinary *Association* football.

1. The ball may be thrown in any direction with one or both hands.

2. The ball may be batted in any direction with one or both hands (never with the fist).

3. A player cannot run with the ball. The player must throw it from the spot on which he catches it, allowance to be made for a man who catches the ball when running if he tries to stop.

4. The ball must be held by the hands, the arms or body must not be used for holding it.

5. No shouldering, holding, pushing, tripping, or striking in any way the person of an opponent shall be allowed; the first infringement of this rule by any player shall count as a foul, the second shall disqualify him until the next goal is made, or if there was evident intent to injure the person, for the whole of the game, no substitute allowed.

6. A foul is striking at the ball with the fist, violation of Rules 3, 4, and such as described in Rule 5.

7. If either side makes three consecutive fouls it shall count a goal for the opponents (consecutive means without the opponents in the meantime making a foul).

8. A goal shall be made when the ball is thrown or batted *from the grounds* into the basket and stays there, providing those defending the goal do not touch or disturb the goal. If the ball rests on the edges, and the opponent moves the basket, it shall count as a goal.

9. When the ball goes out of bounds, it shall be thrown into the field of play by the person first touching it. He has the right to hold it unmolested for five seconds. In case of a dispute the umpire shall throw it straight into the field. The thrower-in is allowed five seconds; if he holds it longer it shall go to the opponent. If any side persists in delaying the game the umpire shall call a foul on that side.

10. The umpire shall be judge of the men and shall note the fouls and notify the referee when three consecutive fouls have been made. He shall have power to disqualify men according to Rule 5.

11. The referee shall be the judge of the ball and shall decide

The campus, 1893.

when the ball is in play, in bounds, to which side it belongs, and shall keep the time. He shall decide when a goal has been made, and keep account of the goals, with any other duties that are usually performed by a referee.

12. The time shall be two fifteen minutes, halves, with five minutes' rest between.

13. The side making the most goals in that time shall be declared the winner. In case of a draw the game may, by agreement of the captains, be continued until another goal is made.

The position of umpire is a very responsible one, and on his ruling depends, to a great degree, the value of the game. If he deliberately overlooks violation of the rules he is responsible for a great deal of unnecessary roughness and consequent ill feeling, but if he is firm and impartial in his decisions he will soon win the respect of all, even those who suffered at the time.

When a goal is made it does not cancel the fouls made, neither does half time.

Any player has a right to get the ball at any time when it is in the field of play, provided only that he handles the *ball* and not the opponent. He may slap or pull the ball out of another's hands at any time while in the field of play.

A player may stand in front of the thrower and obstruct the ball, but he must not violate Rule 5. One aim of the rules has been to eliminate rough play, and for this reason the umpire must interpret them with this aim in view.

Any side which persistently makes fouls is working against its own interests, as three consecutive fouls count a goal for the other side. This seemed the best way for compensating those who play a good clean game, and it has proved of value already, for many a team has had two fouls called on them, but very seldom do they make the third, for a team is then on its good behavior, and thus shows that it is possible to play without making any fouls. Setting the number at three gives plenty of room for those made by accident.

Dudley met head football coach W.J. Keller that afternoon or the next and chuckled about this unusual new game. It'll never catch on with *serious athletes* at Vanderbilt, they probably agreed.

Each returned to his office, no doubt more concerned about an upcoming tuition increase to the $65.00 two-semester fee charged that year. Dudley was on the eve of forming the 19-school Southern Intercollegiate Athletic Association, one of the country's first athletic conferences. For the 20 years during which Dr. Dudley would serve as its president, the SIAA was a great reservoir of football enthusiasm. And at Vanderbilt, the legendary Dan McGugin was forging a remarkable football record not to be equalled by any modern Commodore coach. There was simply no room for this new game basket ball.

Eight decades later the University would field a team to play Basket Ball, attracting nearly 200,000 frenzied spectators to its magnificent gymnasium, reaping financial rewards several times that of the operating budget for the entire university in 1893.

How did it all happen? Read on.

2. 1901

Music, tumbling, and introducing . . . Basket Ball

A university society is not unlike its greater life counterpart: before a concept may be adopted as an established activity, it must challenge the conservative traditions of its day. In other words, Basket Ball would first have to pay its dues.

Vanderbilt near the turn of the century looked to the Ivy League for its academic—and athletic—models. If it was good enough for Harvard, Yale and Princeton, then it was good enough for Vanderbilt.

And for a decade after Naismith's invention, only gymnastics were accepted readily at those schools in the winter months. (Indeed, years later when Harvard first included basketball as a varsity sport, University students submitted that decision as principal reason for expanded support for the game at Vanderbilt).

The league mentioned in the 1893 *Hustler* article never materialized, but basketball grew in popularity among members of the Athletic Club, many of whom were Vanderbilt graduates.

Students, however, will try anthing once. In what must be the briefest season ever, a group of Vanderbilt students formed a team upon challenge from the Nashville YMCA.

The nine-man starting lineup for Vanderbilt: E.H. Hawkins, B. A. White and J. P. Hanner in the "home court" (nearest the Vanderbilt goal); H. A. Davis, R. W. Greene and W. W. Newberry in the "centre court;" and F. L. Day, L.J. Loventhal, Jr. and G. L. Williamson as guards in the opponent's court.

The team took the trolley downtown to the YMCA gymnasium to meet their opponents in one of the first basketball games involving a college team. Using Naismith's two-year-old rules and a soccer ball, Vanderbilt defeated the YMCA 9-6.

BASKET BALL OUTFITS.

INDOOR BASKET.

The baskets are strong iron hoops, with braided cord netting, arranged to be secured to a gymnasium gallery or wall for indoor use, or on an upright pipe the bottom of which is spiked to be driven into the ground for outdoor use. By means of a cord the ball is easily discharged after a goal is made.

Indoor Goals, per pair,	$15.00
Outdoor Goals, per pair,	30.00
No 10 Association Foot Ball, each,	3.25
American Rubber Foot Ball,	1.25

Prices for Special Portable Baskets for Exhibitions in Halls or low priced outfits given on application.

OUTDOOR BASKET.

An 1893 advertisement for a new device—a basketball goal.

The *Comet* reviews the 1893 season.

BASKET BALL NINE.

B. G. WHITE, ...	Centre Home.
E. H. HAWKINS, ...	Left Home.
J. P. HANNER, ...	Right Home.
H. A. DAVIS, ...	Centre.
R. W. GREENE, ...	Left Centre.
W. W. NEWBERRY, ...	Right Centre.
F. L. DAY, ...	Guard.
L. J. LOVENTHAL, JR., . . .	Right Guard.
G. W. WILLIAMSON, . . .	Left Guard.

Result of Game Played.

Vanderbilt vs. Nashville Y. M. C. A., . . .	9—6.

Later that month, students formed the University League, gathering teams from the dental school and the undergraduate classes. Games were played as part of an afternoon extravaganza in the gymnasium (The Old Gym, which now houses the Fine Arts Department, is in 1975 the oldest standing building at one time used for college basketball).

Over 100 students paid a dime and packed the small West End facility for this program:

    I.   Overture by the Orchestra
   II. Springboard demonstration
  III. First half of the basket ball game
  IV. Tumbling exhibition
   V. Second half of the game
  VI. Music

That first organizer of basket ball events at Vanderbilt was the predecessor of today's entertainment promoter: If you've got a talented, but unknown performer to push, bill him with an established winner. Get that visibility.

It was a time of innovation that gave us the automobile, dirigible, movie machine, rayon, vacuum cleaner and the zipper. People were receptive, too, to new diversions. If the officials of academe were not ready for Basket Ball, the students were.

Intramural games and informal contests were played almost daily in January and February until 1900, but not without a negative glance from the University administration.

In February 1899, this letter appeared in the *Hustler:*

The Executive Committee of the Athletic Association desires to express the hope that all students who expect to be candidates for the track, baseball and football teams of the University, in fact, all who have athletic ability, will avoid the game of basketball as played in our gymnasium.

Our athletes have had bitter experiences with this game in the past, and therefore the committee desires to give warning in due time.

The gymnasium is not adapted to the game, and the practice of playing it in their gymnasium suits is considered unsafe by all experts.

This game cost us the track championship of the Southern tournament last year and it is hoped that this year we may have winning teams in the field. To bring this result about we must have the hearty cooperation of every student, and no chances should be taken in a game like basketball in which there is nothing at stake.

Wm. L. Dudley, President
Athletic Association

Thus, Dr. Dudley had participated in Rule No. 1 for the Frustrated Fan: When you lose, find a scapegoat.

Basket Ball was now nine years old. The Nashville Athletic Club and the YMCA had taken quickly to the sport, but it had remained an intramural affair at Vanderbilt. The challenge was issued and the University obliged. A varsity team was organized after an announcement in the *Hustler* and with only one week of practice met the YMCA Ramblers on the opponents' floor December 15, 1900.

The YMCA gym was equipped with wire mesh for backboards and the home team made quick use of this advantage. Vanderbilt, accustomed to the firm rebound of its wooden backboards, shot poorly, trailing 16-4 at the half.

Coach W.D. Weatherford and his starters—Walter Simmons, Ernest Reese, Tom Motlow, Herbert Gannaway and E.L. Woolf—reasoned that a more aggressive approach was needed. Weatherford made the game's first substitution, inserting forward Grinnell Jones into the fray.

It almost proved too much for the Ramblers, who saw their lead diminish to a single point with 60 seconds to play. Experience, however, prevailed as a Rambler found the mark in the dying seconds to insure a victory, 22-19.

A student reporter observed that, with practice, the Vanderbilters should soon be a winning team. With that encouragement from the press, Vanderbilt won its next two games with the Ramblers, 24-9 and 14-12.

The season was closed with a trip to the Nashville Athletic Club to play a team reported to be giant by the standards of the day—each over six feet and outweighing the Vanderbilt squad twenty pounds to the man.

Simmons, a forward, ended his brief basketball career in style, as, according to the *Hustler*, he "brought down the house figuratively, and almost literally, by throwing over his shoulders two of the N.A.C. men at once, each of whom was larger than he, in a way that was rather humiliating to the N.A.C. rooters."

Losing 13-11, the squad returned to the campus and many of

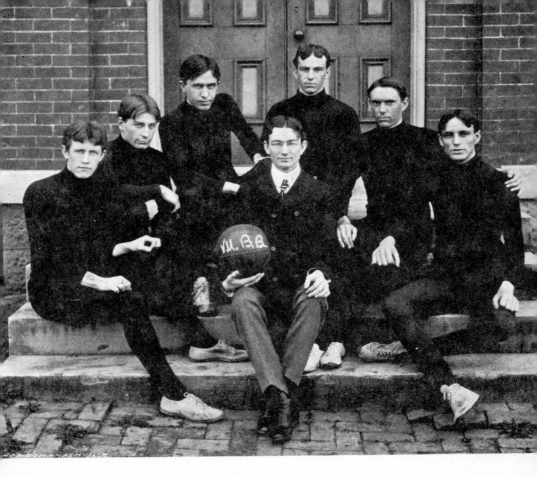

The 1901 varsity squad. (From left) Grinnell Jones, Walter Simmons, Ernest Reese, coach-manager W. D. Weatherford, Herbert Davis, Tom Motlow, Alexander Perry.

the players to baseball or track season. Simmons, Reese, Motlow, Gannaway, Woolf, Perry, Jones, and coach Weatherford had won two games and lost two.

It was a start.

3. 1902-07

On the road; an interim setback

Getting there is half the fun.
    —Advertising slogan for Cunard Steamship
    Company, 1950's.

The new century brought an almost overnight interest in the game. In December 1900, Harvard turned out 25 players for varsity practice, Yale traveled to Chicago University for a Christmas game, and Purdue came to Nashville to play the Athletic Club. Only a year earlier, eastern professional teams had formed the National Basketball League.

Facilities were, however, an ever-present problem, both in size and basic equipment. Malcomb W. Ford, writing in the New York Mail and Express, explained why basketball was played with only five men instead of football's eleven: "More than five men would crowd most gymnasiums where play is held."

In the decade since its beginning, several rule changes had come about. Each half was lengthened from 15 to 20 minutes and a uniform four-by-six foot backboard was required. Basketballs produced specifically for the game were introduced and the baskets were enlarged from 15 to 18 inches.

In February, 1902, Vanderbilt took its first "road trip," traveling by train to Birmingham to face Howard College and the local Athletic Club.

They found what is now fully understood: it's tough to win on the road. Bizarre things happened that would never occur at home. For instance:

Birmingham's gym was an old store warehouse fitted with baskets the opponents had nailed so close to the ceiling that a ball tossed with any arc would strike the ceiling first and fall into the hands of rebounders. It was, in short, impossible to score unless you knew how to bank the ball softly off the rafters, at which, of course, the Howard players had been practicing all winter.

By the time Vanderbilt had figured this out, Howard had surmounted a sizable lead and won the game 33-23. It was, for the record, Vanderbilt's first home job. It would not be the last.

Although they won the next game with Howard and lost the final contest to the B.A.C., the trip was a resounding success, experience-wise and financially. Howard paid the Commodores' travel expenses to Birmingham and through Sunday morning, at which point the Athletic Club picked up the tab for the remainder of the trip. This tradition made possible those early travels and before the construction of mammoth facilities and large paying crowds, it was the only way a basketball program could balance its budget.

Coach Weatherford's squad finished the season 5-2 and outscored opponents 158-125, an average of almost 23 points per game. Shooting was far from a polished art—all shots were stationary, two-hand push shots. No fast breaks, no layups, no jump shots and almost no coaching, not so much because of rules, but because these techniques were not yet known to the game.

An undefeated 6-0 season came in 1903, made possible mostly through the solid efforts of the Clary brothers—John, Lawson and Ben. They braved such problems as oil-lamp lighting in the Cumberland College (Lebanon) gym while scoring a then-high total of 44 points to Cumberland's 14.

Their play inspired a *Hustler* editorial demanding that the team be placed under Athletic Association guidance for more financial support. "If the quality play of these fine men is to continue," the writer surmised, "the university must now face the responsibility of adequate support."

That support came and the games soon became regular events, as well as social affairs. An announcement was posted, encouraging all men to come to the games with a member of "the fair sex. The team manager desires this not only to increase attendance but understanding that through the coeds and town ladies, the interest in the game will grow. Incidentally, it may be mentioned that he also wants to make it a success financially." Besides, the writer stated, "it is a good way to keep up the enthusiasm from the recently-completed football season and conserve it for track and baseball."

The 1903-04 season brought additional rule changes. A wooden ¾-inch backboard was now required. Dribbling was better defined, thus preventing the "double-dribble." Officials were now expected to eject any player using profane language. Prior to this, pursuit of the ball was mostly a free-for-all, resulting in numerous injuries on hard floors. Another new rule limited tackling the ball to one player at a time.

While the rules were beginning to more closely resemble the present game, action was still inconsistent and usually unplanned. Fights were not uncommon—players vs. players, players vs. fans, and fans vs. fans. Rules were unevenly applied in gymnasiums that would vary widely in dimensions, from converted classrooms to huge meeting halls.

But these factors were secondary to early players. This was a new game and it was great fun.

The 1904 team posted a 6-1 mark that spring, but returned to school in the fall to find that varsity basketball would be abandoned that winter. The University's terse announcement stated that the gymnasium was now being used far too often for basketball, shoving out gymnastic activities. So there would be no basketball practice facilities. In 1904, students had little voice in University policy, so the administration's word was law.

Significantly, 1904 was the year McGugin became head football coach, outscoring opponents 474-4 while producing an undefeated 9-0-0 season. There is no record of McGugin's involvement in the decision to drop basketball, however.

The policy held through the following year and would possibly have continued for several more years had an eager group of students not have pressed their case to the Athletic Association through the makeshift team's coach, captain and starting center, J.N. "Stein" Stone. The University relented and allowed Stone to arrange a seven game schedule, including two contests with the New York Professionals, a traveling group with great advance billing but little talent. Vanderbilt disposed of the visitors 30-18 and 38-23.

The '06-07 team finished 6-1 and opened the door for the school's first competitive schedule the following year. More importantly, basketball, only 15 years old, was now a fixture at Vanderbilt.

4. 1908-15

The Hippodrome, fights and the Ramblers

On a cold December afternoon in 1907, A.G. Adams, newly-appointed manager of the Vanderbilt squad, carefully measured the floor space in the Hippodrome skating rink, marking where each line would be painted. The site (in 1975 a Holiday Inn) was to be a new home for the Commodores. It was cold and drafty, ill-equipped for large crowds, but it was an improvement over the Old Gym. University officials, too, were pleased to have the gym free for more important events, such as tumbling and springboard.

"Lep" Adams knew, however, that there were new horizons for the game, which had now grown immensely in popularity in the East and Midwest.

"I had managed to talk Shorty Brown in the Athletic Association out of $34.00 for equipment, and that was our budget," he recalled from his home in retirement in Coral Gables, Florida. "We really had no coach. Willard Throop, the captain, recruited me as manager and he ran the team. We made do and never thought we didn't have what we needed. It was a game back then, and we played it for fun."

Adams wrote to officials of several schools in the East, inviting teams to Nashville. Columbia and Yale responded and later defeated the Commodores in the school's first intersectional games.

A Christmas trip was becoming standard for college basketball squads everywhere. It was for most of these young men the first long trip away from home or school and was a fine incentive for students to respond to the call for participation.

Players would soon discover the wonders of the Gulf coast town of Mobile, the awesome size of Chicago and New York and the sins of New Orleans. The road trip was, and still is, one of college basketball's most pleasurable experiences. Unlike football, where armies of tense specialists bury themselves in hotels hours before the games, rarely participating in sight-seeing, basketball teams have always taken a more lighthearted view toward their travels. A football game in New Orleans, even in 1975, means a trip to a motel that just happens to be located in the town. Fly in, see the playing field, back to the motel for sleep, up for pre-game meal in the motel, team meeting, play the game, on the plane, back to Nashville. All work and no play...

Basketball is another matter, at least at Vanderbilt. For nearly 70 years teams have journeyed to these cities, winning more than their share of road games. Morever, they know where they have been. From Lep Adams and his touring squad in 1906-07 to the "F-Troop," and jet travel in 1975, basketball players have found that there is more to a town than its gymnasium. Even in Kentucky.

Most early road trips, however, involved towns like Clarksville, Lebanon and Chattanooga. It was on these occasions that Vanderbilt encountered very unusual basketball facilities.

Southwestern Presbyterian University, the forerunner of the Memphis school, was then located in Clarksville in buildings that would later become Austin Peay State College. The gymnasium was a nightmare—enormous supporting columns stood throughout the building, as many as 12 on the playing floor. These were large enough to conceal a man and the S.P.U. team exploited this situation.

"It was a tough game, to say the least," remembers Adams. "You'd get the ball and start to your goal thinking you had clear sailing, but out of nowhere, one of the opposition would jump from behind one of those damn columns, knock you down, steal the ball and go down to score. I can tell you that wasn't very fair."

The game was roughing it at its worst, and the Clarksville experience was not unusual.

The game was still a "physical" contest. Finesse was unheard of, and teams were more adept at muscling for goals. Indeed, this aspect of the game led a group of Vanderbilt students to call for a downgrading of the varsity letter in basketball. To award the "V" for basketball was an insult to those great outdoor contests, they editorialized. But interest continued to build. The daily newspapers in Nashville and in towns where Vanderbilt played

The 1908 Coed team: (from left) Annie Mason, Ada Raines, Elizabeth Young, Florena Gates, Virgie Black. Vanderbilt women fielded teams from 1902-1933.

began to send reporters to the games. Coverage included not only scoring—indeed, that was a minor element in most stories—but often long rambling commentary on a player's style ("he tossed in baskets with grace and ease"), physical appearance ("...the opponent's forward, who must be the prettiest player in the South") and the fans ("...an audience which included young ladies comparing favorably with the hometown coeds").

The '07-08 squad produced the first losing season, 6-10, but it had broken new ground with the Columbia and Yale games, the Mobile trip and a move into the Hippodrome.

Coach Ed Hamilton and captain Bill Neeley improved the record in 1908-1909, winning 11 games and losing only 4 in a year which had an overflow of varsity applicants for the first time. A "Reserve Squad" was formed and won its two games while the varsity was averaging 33 points per game and topping the 50 mark for the first time in defeating the Chattanooga Ramblers, 52-23.

The rivalry with the local athletic clubs was still top billing, however. The season's final game found Vanderbilt "tied" with the N.A.C. for the Tennessee Championship and the game virtually decided the best team in the South, according to Nashville reporters.

Playing in the Hippodrome, Vanderbilt had already beaten the N.A.C. twice, but fell victim to the shooting of a former Commodore forward Eugene Lockhart, and N.A.C. won, 25-24.

The loss left the two teams tied in official "standings" and when N.A.C. refused to playoff the tie, writers reported that they then shared the Southern crown with the Mobile Athletic Club. It was now a regional game and players were getting a taste of what ratings were all about.

For the first time, accurate game statistics were maintained and players had another, personal facet to watch. Center R.B. McGehee averaged 9.2 points per game to lead the '09 squad, and the assault on the Record Book began.

McGehee returned to captain the 1909-10 team which finished 10-3 despite nine rigorous road games. The Commodores had developed a reputation of sorts by this time, mostly due to the fielding of star football players. Vanderbilt was still, after all, a football school and a very successful one at that. Names like Ed Hamilton, "Zeke" Martin and later Josh Cody, Lynn Bomar and others were terrific drawing cards. On the football field, these gridiron aces were only numbers, but in a gymnasium there were facial expressions, voices and other personal characteristics to be enjoyed. They were real.

When Carl "Zeke" Martin assumed his role as coach and captain in the fall of 1910, he reminded his players that this would be a season to be enjoyed. On the trip South in February, they would take a few extra days off, lay on the sunny Gulf coast beaches and forget Vanderbilt for awhile.

They were a high scoring team, averaging 43 points per game with a season high of 74 against the YMCA Ramblers. Martin and manager Woodall Rogers had forgotten one thing, however: the University frowned upon frivolity and irresponsibility, even among its athletes. The trip South lasted two extra days, beyond the firm rules of the University and disciplinary action was taken. Martin and his manager were suspended from play for the season.

This set the stage for the first "team meeting" for an emotional cause. The squad decided to win one for the coach. They hosted a team from Wetumpka, Alabama and crushed the visitors 60-7 in a spirited overkill. The psychology of adversity became a regular tool in getting ready for battle.

After an 8-2 season, Martin was returned to action in 1911-1912 and coached the first Commodore team to journey to Kentucky. Starting such a tradition was perhaps a mistake, for 20 years later a militant young coach, Adolph Rupp, would make basketball a truly national sport and for many years humiliate his Southern neighbors.

33

Schedules were still inconsistent and other than regular games with the Nashville Athletic clubs, there were few actual rivalries. Martin guided the '11-12 team to a disappointing 9-9 record, although playing a travel schedule that would carry the team 1,800 miles by rail and bus. The Kentucky trip was disastrous, the Commodores dropping games to Ky. State (later U. of Kentucky) 28-17 and 22-18 and to Christ Church of Cincinnatti, 47-27. This closed a roller-coaster season that saw Vanderbilt demolish Union College 95-24, the Jackson YMCA 81-13, and Cumberland 78-10, yet drop six games to underdogs.

The students had grown restless while they had become more sophisticated about what materials were required for success in college basketball. "The Team Needs Its Own Coach!" read one editorial. Team captains had been forced to double as coaches, and the undergraduate manager served as principal planner for all trips and budgets. There was little financial support from the University.

The faculty leaves for the Front, 1917.

This routine continued through a 3-4 season in 1912-1913 led by Oscar G. Nelson. Games with the local YMCA and Athletic Club were suspended during that year and with them, much of the spectator interest.

So, in the fall of 1913, the team got its first full-time coach, of sorts. G.T. Denton, a football assistant under McGugin, was handed the assignment as an additional duty. Not much changed, except that now Vanderbilt had a regular coach, on paper at least.

Denton's first team, led by captain Tom Brown, played well through an abbreviated nine-game schedule, losing the "city championship" to the YMCA Ramblers in the final game and finishing the season 6-3. The highlight of that year was the formation of a "Co-Ed" team, which even accompanied the men's squad to Memphis. Their organized life was short, for the women soon gave up the game on a quasi-varsity level.

The 1914-15 effort was an unsuccessful campaign, with a 6-6 record, half those wins against YMCA teams which had begun to decline in strength by that time. But emerging on the squad was a player who would one day bring Vanderbilt its finest team until the later scholarship era. Joshuway Cody, an All-American tackle for the famous point-a-minute, 1915 football squad, played basketball with equal fervor, if not skill. Cody was big: 6'4" and 220 pounds, a giant by 1915 standards, but he played smoothly, a natural athlete, as they say.

Cody and another footballer, Tommie Zerfoss, teamed with former captain Bob Davidson to produce an acceptable 11-3 record in 1915-16. The previous season had given Vanderbilt its first win over Kentucky and in 1916 the Commodores won two, 39-25 and 23-20.

The first overtime-decision was played that year, a 41-39 loss to Columbus, Ga., YMCA, and Vanderbilt approached the season finale with the Nashville YMCA Ramblers as heavy favorites. The rivalry had been revived in recent years with the filling of Rambler teams with ex-Vanderbilt players. Too, the YMCA had a spacious new gymnasium, with over 1,000 excited fans packed for the final game, a new high in attendance for the game.

The atmosphere was tense and two fights erupted as Vanderbilt was pulling away to a big lead. The Ramblers fought back and won the game, however, 25-23 in the most exciting and well-publicized game to that date. Interest in basketball was rampant and it would take a World War to slow the growth of the game.

5. 1916-20

The Kaiser, tittybums and That Championship Season I

On May 7, 1915, German submarines sank the Cunard liner *Lusitania*, killing 1,198, including 124 Americans. With the war heating up throughout Europe, university students began to realize that their time was soon to come.

The fall of 1916 brought another outstanding football team for McGugin, finishing 7-1-1 with a lone loss to Tennessee. Coach Denton's 1916-17 basketballers struggled to a 3-8 campaign and closed the year with a disappointing loss to the YMCA Ramblers.

Tensions had begun to focus abroad. President Woodrow Wilson asked Congress to declare war on Germany. Vanderbilt athletes volunteered in numbers and were off to the front within weeks, joined by the now fabled McGugin. Wars tend to take precedence even over football seasons.

New coach Ralph Palmer fielded a basketball squad for the 1917-18 season with only one varsity player with any previous playing experience, captain Alf Adams. Adams, who had starred as an All-Southern end, led the Commodores through a 6-3 season, during which campus and community interest had naturally ebbed.

Meanwhile in Europe the Yanks were battering the Kaiser on all fronts. The Armistice was finally signed on November 11, 1918, ending the brief but dramatic World War I. Americans lost nearly 117,000 men, among them Vanderbilt's great running back Irby Rice (Rabbitt) Curry, who would serve as an inspiration for many post-war teams.

The boys came home with new enthusiasm for games, anxious to put the grisly memories of war behind them. Ray Morrison, interim football coach during McGugin's absence, was assigned the duty of basketball coach after Christmas, but the actual work

36

fell to Tommie Zerfoss. Zerfoss soon tailored the squad into a unit and led all scorers with a nine-point average as they completed an 8-2 season.

The group restored credibility to the game at Vanderbilt and played with intensity. "Of course, no one had any money then," remembers Zerfoss, in 1975 a retired physician living in Nashville. "But you'd get a quarter or so, walk to town and gamble it away at Jew Sam's establishment." Sunday afternoons found Zerfoss and teammates making the rounds of sorority houses for dinner, an occasional horse-and-buggy ride for courting.

On the road, players would repair to the train's ladies' powder room for a heated crap game, if they could squeeze out the "tittybums" that would stowaway on these journeys.

"A tittybum," explained Zerfoss, "was a student who would hide away in the train without paying. He simply wanted to see the game and would even ride in the well between the steps and the door of the coaches. We'd hide them out in our berths, too." This was not exactly an activity endorsed by railroad officials, so there were sometimes brushes with the law. One such experience came in Mobile after a long train ride from Nashville.

"They caught two students who were stowaways," recalls Zerfoss, "and locked them in the stadium men's room before the game. Well, two of our players were quicker witted than the guards, obviously. They demanded to use the restroom and while inside, changed clothes with the student-prisoners, the students donning the uniforms and walking away unmolested. Several minutes later the players came out and confronted the guards, who were then convinced by the coach that they were legitimate. This infuriated those fellows to say the least." Such was the excitement that made collegiate sports in 1919.

Zerfoss, a forward, was joined by captain L.M. Graves, Senter Crook, manager "Dooche" Sherman (who, as manager was also the team's second leading scorer), and a second-year man, Garland "Chicken Foot" Morrow. Morrow, scoring only four points during the season as "standing guard" (this player position was primarily a defensive player whose responsibility was to prevent the easy basket by an opposition after a rebound), still came into his share of post-season laurels. "Morrow," concluded a writer for the University's *Commodore*, "proved to be a tower of strength that was well-nigh impregnable, and it was largely due to his efficient repulsing of hostile attacks that Vandy made such a splendid record."

Alf Adams, also a standing guard, recalls this assignment in less colorful terms. "It was our job to simply see to it that the opponent did not advance past us and that meant knocking him down, if necessary, to sort of *educate* him. You did that a couple of times and a player wouldn't want to get near you. It was plenty rough, for sure, but we thought nothing of it. It was fun."

The stage was now set for the school's first serious run at the SIAA championship in the winter of 1919-20. Zerfoss, now captain and coach, Adams, Morrow, Graves and "Rollie" Norton returned from the previous team. Rookie guard Dick Gleaves joined the team as did football aces Johnny "Red" Floyd and Josh Cody, who had returned to school the previous year and earned All-American gridiron honors.

The SIAA was in 1920 an unwieldy 30 teams ranging from Virginia to Texas, so the basketball race of that school year was, in essence, for the championship of the entire region. The title was based upon season record; and the Commodores, who had finished 14-4 overall, waltzed through the conference schedule, defeating Georgia (40-18), Georgia Tech (39-21), Centre (29-18), and Georgia Tech (32-3). The Yellow Jackets managed only one field goal in the season finale.

The title fell to Vanderbilt, the trophy was received by mail and placed in an appropriate spot in the Athletic Association offices on 26th Ave. South. There was little more fanfare than that.

"You've got to understand," remembers Morrow from his ranch in Abilene, Texas, "that since there was no real seating for

Introduction to *Commodore* Season review, 1920.

Alf
Adams

Tommie
Zerfoss

Dick
Gleaves

Josh
Cody

The 1920 Commodores: Southern Intercollegiate Athletic
Association Champions.

Rolly
Norton

L.M.
Graves

Johnny
Floyd

Gus
Morrow

39

students or fans at games, we really didn't have much interest. It was fun to win, of course, and the conference championship was a real thrill for the players, but it was no big deal for anyone else."

Nashville's daily sports pages dutifully reported the title, but with none of the flare in which it covered the controversial decision earlier in the year to forbid Zerfoss to finish the season. It seems that the medical student had played for a year in Kentucky before transferring to Vanderbilt and was thus ineligible for another season as a Commodore guard. "Meet Mr. T. Zerfoss, Ex-Commodore Star!" was the *Nashville Banner* headline after the conference banned him from further play. Zerfoss then jumped to the rival YMCA Rambler squad in mid-year. "Sad things await the future foes of the Ramblers," read sportswriter J.L. Ray's lead. "The Memphis 'Y' is in mourning. The Chicago Athletic Club sheds buckets of tears. And Vandy is silent." The Commodores had lost its star and this was big news.

The *Commodore* would later memorialize the 1920 SIAA champions with flowing praise: of Zerfoss, "the greatest of great forwards;" of Graves, "The high-jumping medico . . . this young Apollo;" of Adams, "a militant and pugilistic physiognomy, (he) hurled back the hostile onslaught of all comers, big or little;" of Morrow, who "shifts quickly, pivoting, dodging, dribbling, or passing to the constant discomfort of the enemy;" and of Cody, "This isn't Hercules, nor his side-kick Atlas, nor old man Samson. Just to relieve the suspense, we'll announce that this is Joshuway Cody, the intereference-smashingest, goal-cageingest, home-run-knockingest, super-athlete in all Dixie." Alas, they don't write like that anymore.

6. 1921-26

A new conference, Josh takes the boys to New York

In December 1920 the 16 larger schools of the SIAA pulled out to form the Southern Conference. McGugin continued to contend regularly for the football crown, but basketball was faced with a rebuilding job. Zerfoss was now the full-time coach while finishing medical school and he had only captain Gus Morrow returning from the 1920 championship team.

Michigan and Marquette traveled to Nashville to defeat the Commodores 21-7 and 29-6, respectively, in the Hippodrome. These incredibly low scores were due to the fact that the game was still a rough, unscientific contest; and Vanderbilt, to boot, had few real "shooters." Michigan introduced Vanderbilt to its pressing "5-man defense," which obviously caught the Commodores off-guard. In those pre-television days, a player learned what other players were doing only by actually engaging an opponent on the floor. There were no elaborate scouting reports to prepare a team for what the opponent might offer; adjustments were made on the spot. Zerfoss and Morrow struggled through an 8-14 losing season which included a loss to new opponent Auburn and a victory over Tulane.

Wallace Wade, another assistant to McGugin, accepted the basketball coaching assignment the following year as collateral duty, still all the University would provide the now 30-year-old sport. Wade had fielded great prep-school teams in Tullahoma, but he had little talent for his first college season, finishing 8-8 for the year.

Captain Jule Thomas led scoring with a nine-point average while Vanderbilt managed to dispose of Kentucky but lose twice to a new opponent, Tennessee, 20-5 and 16-15.

Vanderbilt traveled to Atlanta for the first conference tourna-

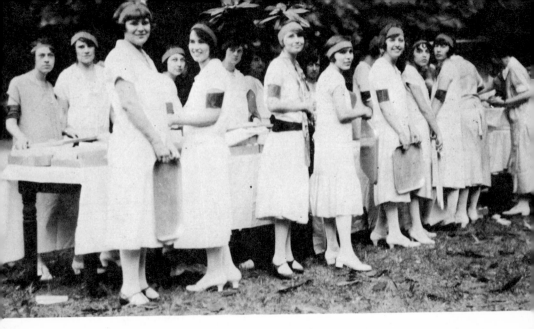

Campus life, the Twenties.

Reunion.

ment amid much hoopla for the new event. Winning its opening game over The Citadel, the Commodores then met Mercer, whose new coach Josh Cody had taken his team to the tournament finals the previous year only to lose to Kentucky. Cody capitalized on late Vanderbilt mistakes and Mercer won the game 27-26 to end the Commodores' first tournament experience.

Wade took his 1922-23 charges North for its first five games. Losses to Wabash, Cincinnati, Wittenburg and Ohio State were capped by a win over Chicago before the Commodores returned to a predominantly YMCA-filled schedule. A season-ending win over Tennessee, 28-25, sent the Commodores off to Atlanta, again full of hope for a shot at the tournament title.

The first game victory over L.S.U., 39-10, was followed by a heartbreaking 26-23 loss to V.P.I.; Vanderbilt had finished an acceptable 16-8 campaign. A team newcomer, football All-American end Lynn Bomar, was a terrific drawing card and crowd pleaser.

"He was a great attraction," said Ray Foster, a "running guard" that season. Foster, a retired Dupont Company official living in Nashville, recalls large crowds hanging on Bomar's every play. "Actually, he wasn't much of a player but with that kind of interest in him, he was important."

The two-hand push shot was still the principal means for scoring baskets, with the between-the-legs foul shot the only other scoring technique. The center jump after each basket slowed the game pace considerably. In 1923 the Commodores saw glass backboards for the first time in Chicago. Back home they watched a traveling professional team, the New York Celtics, defeat the local YMCA squad and produce a $600 profit. The game had now gained interest nationally, and young players were starting to recognize names—Joe Lapchick, Nat Holman, Dutch Dinnert and others.

Wade completed the season very involved in his plans to take the head coaching job at Alabama the following season. "That was all he could talk about," remembers Foster. "We could have used a more interested coach about that time during the tournament." The next season would bring just that.

Josh Cody returned to Vanderbilt from Mercer in the fall of 1923 to become McGugin's Number One assistant, and it was generally expected that he was to be groomed for McGugin's retirement. Basketball was certainly secondary to McGugin, but Cody relished the challenge of producing a winner for his alma mater.

At that time sports seasons did not overlap as greatly as in 1975, so when football was completed in late November, Cody could address his total effort to the upcoming basketball program. Practice did not usually begin until December 1, but Cody instructed non-footballers to begin drills early in November.

Cody moved quickly to broaden Vanderbilt's intersectional experience, though it would result in a poor 7-15 record in 1923-24. A Christmas trip to New York found the Commodores more involved in visits to the Zeigfield Follies than the game of basketball, for they dropped all three games in the city to the Crescent Athletic Club, City College of New York, and the Buffalo All-Stars. Cody knew, however, that playing on the road served to strengthen a team and to provide competitive experience not to be found any other way.

A win over Clemson, 42-14, in the conference tournament preceded a loss to North Carolina, 37-20, as captain Alvin "Pep" Bell and Bomar finished their careers.

The 1924-25 edition fared little better, with a 12-13 mark, but Cody was beginning to gather talent for another run at the title. The '24-25 team was captained by Gil Reese, who was classified in the *Commodore* as "everything in the University except the chancellor." Reese was joined by a talented newcomer, Jonas Coverdale, and three exceptional sophomores—Jim Stuart, John McCall and Malcolm Moss. An early trip through the Midwest—Drury, Kansas City A.C., Butler, Franklin College, and Wabash—produced only one win, but the squad posted impressive wins over Georgia, Georgia Tech and Tennessee.

Coverdale provided most of the scoring that year, as well as considerable controversy. He had been a high school star and was a prized prospect at Vanderbilt. Since it was still a time when no scholarships were offered for Vanderbilt athletes, however, Coverdale was forced to work at the local YMCA. This activity led to a Southern Conference decision to rule him ineligible after his second year of varsity play.

For Coverdale, memories of those two years are warm and bring back images of high times in New York ("Jody Cody loved burlesque—the rougher the better!"), irrepressible Bomar ("his size was so impressive—he charged the ball like the football player he was. What a drawing card!"), and the game in general ("Gosh, it was rough! Everyone always diving for the ball, knocking each other out."). Coverdale lives in retirement in McMinnville, Tennessee, after a long career as a youth-camp

44

director and prep school headmaster and teacher. Those early sports experiences were the events that would shape his life. "It taught you how to work as a team, to accept defeat and hard work as facts of life. You can't get better lessons than that."

Cody's 1925-26 team continued to have problems, winning only eight games while losing 18. Coverdale was gone, Reese left school and a new rule prohibited football players from participating in basketball unless they maintained "B" averages. This ultimately destroyed the squad's slim chance for the Southern title, for after several games McCall was also lost to poor grades. But the annual chant, "Wait 'till next year!" would be for real.

7. 1927

That Championship Season II

You done splendid.
> —Casey Stengel
> describing his best players

The 1926-27 team turned out in full force, grades and abilities intact and with a new motivation for a winning year. Cody had announced his decision to leave Vanderbilt for the head football job at Clemson prior to the start of the basketball season and the team promised a great farewell effort. Cody had been a favorite among Vanderbilt athletes, for he was still young and brimming with optimism for each new season that would come along. Moreover, as primarily a football coach, he had nevertheless given basketball what it had needed—a full-time effort.

With Stuart, a 6'4" center, the six-foot Moss and 6'3" McCall as guards and 5'10" Frank Bridges and 6'1" Dave Baker as forwards, Cody had a winning combination. After an opening game loss to Evansville and an early humiliation by Loyola (31-7), the Commodores righted themselves for wins over powerful St. Louis, Western Kentucky and Kentucky.

"We were panicked and demoralized after the whipping Loyola had given us," recalls Moss, who is a practicing attorney in Chicago and former president of the Alumni Association. "Loyola had stalled the ball in the backcourt (there was no 10-second rule then) until we had grown so frustrated we committed mistakes, and they scored easily. We sat in the locker room for nearly an hour without talking. Cody said nothing. We simply had not been able to adjust. But we learned a lot that night."

Two losses to Western and Georgia Tech worked out remaining problems, and Vanderbilt was not to be defeated again. The team

46

The 1927 Commodores, Southern Conference Champions. (seated) Dave Baker, Jim Stuart, Malcomb Moss, John McCall, Frank Bridges. (standing) Manager Alfred Benjamin, Allen Sharp, Vernon Sharp, Willie Martin and coach Josh Cody.

went to Atlanta seeded no higher than fourth for the Southern Conference tournament, but determined to give Cody a title.

Opening victories came surprisingly ease—44-32 over Washington and Lee and 32-20 over Ole Miss. South Carolina challenged Vanderbilt in the semifinals, but Baker and Bridges consistently shot the Commodores out of range, winning 31-26 and setting the stage for the title bout against Georgia. The Bulldogs had traveled this far by defeating tournament favorite North Carolina in the semis, thus establishing themselves as the team to beat.

Georgia moved out quickly and led 26-18 at the half, but baskets by Baker and Stuart soon had Vanderbilt in the lead. Georgia called timeout; and the largest crowd to ever see a basketball game in the South—partisan Bulldog fans—was on its feet. The lead changed hands several times before Stuart struck again for five consecutive points late in the game, and Moss hit critical free throws when Georgia began fouling. It was, for sure a "barnburner" as the Commodores held on to win, 46-44.

Ralph McGill, then *Banner* sports editor, prepared an inspired game story, eager to relate to the Nashville following the sense of drama that filled the Atlanta arena.

> *"There was a stinging about the eyes for the Vanderbilt men here last night when the crack of the timer's pistol ended that titanic struggle and Josh Cody's last appearance as a Commodore coach and his boys had brought him a Southern championship. He rushed out and caught the tall form of sweaty Jim Stuart in his arms. He grabbed the others as they came off, their faces strained, their eyes deep set. The strain of tournament play all the way to the finals is no small thing. These boys had been through a week of terrific effort that reached its climax in the nerve-wrecking, pulse-shattering thing of last night, when the Georgia Bulldogs were battered down in that test to determine who could take it the longest and not break."*

Stuart, one of the earliest one-hand shooters, and McCall were named to the All-Southern team, Stuart scoring an impressive 19 points in the finals and leading all scoring in the tournament. A large crowd met the Pullman as it rolled into Union Station the following evening, welcoming Vanderbilt's most successful team ever. For Cody it was an especially sweet moment.

"He was an excellent coach," said Moss. "No razzle-dazzle, but great fundamentals and strong on conditioning. He was truly a motivator out there."

The 1927 title ended an era in Vanderbilt basketball. Although it would be 20 more years before the first scholarship was awarded and 25 years before a legitimate facility would be built and another title won, the '27 season saw University ambivalence to the program diminish and a new interest grow out of success. Vanderbilt football would soon begin a decline into a position of lesser stature among southern teams just as schools such as Alabama, Tennessee, LSU, Auburn and Georgia began their rise. The Southern Conference, which in 1927 contained 23 teams, grew unmanageable and would soon dissolve into a smaller Southern loop and the Southeastern Conference. For football, it was a transition to which Vanderbilt would never quite adjust, but in basketball this new organization would become a vehicle for growth and national recognition.

8. 1928-36

New rules, Cody returns, and Cody leaves

When Red Floyd replaced Cody in the fall of 1927, he was faced with a difficult, if not impossible, act to follow. Floyd had played for the 1920 championship team and was versed in the game's fundamentals, but graduation and ineligibilities had taken their toll on the squad he fielded that winter.

Bridges returned to captain the team through an abbreviated 5-7 record, and Floyd was so pessimistic of his depleted squad's chances that he declined to take the group to Atlanta for the conference tournament. From the pinnacle to the pit they tumbled. The next season offered little hope for improvement.

The team, composed mostly of sophomores, managed only four wins against 12 defeats in 1928-29. That spelled Floyd's doom as cage coach. Dan McGugin, who also served as athletic director, turned to another former player from the '20 squad, Gus Morrow, to rebuild the program after finishing his duties as line coach in the fall.

Morrow had enjoyed considerable success coaching prep basketball teams in Atlanta after his graduation and even helped McGugin scout Georgia Tech football teams. "The Depression had begun and there wasn't much money, so basketball was pretty much a rag-tag affair. We traveled by broken-down buses and counted on guarantees from other teams to make expenses, maybe two or three hundred dollars a game at the most," recalled Morrow. "The most disappointing thing was losing all those close overtime games." Clemson, Tennessee, Duke and North Carolina took those decisions from Morrow's teams during a two-year stretch which saw game scores still averaging little more than 30 points per team. "We were still using the two-hand push shot from the chest and the underhand sling shot for foul shots," said Morrow. Jim Stuart had been the first to use a one-hand shot in 1927, but most coaches forbade players from experimentation. So, what was good for the old timers . . .

Shelby Coffey and captain Donald Cram provided much of the offensive punch, although not enough to prevent the Commodores from slumping to 6-16 for the '29-30 season. Vanderbilt was the only Southern Conference school observing the controversial "two-sport" rule, which required athletes playing more than one sport to maintain exceptionally high grades. Morrow, then, was faced with "Catch 22," which dictated that while he must draw most of his basketball players from the football ranks, he couldn't use them unless they were top students.

The 1930-31 edition was vastly improved, and it entered its home stretch with a 15-2 mark. The overtime loss to Duke began a slide that would drop the Commodores to 16-8 for the year. A mid-season win over Tennessee, 41-40, presented local followers with one of the finest-played contests ever in the Old Gym. A tradition had begun: when Tennessee came to Nashville, things would happen, and the game was not to be missed.

Gus Morrow had another special distinction during the '30-31 campaign. When Vanderbilt met Kentucky twice that year, there was a new face on the Wildcat bench, 28-year old Adolph Frederick Rupp. John Mauer had taken the Miami of Ohio job after producing three good seasons for Kentucky, so the school turned to a fresh young high school coach who had been a guard on Dr. Forrest "Phog" Allen's undefeated 1923 Kansas team. Rupp made his mark on college basketball immediately.

"I'm pleased to say my teams gave him a run for his money," (although losing by margins of five and 20 points) said Morrow, who would be the first of seven Commodores coaches over the next four decades to face Rupp, usually without success. But Vanderbilt coaches were not alone, for Rupp was destined to become the game's biggest winner, dominating not only Southern basketball but also often the entire country. It was Adolph Rupp who made college basketball a truly national major sport.

Morrow's stint as head coach was short lived. When Josh Cody returned to Vanderbilt as top football aide, the basketball job naturally fell to the man who had worked such miracles with the 1927 champions. Returning from the '31 squad were captain Bill Schwartz, Jule Foster, and Tommy Henderson. Although they finished the season only 8-11, they had their moments.

After a 61-37 trouncing by Kentucky, the Commodores upset

undefeated Alabama 39-32 and later shocked the Wildcats 32-31 in Lexington for the first Vanderbilt win in that gymnasium.

Tournament hopes were quickly dashed, however, when Duke won the opening round game from Vanderbilt in overtime, 41-32. The annual event in Atlanta signaled the end of the Southern Conference basketball organization (football teams continued in the SIC through the '32 season). Vanderbilt, Alabama, Auburn, Florida, Georgia, Georgia Tech, Kentucky, LSU, Mississippi, Mississippi State, Sewanee, Tennessee and Tulane formed the new Southeastern Conference while ten Coast schools remained in the Southern Conference

That same year brought new rule changes, particularly the introduction of the "3-second" rule, which prevented a player from standing in the free-throw lane. Primarily adopted due to increasing rough play by bigger men under the basket, the new rule was another way to minimize a height advantage. The 5-second backcourt rule in 1930, to prevent offensive stalling, was followed by a 10-second version in 1932. But the center jump after baskets remained; moreover, many rules were still being enforced selectively according to regions. The Joint Basketball Committee had been formed in 1915 with representatives of the National Collegiate Athletic Association, the Amateur Athletic Association and the Y.M.C.A. But the problems of legislating various levels of play would remain even to the present. In fact, college coaches found that they were not actually in control of their game but that rather that the vast number of high school representatives dominated new rule changes. Thus, a conservative approach more adaptable to the high school game became the norm, even as basketball players grew more proficient and imaginative.

Cody's 1932-33 team featured experienced players— Henderson, Foster and Harold "Skinny" Huggins. After an opening loss to Big-Ten-Champion Ohio State, Vanderbilt won easily over Clemson and took a double-overtime decision from South Carolina. As if that were not enough tension for Cody, his Commodores followed with a 37-32 overtime win over Tennessee. The two SEC wins sparked an eight-game winning streak over Conference opponents. Late road trips to Knoxville and Lexington, however, jolted Vanderbilt with two losses. They ended the regular season ranked second behind the Wildcats.

The first SEC tournament was a romp for Kentucky after Vanderbilt had been eliminated by Mississippi State, 48-36. The

Cody with tryouts, 1932.

Starters, 1931: (standing) Bill Schwartz, Shelby Coffee, Bertram Chalfant, (kneeling) Tom Henderson and Bill Young.

Commodores had eased past Tulane, 28-25, in the opener, but State out-ran and out-maneuvered a slower, although more experienced, Vanderbilt five. It was a disappointing end to a 14-8 season that had, overall, been very successful.

The 1933-34 team was less-talented but thrilled followers with a 31-26 win over Tennessee and opening wins over Auburn and Georgia Tech. A frustrating last-second, 24-23, loss to Florida in the second round of the SEC tournament ended the year. Cody, however, continued to win the admiration of students, as noted in the *Commodore's* season wrapup:

> *"Those of you who rub your eyes in complete bewilderment when a so-called dispenser of black magic pulls the proverbial rabbit out of the silk hat will be surprised to find that this same trick is being pulled year after year on our campus in the little box-car affair labeled 'Gymnasium' which the 'maestro' of Southern basketball coaches is forced to use as a practice floor.*
>
> *The average coach would throw up his hands in dismay if he were confronted with the problems that face the Vandy mentor at the start of the season. Green material, ineligibilities, insufficient practice space, and various other handicaps to be overcome. 'Engineer' Cody puts that fine analytical mind to work and the result is another excellent team."*

Vanderbilt's 1934-35 basketballers managed to win regularly from SEC opponents Auburn, Tulane, Sewanee, and Georgia Tech; and the Commodores finished fourth in the Conference. Kentucky and Tennessee fielded powerful teams and won all four contests with Vanderbilt en route to sharing the loop title. Low-scoring games were still routine, but a 53-19 loss to Kentucky in the closing contest signaled a new problem: the Wildcats were not to be temporary winners.

Willy Geny, a 6'4" All-SEC football end who had also won second-team honors in basketball the previous year, joined 6'5" center Dick Plasman on this squad. Vanderbilt's cage fortunes were bright for the 1935-36 season.

A defeat at the hands of Georgia Tech in the Conference tournament capped a year that saw Vanderbilt finish second in the SEC behind Tennessee. The Commodores managed to upset Kentucky in the Hippodrome, Rupp's first loss in Conference play. This provided additional ice to the cooling of relations between The Baron and his fellow coaches around the league. Rupp had worked surreptitiously the previous year to have the tournament format discontinued, and he soon had the reputation as a manipulator and intimidator of both officials and league representatives.

The Kentucky win was the season highlight, but Tennessee also fell once to Vanderbilt, 33-30, before returning to Knoxville two days later to avenge that loss, 34-33. The Commodores had earned a spoiler role in those years and would continue to decide league races from a distance for many years to come. Unfortunately, to become a spoiler is not what a team sets out to accomplish each season.

Cody had been passed over for the head football job in 1935 upon McGugin's departure; the University chose instead Ray Morrison, a 1911 All-American Commodore quarterback. Cody quickly grabbed the opportunity to become Florida's head coach and left Vanderbilt for good after the '36 basketball season. Josh Cody continued to field competitive basketball teams in his later years at Temple, and many friends felt that he grew to love the indoor game even more than football, which had given him such fame. Indeed, he left an indelible mark on Vanderbilt basketball during his 13 years as a player and a coach.

9. 1937-41

Pinky, Hanna, and the phys–ed coach

Ray Morrison had his problems in the fall of 1935, producing the first losing football record, 3-5-1, in 23 years. To complicate matters, two of his assistant coaches had the undiplomatic habit of disappearing off to Texas after the last football game in November. The coaching vacancy in the basketball program was not a problem Morrison needed at that time, so he hired a non-coach.

Jim Buford and trainer Smokey Harper had managed the team for the final games of the previous season, with loyal Cody joining the squad for road games even after he left for his new position at Florida. Buford's only playing experience dated back to his high school days in Franklin, Tennessee. He had served as intramural director at Vanderbilt and had assisted Cody with the basketball duties before Athletic Association chairman Madison Sarratt approached Buford with an offer of a $500 raise to replace Cody.

Buford took the reins with shocking authority, creating early morale problems among the players. Team captain Ken "Kayo" overly, a Phi Beta Kappa student, had played three years under Cody and was expected to be an important starter for the '36-37 squad. Instead, Buford booted Overly and another starter, Dave Coleman, off the squad.

"We'd been beaten down at Georgia Tech in the fifth game," recalls Overly nearly four decades later. "And Buford had pulled Coleman for no reason. I went to him and insisted he play Dave, who was one of our best players. Well, Buford then told us both not to come back. Things went from bad to worse after that."

The Commodores plodded through a 6-10 season and were not invited to the SEC tournament.

55

Six lettermen returned for the '37-38 season, again a losing venture with ten wins and 11 losses. Captain Ed Hunter, Bob Rymer, and Ross Hanna were sporadic scoring threats, but Vanderbilt failed again to win in its contests with Tennessee and Kentucky. The two schools were, by this time, Vanderbilt's major rivals and to lose these games regularly generated little good will among alumni and friends.

"I was a maverick among coaches," recalled Buford. "While Rupp and the others were planning special, disciplined patterns, I was letting my boys free-lance." Free-lancing rarely worked, however, and Buford's loose "style" was infuriating for a team which felt it deserved better guidance.

"He was a remarkable gentleman, though," said C.W. Metz, a standout guard on a later Buford team and now a Memphis physician. "Of course he wasn't emotional and didn't have Rupp's dynamism." Other players remember Buford as insensitive to the modern demands of the game as played in the late Thirties. But the scholarly Princetonian tried in the face of adversity; the University still wavered in its support for basketball, and Buford was the best talent available as far as they were concerned.

"Dean Sarratt bailed me out of trouble frequently," continued Buford, watching his Golden Retrievers gambol across the beautiful Williamson County farm which, at 75 years of age, he still manages. "I fought for those players at a time when everything was secondary to football." It was rumored that Buford had even challenged Rupp to fisticuffs once after a Wildcat had roughed up a Commodore player and the Baron had not intervened for justice.

Superior coaching or not, the 1938-39 squad gave Vanderbilt its finest effort since the 1927 Championship Five. Hunter, Rymer, Hanna and Joe Little were returning standouts and were joined by a young sophomore pre-med student, Brant "Pinky" Lipscomb.

"He was an unorthodox-looking player," offered Buford, "but Pinky was a great natural athlete; he did everything well. When he got the ball and started down the floor, nothing could stop him." Lipscomb led all scorers through a 14-7 season that now showed the Commodores averaging 45 points a game. They entered the S.E.C. tournament in Knoxville with legitimate optimism for the first time in 12 years.

Vanderbilt destroyed Mississippi State in the opener, 73-40, setting a tournament scoring record. An eight-point win over

56

Alabama moved the Commodores into the semi-finals against a host Tennessee team.

"General Neyland, the tournament director, made sure we wouldn't get a break," remembers Lipscomb. "He literally hated Vanderbilt and so we were forced to play twice in one day after winning the Alabama game. To top it off, we got a terrible call from Bowser Chest (an official) late in the game that gave Tennessee the ball. They scored and we lost." The 34-31 defeat ended a splendid year, however, as Lipscomb led all tournament scorers with 42 points and was a first-team all tournament selection.

Play improved early for Vanderbilt with a 53-49 win over powerhouse Western Kentucky. "Ed Diddle (Western coach) drew three X's on their floor before the game to indicate the points at which plays were to originate," said Lipscomb. "It didn't help much, though. We beat them good. There was Old Man Diddle, all the basketball scholarships he wanted, tossing that towel and crying. It was a sight to see."

Lipscomb, an orthopedic surgeon, was to become the Commodore's first superstar. He has colorful memories of his varsity career.

"We practiced in the Old Gym, of course, and played in the Hippodrome, which was completely inadequate for the game. After all, it was a *skating rink.* Crepe paper hung from the rafters during some games and the ball would strike the paper if shot with any arc. The floor had an oil-slick coating for the skaters and that was hell for rubber-soled basketball shoes. And road trips were definitely second class—we were driving about in old buses while other schools took the train. Buford was really tight-fisted."

The left-handed Nashvillian utilized an unusual shot to rise to the top of Southern scorers. It was basically a moving, jump-hook shot and it was impossible to defend. "Pinky was undoubtedly one of the best players I ever faced," praised Rupp, who later chose Lipscomb for his list of top-five opponents. "He had that funny little shot and he gave us hell."

On at least on occasion, Kentucky returned the favor. Playing in Lexington, Pinky stole a pass from Wildcat Carl Staker and dribbled toward an easy layup that would have increased a Commodore lead. Staker's frustration was out of control and the Kentucky guard took a dangerous "cheap shot" at Lipscomb, slugging him in the back of the head just as Pinky was shooting. Knocked cold, Lipscomb missed the ensuing brawl, but returned

The 1939 starters: Joe Little, Ed Hunter, Bob Rymer, Pinky Lipscomb and Ross Hanna.

Jim Buford and Red Sanders.

to finish the game, which Vanderbilt finally lost, 51-37.

"I just couldn't understand how Rupp could sit there and not pull his player from the game," recalled Buford, still livid when remembering the incident. Buford, like most other S.E.C. coaches, felt that Rupp so intimidated game officials that the Wildcats had an advantage at every outing.

"That's goddamn crazy," proclaims a newly-retired Rupp from his Lexington horse farm. "I just always beat them so bad those coaches were jealous. For our opponents, Kentucky was always the biggest game, but for us, they were all the same."

Lipscomb and teammates Hanna, Little, Maurice Holdgraf, and Jack Irby led an effort which Rupp would not quickly forget in 1940. Building an early lead in the Nashville contest, Vanderbilt gradually pulled away at the end to hand Kentucky a 40-32 defeat. "Don't let Rupp kid you; that hurt him," said Lipscomb, sidelined with pnuemonia after that for the final seven games.

Vanderbilt topped Mississippi State in the S.E.C. tournament's opening round, but then faced the Wildcats only hours later in the quarterfinals, losing 44-34 to the eventual champions. Hanna offered a stirring performance and was named to tournament second-team honors.

"We were midgets," Lipscomb confessed, recalling the 8-9 season. "Alabama had started recruiting basketball players and giving scholarships. Tennessee and Kentucky were, of course, already doing so. In fact, what we were able to learn was from watching Kentucky. We had great respect for Rupp and his players. We had to admit that all that national prestige Kentucky enjoyed spilled over on us when we played well against them."

Lipscomb was not a football player, and that was to his advantage with Buford, who had a decided dislike for the cocky gridiron stars who might plan to dominate his basketball teams. His "techniques" were, at times, pure misery for a group of experienced, competitive players. This was never more evident than in the 1940 Alabama game.

"Coach Buford, smoking those cigarettes incessantly, came to us before the game," said Lipscomb, trying hard to supress a bellylaugh. "He had a special play, he said, which was this: the 'Pygmies' on the team—all substitutes under 5'5"—would start the game, wear down the taller, stronger Alabama players, after which the starters would enter and finish off the opposition.

"Well, we couldn't believe what we were hearing. Those little guys went out there, didn't score the first quarter and we were down 13-0. Now we were on the bench trying to take this stuff quietly, but Hanna couldn't stand it. He ran under the bleachers screaming and calling Buford everything in the book. Boy he was mad!

"When the quarter ended, Buford beckoned to us and said, *Now we've worn them down, get in there and finish the job.* Somehow Hanna did finish the game, hopping mad, and we almost won, but this was the last straw between Hanna and Buford."

Pinky, Holdgraf and Joe Davis formed the nucleus of Buford's final team in 1940-41, resulting in a mediocre 8-9 season which failed to produce a major victory. Lipscomb set another tournament record with 29 points in the win over L.S.U. and 25 against Florida in a losing effort. This brought to an end an exceptional career. Too, he repeated his '39 honor when he was chosen among first-team all-tournament players.

Buford was replaced by football assistant Norm Cooper the following year; the controversial coach became director of the Student Union and later Director of Admissions. In that capacity, later coaches would have to deal with Buford in their efforts to admit student-athletes. He remained a faithful follower of basketball and would later become trusted advisor to Bob Polk. Misunderstood as a coach? Probably not, but he deserves a better place in Vanderbilt cage history than some would suggest.

As World War II approached, players began to realize their schoolwork would be cut short if the U.S. did, indeed, enter the conflict. Cooper's 1941-42 squad had hardly opened practice in December when the news of Pearl Harbor jolted the country.

Ross Hanna (17) scores against Austin Peay in Clarksville.
Bill Harlan (18) and John Milliken (19) watch, 1940.

10. 1942-47

Hitler, Rupp, Ol' Norm, and the 98–29 disaster

The lion and the calf shall lie down together but the calf
won't get much sleep.
                    —Woody Allen
                    Without Feathers

Nothing inspires the typical American Male more than war and
athletic competition. The pursuit of personal fortune, for
example, is the elixer which moves men toward great heights in
business, but fortune is an elusive target. War and sports, on the
other hand, are universally available proving grounds for virility.
They offer, in short, something for everyone.

When World War II began to take its toll on smaller college
sports programs in this country, there was concern among
alumni, sportswriters, and fans that it would take years to rebuild
teams into proficient, working units capable of competing with
the major athletic powers. Vanderbilt University officials, headed
by then Chancellor O.C. Carmichael, were adamant about dropping football entirely from varsity competition. Several players
still in school schemed with a local sportswriter to petition
Athletic Committee Chairman Madison Sarratt for support to
field a team in 1943. Head football coach H.R. "Red" Sanders
was in the Navy, but the autumn air meant football and these
students wanted to play.

For two seasons, 1941-42 and '42-43, the basketball schedule
was virtually unchanged. Norm Cooper, named to suceed Paul
"Bear" Bryant as football head line coach under Sanders, had
played and coached basketball at Howard University. As usual,
basketball was still a "filler" between football and baseball

seasons. For Cooper, as with past double-duty coaches, basketball offered a relief from the intense pressures of the gridiron. Little was expected from the basketball program in the area of ticket sales or tournament success. If a coach produced a winner, that was nice. If he failed, no one was after his job. The situation was one of non-tradition. A multi-million dollar facility, escalating budget, and three SEC championships would change that.

The '41-42 squad proved again that winning wasn't *everything.* The *Commodore,* in summarizing the 7-9 season that produced only three SEC wins, had something nice to say about every player. For instance, concerning captain Harrison Rue:

> *"Rue proved to be an ideal and outstanding captain. While not possessed with above-the-average basketball ability, Harrison held the highest possible respect of his fellow players. He was the first out of practice, worked as hard as any member of the squad, and was the last to go to the showers after the daily workout."*

Not exactly probing journalism by 1975 standards, but *nice.*

The year did, however, give local fans one of the more exciting contests with rival Tennessee. Sporting the best team during his famed career in Big Orange Country, Johnny Mauer brought Tennessee into the Hippodrome with expectations of an easy romp over the inexperienced Commodores.

Leading 34-32 with a minute to play, Mauer was charged with a technical foul and Vanderbilt forward Julian Olsen made a free throw to cut the margin to one. The Vols held on to win, but it was one of Mauer's toughest games en route to the regular season SEC title.

The '42-43 team, led by Olsen and David Lipscomb transfer Dave Scobey, managed to upset Tennessee, the eventual tournament winner, 30-27. Vanderbilt missed nine of 11 free throws in the game, but Tommy Owen made 14 points and held the Vol's star center, Dick Mehen, to four points. Earlier in the season, Vanderbilt had scared Kentucky in Lexington before losing 39-38, with Scobey leading all scorers with 14 points.

For the next four years the Vanderbilt basketball coaching job was like musical chairs: trainer Smokey Harper fell heir to the position in '43-44; Gus Morrow, then a physical education instructor, took over for '44-46; and Cooper returned to coach in 1946-47. Continuity was impossible, and the records of those teams showed it.

Harper's makeshift wartime group won 11 games and lost only four, but the schedule was packed with military teams. The SEC played only an informal schedule that year. Dave Scobey, scoring a ten-point average, captained a mixture of untested players through a 6-6 season that included no SEC schedule. As guard Ben Robinson confessed, "We were lucky to find ten guys over 5'6" that could walk and chew gum at the same time."

The '45-46 effort included a return to SEC competition, but Vanderbilt managed only two conference victories, over Georgia and Ole Miss. Tennessee swept three games from the Commodores, including a 46-32 decision in the opening round of the newly-resumed SEC tournament at Louisville. Navy trainee John Dalton's 11-point average led Vanderbilt scorers.

Norm Cooper's '46-47 team was again shutout by Tennessee (54-47 and 84-41) and Kentucky (80-30 and 84-41) in regular season play. "Some of us had never even played high school basketball," said Hank Duvier, attending Vanderbilt through the Navy V-12 program in 1945. "I didn't even know Vanderbilt University existed until the Navy sent me here." Duvier, in 1975 a chemical engineer working in Nashville, remembers long, tiring bus rides to "dinky hotels in awful places like Oxford and Starkville."

Cooper provided the players with ample "color" to make these trips tolerable, if not downright exciting. He feuded with fire marshalls in the tiny Auburn gymnasium over his cigar.

"For the last time, Coach, put out that cigar or you're going to jail," warned the official as Cooper took his team into the locker room at halftime.

"Old Norm told the fire marshall in so many words," recalls Hayworth Parks, then a sophomore guard, "to use his hat for a restroom. We didn't see that guy for the rest of the evening."

Insult was added to injury in Auburn that night. Returning to a makeshift classroom dressing room after the game, Vanderbilt players found their clothing rifled and wallets, watches and pocket change stolen. "Not exactly 'class' facilities," said Parks.

According to his players, Cooper developed a reputation as "an ornery 'cuss who would fight for his team." At Lexington, the Kentucky band was strategically positioned behind the visiting team's bench, booming out their "fight songs" during timeouts, much to Cooper's disgust. "Instead of talking over plays in the huddle," recalled Parks, "Norm would carry on a name-calling contest with the band, shouting and shaking his fist. He was something to watch."

Gus Morrow, 1945.

Flamboyant, maybe, but could Cooper coach basketball?

"Hell, no!" he boomed into a telephone during a 1975 trip to Nashville for a Vanderbilt football game. "You want to know how we decided who would be basketball coach? Jim Scoggins (another football assistant under Sanders) and I would flip a coin before the season; the man that lost got to coach basketball.

"Red Sanders was always telling me what a great job I was doing. *Bull!* I'd tell him. *You just don't want me to quit!*

If Jim Buford had frowned upon the use of football players for his cage teams, Cooper was just as adamantly in favor of the practice. Several of his players were also prominent footballers, and they rarely worried about rules.

"Sanders always told me," remembers Cooper," that you shouldn't put too many rules on a player because sure as hell the first one you catch is the one you can't do without. Sanders' curfew regulation was simply *Get in at a reasonable hour.*

"One night I caught Jack Jenkins (football and basketball star) coming in at 2 a.m. a couple days before we had to play Alabama in football. I reported this to Red and told him I thought Jenkins should be supsended. *Dammit, Norm,* he said, *forget the rules! If Jenkins doesn't play for us against Alabama, they'll beat the hell out of us!*

"He was right. And so was Dean (Madison) Sarratt. Dean Sarratt made a big impression on me. He told me *It's easy to run off an athlete for mischief, but if you keep him, coach him and help him, you've done everyone a great service. Besides, if you do let one go for misbehaving, he'll be the first one in his class to make a million dollars.*

In the 80-30 win in Lexington, Rupp not only played reserves the second half, he instructed his famous starting lineup of All-Americans Ralph Beard, Alex Groza, Wallace "Wa Wa" Jones, Ken Rollins and Joe Holland to get dressed and sit out the remainder of the contest.

"Here we were, leaving the locker room to start the second half," remembers Parks, "and Kentucky's entire starting five are in street clothes passing us on the stairs. And there were twenty players—all on scholarship—sitting on the Kentucky bench. Don't think we didn't know who we were playing!"

"We did anything to play," recalled Duvier. "I can still see Bill Evans (a player and medical student then) coming to games with blood on his shirt after delivering babies. Sure we were unskilled—the two-hand push shot was still our main weapon—but playing was everything. It was great to just be on the same floor as those Kentucky teams. It wasn't embarrassing; we were just a bunch of guys who enjoyed basketball and they were *Kentucky.*"

The Wildcats were rolling toward the finals of the National Invitational Tournament championship in the post-season play, but not before they made one last crushing blow to Vanderbilt basketball. Playing in the opening round of the SEC tournament at Louisville, Kentucky built a 35-point halftime lead. Rupp dismissed his starting lineup for the evening. The demolition of Vanderbilt's inferior forces continued, however, and Kentucky fans roared in anticipation for the Wildcats' 100th point with seconds to play. Parks blocked a Buddy Parker shot to end the debacle as the gun sounded.

Kentucky 98, Vanderbilt 29. It became the most important game in Vanderbilt's struggle out of basketball obscurity.

Part Two
The Bob Polk Era

11. 1947-48

Billy Joe, walk-ons, and Red finds a coach

Southeastern Conference basketball tournaments served as vacations for football coaches, athletic directors, and sportswriters. It was a chance to see old friends, talk about the recent football season, spring practice and the upcoming fall prospects. It was a good place for writers to find copy for hometown readers hungry for gridiron news, even in the off-season. As far as the tournament went, the writer could simply fill in the blanks representing opponents that Kentucky would be defeating on its certain way to the title.

Red Sanders attended the 1947 event with similar plans for a pleasant reunion. What he saw during Kentucky's 98-29 annihilation of Vanderbilt's outmanned basketballers was too embarrassing to ignore as a typical loss to the Wildcats. He returned to the Louisville arena hospitality room and to condolences from fellow coaches. Although not a "basketball man," Sanders was grim and shaken by what he had seen. This sort of thing shouldn't happen, even at the hands of Kentucky, he thought; we must at least be competitive.

Indeed, several years later Adolph Rupp would tell friends: "It hurt me to beat them so bad, but I had to teach those folks in Nashville a lesson, so maybe they'd get interested in basketball and do something about the program."

The problem was apparent to Sanders: Vanderbilt needed 1) better players, 2) a better place to play, and 3) a real basketball coach. In the summer of 1946, the University Board of Trust had recommended construction of a new gymnasium and had appointed a committee to seek funding for the planned facility.

That same summer Sanders had offered a Nashville West High School star a scholarship to play basketball—and football—at

Bob Polk, instructions, 1949.

Pete Robinson hooks, Kelley waits,
East High gym, 1949.

Vanderbilt. Billy Joe Adcock vacillated among Tennessee, Western Kentucky, Kentucky, and Vanderbilt before finally accepting Sanders' offer, but with qualification.

"He called me into his office one day and sort of made me stand at attention," said Adcock from his 1975 home in St. Louis "He said, *Son, we have no basketball scholarships, so when you come to Vanderbilt, you'll be expected to play football, too.* Well, I had played some football, at West, but I told him first, I hadn't even decided I would come to Vanderbilt and second, wherever I did go, it would be on a basketball scholarship and nothing else. That's what I did best, so that's what I was going to do.

"Sanders said, *Well, I guess that's that. Goodbye.*

Adcock returned home to find a message from an alumnus encouraging him to talk to Sanders again. This time, it would be basketball only. Adcock accepted and became the first scholarship player for the Commodores. It was a giant step.

Sanders had made a dent in his first two problems. Now to find a coach. He interviewed several candidates, including Western Kentucky assistant Ted Hornback and Georgia Tech aide Bob Polk. Despite a glowing recommendation for Polk from Rupp, Hornback was Sanders' choice. The selection was duly acclaimed in the sports pages as a step forward, citing Hornback's outstanding credentials as a successful high school coach and as an assistant to the venerable and nearly unbeatable Ed Diddle at Western. Sanders, figuring his last basketball problem solved, returned to his plans for the upcoming football season. After mediocre 3-6 and 5-4 seasons in 1945 and '46, Sanders was under pressure to produce winning football again at Vanderbilt.

Hornback came to Nashville in the spring of '47 to meet with his players—Adcock, Parks, Andy Todd, and war veterans Pete Robinson and Mike Craig (a former P.O.W.) and several "walk-ons." He later recruited Bobby McGuire with an offer of scholarship assistance and began to hold drills to build the '47-48 squad.

"Things changed immediately," said Parks. "Hornback had us doing things we didn't know existed—special conditioning drills, team discipline and play patterns. He really took over."

"I liked Nashville and coach Sanders did all he could to make things right for me. He had hired me over some good applicants— like John Wooden, then at Indiana State (later of UCLA fame). But, you see, I couldn't find a house. Red took me to see

Chancellor Branscomb, to see if the University might build a house on campus and rent it to me. Red told him—*Hell, we've been losing all these guys, Bryant and the others, to places that would take care of them, and we're going to lose Ted if we don't do something.*

"Well, Branscomb didn't go for it, said it would be economically unsound. Sanders raised hell, but I was back where I started. The president up at Western and coach Diddle were trying to get me back there and offered me more than the $400.00 a month Vanderbilt was paying. And then Vanderbilt didn't even have a gym; I knew I could go back to Western where they were sure to have a good program."

So almost as abruptly as Vanderbilt had found a coach, they lost him. Hornback commutted back to Bowling Green for the last time that spring. He remains an enigmatic figure in the development of Vanderbilt basketball. Instead of becoming known as the coach who "got away," Ted Hornback's name dissolved into the nebulous territory reserved for sports unknowns.

It was back to the interview table for Sanders, but this time there was only one real applicant to consider.

Polk had visited the campus several weeks earlier upon invitation from Sanders. He walked from Union Station 15 blocks out West End to the athletic offices, finally meeting the football coach outside Dudley Stadium. Sanders introduced Polk to the right people and showed him the campus. "I asked him — 'Now where's the gym?' " remembers Polk. "This wasn't a question Sanders wanted to hear. When we finally walked over to the Old Gym and that annex they had built for it, I thought — *You've got to be kidding!*

Polk was accustomed to the fine arena the Yellow Jackets maintained for its teams. Georgia Tech had not played Vanderbilt during the two years he had served as a Yellow Jacket assistant; he was not ready for the Old Gym. After two days as Sanders' guest, he returned to Atlanta certain he would not be chosen for the job. Moreover, he was happy at Tech and making more money than Vanderbilt was offering anyway. It was a good rationalization, but Polk was anxious to have a team of his own.

"I was visiting in Tell City, Indiana that August," said Polk, "and read in the *Louisville Courier-Journal* that Hornback had resigned and that the job was Bob Polk's if he wanted it. By that time, though, I wasn't sure if I did want the job. Alex Alexander

Billy Joe Adcock: the layup, 1949.

(athletic director) had been like a daddy to me and he didn't want me to leave Georgia Tech. He said I'd be next in line for the head job there. On the other hand, Bobby Dodd (who was soon to become Tech head football coach and athletic director) encouraged me to take the Vanderbilt job so I could come back to Tech in a few years with experience as a head coach. It was a tough decision."

Polk's coaching career to that point had been an unpublicized climb from a position as an Indiana high school assistant at ten dollars per month to a Navy assignment teaching swimming to hundreds of Georgia Tech men. "Burned-out" on that routine, he had applied for a Navy commission, but Alexander summoned Polk back to Atlanta to help coach varsity basketball. He quickly won the respect of opposing coaches.

"I liked Bob Polk right away," recalls Rupp. "He was enthusiastic and did a good job in preparing Georgia Tech for us. Of course, they never beat us in those days, but not many people did." Rupp's reflections, though almost without exception self-serving, can rarely be argued. From The Baron, you take whatever kindness you can find and run with it.

Polk's eventual hiring did not come without some controversy. "All hell broke loose when we suggested paying this young man five-thousand dollars a year to coach basketball exclusively," said Sarratt, ever the standard-bearer for athletic progress at Vanderbilt. "The Athletic Committee had to be convinced that money should be spent, and it wasn't easy."

To Sanders, the basketball program finally appeared to be headed toward respectability. Polk saw many problems—no real home floor, little community interest, few outstanding players, and no basketball tradition. "It was the challenge that finally appealed to me. I wanted to start something and I thought I could do it at Vanderbilt," said Polk.

He moved to Nashville just in time to begin fall practice for the upcoming season. Vanderbilt had been allowed to use high school gymnasiums the year before, but Polk wanted to avoid conflicts in scheduling. He found a quonset hut on Thompson Lane, the Navy Classification Center, and arranged for its use that winter. Polk marked off the playing floor lines in the cold building. The Old Gym Annex was used for practice, but the Classification Center was now the home court for the Commodores. Some advantage . . .

The same squad which met Hornback the previous spring now

gathered to give their coach his first look at his material. Polk was worried. "I would walk around the campus and ask every tall guy I saw if he could play basketball. You never knew who you'd find."

His first task was to instill confidence in players who had no sense of winning. "He taught us strategy, in addition to basic stuff, like the 'pick-and-roll' and screening on the boards," said Parks. "But most of all, he taught us how to play defense."

Polk fielded against Kentucky essentially the same players in 1948 that had played so miserably in the 98-29 debacle the year before. The new coach, however, had molded this group into a team with a belief that they could, indeed, compete against better players. The 82-51 and 79-43 losses were not pleasant for Polk, but they represented considerable progress. In '46-47, the Wildcats had won by margins of 50, 43 and 69 points. Despite Polk's early results, however, Rupp wasn't concerned about Vanderbilt. Kentucky's '47-48 "Fabulous Five"—Groza, Beard, Rollins, Jones and Barker—swept toward their first NCAA championship and as a unit captured the Olympic gold medal for the U.S.

Certain that the road to improvement lay in tough competition, Polk had arranged a difficult schedule in his first season. Vanderbilt was the only SEC school to play all four top teams—Kentucky, Tennessee, Alabama and Tulane. Although losing seven of these eight games (upsetting Alabama 58-32 in Nashville), Polk coached each contest with intensity and the players responded. An 8-14 final record belied the heartening advance basketball had made at Vanderbilt.

12. 1949

Polk sells the program, one Big Orange comes home

Bob Polk personally sold sixteen season tickets before his first season as head coach. There was nowhere to go but up. The 1948-49 season came on the heels of one of Vanderbilt's best football efforts, an 8-2-1 record which included eight consecutive closing wins.

Polk's off-season recruiting successes in Nashville and the talent-rich Midwest generated considerable excitement in the press. Plans for the new gym had progressed publically to a full-blown scale. Adcock had achieved regional acclaim as one of the South's finest shooters. Polk had managed to obtain the East High gym for home games, a major improvement over the Classification Center. These factors, plus an acceptable improvement the previous year, combined to create the first genuine campus and community enthusiasm for Vanderbilt basketball.

Joining Adcock, captain Craig, Duvier, Parks, and Robinson, was a burly 6'4", 195-pound guard transfer student from the University of Tennessee, named George Kelley. He quickly became the key element in Vanderbilt's turnabout from 8-14 to 14-8.

Kelley had been a reserve center for Tennessee's bowl team of 1944 and 1946 after starring on Nashville West High teams in the early 40's. "I didn't have that killer instinct you've got to have for football," he reflected from his Nashville florist shop in 1975. "Besides, I didn't like UT and Knoxville. It never entered my mind that I was going to a lesser program at Vanderbilt, mostly because I came back to Nashville for an education, not even expecting to play ball."

Kelley spent 18 months in the Air Force between schools and

76

came to Vanderbilt a mature 21-year old. He provided much-needed physical strength to the '48-49 squad, as well as a keen shooting ability. "He was so strong," said Polk, "and that's what we needed under the boards. The other guys had the necessary experience, if not the talent, and I felt we could have a good year."

The Commodores opened with four wins over minor opponents before heading to their first Christmas tournament, the Corn Bowl in Des Moines. Polk's contacts in the Midwest paid dividends, not the least of which were regular winter tournaments, an opportunity for players to enjoy the holidays and receive intersectional experience and publicity as well. Drake and Dartmouth defeated Vanderbilt in Des Moines, but the Commodores stopped in St. Louis long enough to beat Washington University before returning to its SEC schedule.

Two heartbreaking losses to Tennessee, 53-51 and 67-64, dimmed early hopes for a high regular season SEC finish; Kentucky, en route to another NCAA championship, won both games easily, but the Commodores were steadily establishing themselves as a threat. Adcock sparked six consecutive wins, including an SEC record 36 points against Mississippi State (Kentucky's Groza topped that the following week).

George Kelley, rebounding

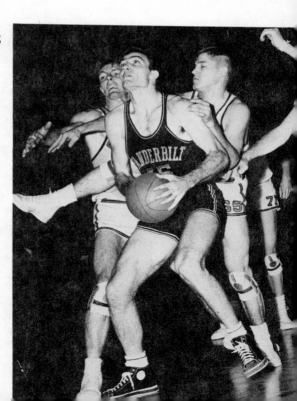

Pep rally, 1949.

Tulane came to Nashville ranked as the sixth best team in the nation but fell 56-54 as Duvier dribbled frantically to run out the clock. Robinson's rebounding, Craig's superior defensive work and Kelley's late basket provided the heroics for Vanderbilt's top performance to that day.

Entering the SEC tournament at Louisville, the Commodores were an even choice against LSU but dropped a disappointing 60-56 decision. Adcock, scoring 18 points in the loss, repeated as a second-team all-tournament selection. Vanderbilt had won nine SEC games, finishing fourth, with two starting guards—Duvier and Craig—who had never played high school basketball. The squad was crushed by the tournament loss. They had tasted a major win against Tulane and were ready for more.

For Polk it meant credibility. He had convinced followers he could win in the "big-time" even with non-scholarship players. "He went out and sold the program to the public and the press," recalled *Banner* sportswriter Dudley "Waxo" Green, who, with the *Tennessean's* John Bibb, was covering the Commodores not only at home but on the road, too. This was a big committment by the papers. Larry Munson was already broadcasting games over a delayed time period for WKDA Radio.

During the season, a provocative question had arisen: If Polk could win with mostly non-scholarship "volunteer" players, what would he be able to do with the talented, confident scholarship players who were happily destroying freshman opponents that year?

13. 1950

Just like Madison Square Garden

A 19, everything is possible and tomorrow looks friendly . . .
—Jim Bishop
New York Journal-American, 1961

"See those goals, boys. They're exactly the same size as the ones in Madison Square Garden, where you'll be playing as sophomores." Polk then opened the doors from the Old Gym into its slightly larger annex and showed his prized Indiana high school prospects the remainder of Vanderbilt's depressing basketball facility.

From Evansville, he brought 6'2" forwards Dave Kardokus and Gene Southwood; from Jasper, Indiana, he lured 6' guard Jack Heldman; and from Nashville he plucked 6'3" guard Bob Dudley Smith. Polk had amassed in one swift recruiting season Vanderbilt's first complete team of scholarship players.

"Dean Lewis, head of the athletic committee, told me, *Bob, we've given you all these scholarships, we now expect you to give Kentucky a run for its money,* recalls Polk. It wasn't that easy. Or was it? Polk had maintained extensive connections with high school coaches since his departure from Indiana, and they served him well when he went hunting for talent in 1948. And Polk did know talent.

Kardokus—"He was a superb ball-handler and great leaper. There wasn't anything he couldn't do and I felt he was possibly the most under-rated high school player ever to come out of Indiana."

Southwood—"He never wasted a step; a great shooter with wonderful poise. That low-trajectory shot was deadly."

Southwood, Kardokus, Weiss, Smith, Heldman.

Heldman—"He was so agile he often played center in high school, but he handled the conversion to guard with ease."

Smith—"What an incredible streak shooter! He could break open a game, score 28 points quickly when he was on."

College recruiting in 1948 had not grown to the monstrous proportions of recent years; but the all-stars of Indiana and Kentucky were still prized catches. Polk used every imaginable sales pitch to interest these four players.

"I understood that Kardokus and Southwood were going to Vanderbilt, and I was flattered," said Heldman, now a food broker in Nashville. "And he showed us the bluprints of that magnificent gym; said we would dedicate it our sophomore year.

80

That was icing on the cake." It was an old recruiting trick—convince a player he will be playing with other great players, get them all thinking the others will be going to your school, and you've got your man.

Fortunately for Polk, those high schoolers knew little about the construction business, for they would only see Memorial Gymnasium as alumni. "He really believed it would be ready," said Kardokus.

Smith was attracted to the idea of playing with his former high school teammate Adcock. "And the thought of a poor boy from a big family attending Vanderbilt was pretty exciting," he recollects.

They began their sophomore season with the same cocky outlook that had made them outstanding prep players. "We beat the varsity all the time our freshman year," remembers Kardokus, a Nashville banker. "We had come to Vanderbilt to win and we didn't know any better."

"They were a bunch of real characters," said Adcock, "but they had absolute confidence in their ability to shoot and win. It's just what we needed."

Vanderbilt moved into yet another home in the winter of 1949, the new 3000-seat David Lipscomb gym. It proved to be a much improved stage for this exciting new group. Football coach Red Sanders had left Vanderbilt for UCLA the previous summer and new coach Bill Edwards had managed only a 5-5 season that fall. Students and townfolk were ready for basketball.

After opening with an easy win over Lipscomb, the team headed for New York to play NYU and Temple. With the assistance of former Commodore Josh Cody, then at Temple, Polk had managed to schedule Vanderbilt's first appearance in the new Madison Square Garden. New York writer Ned Irish had helped make the Garden a reality and it served as the capital of college basketball until later gambling scandals moved many schools to prohibit their teams from playing there. In the winter of 1949, however, Vanderbilt looked upon the Garden as a dream come true; Polk had fulfilled his promise.

Nationally-prestigious NYU was a heavy favorite on their home floor, but Vanderbilt would have none of the gamblers' predictions, winning 65-59 in overtime. "It was a great thrill and it gave us some East Coast publicity," said Polk. What the win over NYU did not do, however, was inspire Vanderbilt against the Cody-coached Temple, and the Commodres fell miserably, 55-33. Two weeks later Vanderbilt stopped Temple in Owensboro,

Kentucky, 49-45.

Oklahoma A&M, coached by the legendary Hank Iba, hosted the All-College Tournament that Christmas and met Vanderbilt in the opening round. A&M, nationally-ranked and runnerup to Kentucky for the National title the previous year, barely stopped the eager Commodores, 62-61. The coaches were beginning to expect exceptional performances from Polk teams. "Hell," remembers Rupp, "*I* knew he was a fine coach and that he'd get the job done fast."

Vanderbilt then launched its finest SEC season performance ever. Two wins over Tennessee, 67-52 and 50-44, topped an 11-3 conference mark in what Polk termed the SEC's "ridiculous square around robin." This was a system which established three divisions; Kentucky, Vanderbilt, Tennessee, and Georgia Tech—four major teams—in the same division. Kentucky, later snubbed by NCAA tournament selection officials, defeated Vanderbilt twice again, but by only four points in each contest. (Post season NCAA competition was on an arbitrary selection basis then. Automatic participation by SEC champions came several years later.)

Vanderbilt had finished the regular season 17-7 for a second-place SEC finish, and entered the tournament as the second-seeded team behind the Wildcats. Several hundred fans made the trek to Louisville expecting to see a repeat of the two earlier wins over Tennessee. Ticket sales were at an all-time high for the contest.

If the season accomplishments had been a brilliant "high" for Vanderbilt, the tournament game with Tennessee was certainly the "low," for the Commodores hit only 16 of 101 field goal attempts and dropped a 50-44 upset loss to the Vols. Bob Dudley Smith's 16 point spurt—11 in the first half-was the only bright spot in an otherwise dismal performance. Heavy criticism was everywhere. How was this team, so magnificent during the season, so bad in this tournament, when all the chips were down?

"Forgotten today is the fact this team boasted the best win-loss record in recent history," wrote the *Banner's* Green. "All you hear is the team hit but 15.8 per cent in losing to the Vols. Forgotten is the fact that this team scored more points than any team in the school's history. You listen to nothing but the team Friday missed ten free throws. Forgotten is the fact that this team beat Tennessee in Knoxville for the first time in 22 years. You get only that Billy Joe Adcock connected with three of 27 attempts from the field."

82

Jack Heldman; defense, 1950.

The graduating Adcock completed a career which at Vanderbilt could readily be described as incredible; seven school scoring records, selection to at least one All-American team his final year, a 14.3 career scoring average.

Adcock, now an official of the Monsanto Company in St. Louis, is quick to credit Polk with success in molding an unusual group of players into a winning combination. "He taught us so much—fundamentals as well as set plays and defensive strategies. We learned to take advantage of the fast break, not just run and shoot." Adcock was later drafted by the NBA's top team, the Minneapolis Lakers, but turned down the $3500 bonus—a good figure then.

With the departure of the '49-50 team, Polk lost his sentimental favorites: "the non-scholarship players who had worked so hard to contribute to this team—Duvier and Robinson and from the year before, Craig and Parks and the others. They were great guys with great hearts."

Polk turned to recruiting with the pleasant knowledge that the Super-Sophs would be back for two more years; and there were other fine players yet to be signed in his home state Indiana and around the South. *Who knows?* he thought, *maybe we can get to the top sooner than even I thought.*

14. 1951

The calf kills the butcher, That Championship Season III

Another season, another gymnasium. "When I first came, I asked people where we would be playing our games," remembered Polk. "*Anywhere you want,* they said, *Just get in a car and drive over to any high school and ask them. It's simple.* Well, that wasn't fun, and it's tough to recruit or get any home floor interest that way, but we had no choice. In '50-51, let's see, I guess it was Lipscomb."

Despite a poor tournament showing the previous year, Vanderbilt opened the season with a new confidence. An important year of sophomore experience behind them, Heldman, Kardokus, Southwood, Smith, and senior captain Kelley, were a formidable lineup. To this group Polk added Iowa transfer Al Weiss, a powerful 6'4" center with excellent player credentials. With Kelley now shifted to guard and with Southwood as the front-line reserve, Polk felt well prepared in his fourth season.

After opening losses to Holy Cross and NYU and a shocking upset at the hands of Lipscomb, Vanderbilt did not look like a title contender. Six straight conference wins later in the season set the stage for what Commodore fans felt would be a great Kentucky game. The Wildcats were unimpressed, winning 74-79. Kentucky won the second contest with equal ease, 89-57, and entered the SEC tournament heavily favored to win a seventh title for Rupp.

Vanderbilt had completed the season 15-8 and faced Tennessee in the opening round. Al Weiss scored 20 points in the first half, and Kelley dominated the boards to lead an 88-52 assault on the Vols. After a 70-60 win over Georgia and another over LSU, 75-63, the Commodores were in the tournament finals for the first time since the 1927 Southern title. The foe would be the same Kentucky team that had convincingly beaten Vanderbilt twice in the regular season. Moreover, this was what Rupp had termed his best team ever.

"I felt like we had a good chance," remembered Heldman, reminiscing with Kardokus in 1975.

"Bull!" said "Hocus-Pocus" Kardokus. "I was absolutely scared to death. I just didn't want us to get embarrassed."

"I was worried," remembered Polk. "We hadn't given them much of a game either time that year. We hadn't had any rest (the LSU game was played in the morning, the finals following only hours later). Joe Worden brought the pre-game meal to the players in their beds. It didn't look good."

Kentucky's overwhelming height superiority, especially in All-American seven-foot center Bill Spivey, was expected to be a major element in the probable Wildcat victory. Shelby Linville at 6'5" and 6'3" Walt Hirsch, guards Frank Ramsey and Bobby Watson, and a young sophomore named Cliff Hagan completed Rupp's awesome lineup that faced Vanderbilt that evening in March 1951. With only one loss during the season (a 43-42 overtime decision to St. Louis), the Wildcats came to Louisville ranked atop the national standings.

The 'Cats led early in the contest, but Vanderbilt cut this to only four points, 30-26, by intermission. "I felt that we would have to control the tempo of the game to have a chance," said Polk. "Kentucky had that awesome ability to destroy a team in a matter of seconds with the fast break. We had to contain this."

Kentucky built a ten-point lead early in the second half, and the 7,000 fans, mostly Wildcats loyalists, were relaxing in anticipation of a romp. Then something went wrong with the 'Cats game plan.

Kardokus, Southwood, and Smith led a rally which soon pulled the Commodores to within a point, 48-47, with ten minutes to play. After nearly six minutes of lead swapping, Southwood scored to put Vanderbilt in front 57-55. Kelley then hit two free throws with three minutes to play to seal the victory 61-57. Kentucky appeared heavy footed, and even the giant Spivey was unable to dominate the boards.

After shooting consistently well during the season, Kentucky managed only 17 percent that night, while Vanderbilt was scoring on 33 per cent of its field goal attempts, 42 percent in the closing half. (Forty percent shooting was considered remarkable in those days.) Kardokus (13 points), Smith (15), South-

The 1951 Commodores, Southeastern Conference Tournament Champions. (seated) Jack Heldman, Bob White, Dave Scobey, Coach Bob Polk, Jimmy Clark, Bob Dudley Smith, Trainer Joe Worden. (standing) George McChesney, George Kelley, Dave Kardokus, Al Weiss, Bucky Herring, Gene Southwood, Manager Harold Lovell.

wood (14), Heldman (11), and Kelley (8) provided all the Commodore scoring. Reserve guard 5'7" Bob White executed an amazing defensive maneuver, jumping high to steal a pass on the fast break to chill a Wildcat rally. Al Weiss, although not scoring, was effective in screening Spivey away from the goal.

The aftermath was tumultuous. "We wandered over to the hotel where Kentucky fans had set up a victory celebration," recalls Kelley. "They even had a trophy already engraved with Kentucky as champion. Boy, was it quiet there!"

"That Vanderbilt game wasn't important to us," commented a still confident Rupp over the telephone 24 years later. "Hell, we'd already won the regular season title, and that's all that counted."

Substitute guard C. M. Newton (now head coach at Alabama) echoed Rupp's memories. "What difference did that game make? Nothing." Such rationalizations ring hollow. This was *Kentucky*, and it killed them to lose, anytime.

Rupp, who praised Vanderbilt's "scrappy play" immediately after the game, later visited the hospitality room "to set the record straight" with writers and other coaches. In so doing, he showed haughty stubbornness, much to the embarrassment of all onlookers. Dudley Green reported in the next day's *Banner*:

> "His opening remark to the Commodore mentor was *Bobby, you made a grave mistake tonight. I want you to make the most of it. It is not going to happen again. You have been getting the best boys for the past three years. I haven't been recruiting but I'm starting tomorrow. I'm going out and get me some good boys.*
>
> "*How can you say anything like that, Adolph,* asked Harry Rabenhorst, LSU coach, *when by your own admission you have the greatest college player in the country in Cliff Hagan performing on your second team?*
>
> "Rupp, sporting a patch over his injured right eye, wheeled to put a falcon-like glare on Rabenhorst.
>
> "*I haven't been out of Lexington in three years to look at a boy,* shot back Adolph."

Kardokus layup, 1951.

Green went on to report the other writers' perspectives on the Vanderbilt win. Among those:

"Jerry Bryan, Birmingham News: *Frankly, I didn't think it could happen . . . Well, Kentucky was beaten and I think it's a fine thing for basketball.*

"Walter Stewart, Memphis Commercial Appeal: *The calf killed the butcher.*"

The tiny DC-3 aircraft returned to Nashville the following day with a cargo of weary Vanderbilt players. Over 1,500 fans jammed the airport to greet their warriors. Many had watched the game on that wonderful new machine, television, the first such broadcast for Vanderbilt basketball.

Players and coaches attached the customary "greatest thrill" tag to the victory. Although a new rule awarded the NCAA tournament berth to the regular season winner, thus sending Kentucky on to higher competition, Vanderbilt nevertheless had won its first SEC title. The team voted not to accept a bid from a post-season tournament at Bradley University, nor an NIT invitation should it come. They were winners, but they were tired.

"It had been exhausting," recalls Kardokus. "All I wanted to do was sleep after that."

The win gave Polk and Vanderbilt even greater visibility not only in the South but throughout the nation. Kentucky, the perennial national basketball power, had been beaten and that was news.

"It was a great boost to the program," said Polk. "Now, when we would be out recruiting, people would know Vanderbilt. Without question it was the most important step in the growth of the program."

15. Adolph Faces the Fix

Not with a ten-foot pole

He that maketh haste to be rich shall not be innocent.
  —*Proverbs 28:20*

I do everything for a reason . . . Most of the time the reason
is money.
  —Suzy Parker, actress
  Newsweek, 1963

Kentucky went on to capture a third NCAA title in 1951, reaping praises as possibly the best team ever assembled on a college campus. As it turned out, it was perhaps too good.

The following August, Rupp addressed a group in Nebraska, commenting on the gambling scandals breaking out across the country. "The gamblers couldn't touch my boys with a ten-foot pole," he said with confidence. Several weeks later the news broke that former Kentucky All-Americans Alex Groza and Ralph Beard had been taken into custody and charged with "point-shaving" in a 1949 game with Loyola in the NIT in New York. Dale Barnstable also admitted involvement in the scheme.

Later, Walt Hirsch and Jim Line were implicated in similar "fixes" during games of the '49-50 season. In another set of charges, Spivey was charged with conspiring to fix games in 1950 and 1951, including the St. Louis loss. Spivey was later acquitted, but his career was ruined.

A disturbing question arose in Nashville. Had Kentucky thrown the game in the SEC tournament? "I talked to some of those Kentucky players over the years," said Kardokus, "and

Polk and the Baron.

they all assured me that there had been no fix in our game. Still, I guess people wonder . . ."

Rupp continued his march in 1951-52, finishing 29-3 with the number one ranking again, although losing in the NCAA regionals to St. Johns. One month later, however, New York Judge Saul S. Streit handed down a scathing verdict that resulted in the cancellation of UK's entire upcoming season, '52-53. He cited numerous Kentucky violations: classroom cheating by athletes, encouraged by university officials; illegal subsidies of players; admission of unqualified students into the school as athletes. Too, he charged Rupp with personally failing "to observe the amateur rules to build character and protect the morals and health of his charges."

The school rebutted many of Streit's charges, but the SEC found Kentucky sufficiently guilty to demand that basketball be dropped at the school for one year. The subsidy issue—giving money directly to players—was the final crushing blow.

Throughout the country, players became suspect. The gamblers had tainted the sport, and it would take years to recover the prestige basketball had begun to enjoy before the events of 1951 and '52.

In 1975, college athletic events still provide a major vehicle for gambling. In Nashville, placing a bet is as simple as dialing a telephone number. Projected win margins—"the line"—are published by the newspapers as reliable measures of team quality. Where there are games with a final outcome, there is gambling. Basketball presents an unusually opportune situation for a "fix." A leading scorer can have a poor shooting night and no one takes particular notice that the team wins by only six points instead of the predicted ten or twelve. One player can easily have such control on the outcome.

Grantland Rice, the Twentieth Century's most famous sports writer, thought there was more to athletics than simply winning. So did the Judge.

16. 1952

Finch, feathers, and the Latvian hostess

The tournament championship was a hard act to follow. Vanderbilt basked in the afterglow of '51 and looked toward another post-season showdown with Kentucky. They opened with six straight wins before losing to a superior St. John's team. A poor showing in the holiday Cotton Bowl tournament preceded impressive wins over Tennessee, LSU, and Auburn. Four consecutive conference losses followed; inconsistency was becoming a problem for Vanderbilt. After a string of seven consecutive wins, Kentucky won its second game of the season from the Commodores, by a 30-point margin. The Wildcats were not fooling around this year.

By the early Fifties, college basketball teams had begun to score, and score, and score. Contrasting the typical 30-point average team totals only five years before, Vanderbilt was now scoring at a 62-points-per-game clip. Accuracy, however, was not the norm. If Vanderbilt hit on 35 per cent of their shots, it was considered a good evening.

Shooting was not a major problem for Vanderbilt in '51-52; rebounding was. Weiss, at 6'4," was the tallest and strongest Commodore. The entire team averaged only 6'1." SEC opponents were not to be taken by surprise by Vanderbilt after its title the year before, and the Commodores entered the tournament as the team to beat in order to reach the finals against Kentucky.

An easy win over Georgia led Vanderbilt into the quarterfinals against Florida. The Gators stayed close throughout the game as Vanderbilt saw easy shots roll out time after time. "I've never seen a team try so hard and not have shots go in," recalls Polk. Florida scored a last-second basket, forced the contest into overtime, and won in the extra period, 66-63.

The loss ended an 18-9 season (9-5 in the SEC) and brought to a close the careers of Vanderbilt's first all-scholarship squad: Kardokus, chosen to the second team All-SEC squad; Weiss, chosen to the same honor the previous year; Smith, Heldman and Southwood. They had put Vanderbilt basketball on the map.

Two years earlier, Polk's recruiting efforts in St. Louis finally paid off. A 17-year-old high school star from Kirkwood High, Dan Finch, was one of the city's hottest commodities. A 6'3" forward, Finch had set a state tournament scoring record and was St. Louis' top player.

"Polk really recruited my parents," Finch recalled from his Nashville law office. "I wanted a school that was good academically, and I wanted to get out of St. Louis. Nashville was a nice little town, coming from there."

Though heavily recruited by St. Louis University, one of the country's top teams then, and by various Big Eight Conference schools, Finch signed a Vanderbilt grant in '51. After a solid freshman year, scoring at a 16-point rate, Finch became a logical choice to lead the Commodores after the graduation of its first exceptional team.

"He was our first boy out of St. Louis," said Polk proudly. "I had known his coach and that helped." (It seemed that Polk knew *everyone's* high school coach!) "Dan was a great jump-shooter and had a good one-hand set shot. He was gangling and went to the boards extremely well. Dan picked up all sorts of baskets by hustling for loose balls. I'd certainly have to put him on any all-time Vanderbilt team."

During his sophomore year, Finch had been the team's fourth leading scorer and rebounder. He followed this with a resounding junior-year 21-point average, including 30 against Duke, and second-team All-SEC honors. His final year produced a 22-point average and a first All-SEC team selection. Finch was Vanderbilt's first consistently high scorer. Too, he added another dimension to the camaraderie that Vanderbilt teams had come to enjoy, especially on road trips.

"Just don't embarrass me, Polk told us. *Do what you want to do, but be ready to play on Saturday and Monday."* recalls Finch. Finch relates tale after tale, some slightly exaggerated by the passing of time, but there is little question that the Commodores enjoyed themselves off the floor.

"We were in New York playing St. John's in the Garden and staying at the Roosevelt Hotel in Times Square. I'm in my room

Dan Finch (45), scoring. George Nordhaus (left), watches, 1953.

that afternoon and somebody knocks on the door. It was Kardokus, who bashed me with a pillow, feathers flying everywhere. Well, we had a hell of a pillow fight; Weiss, too—feathers everywhere. We get back from the game later and here's Polk and a whole army of hotel managers waiting in the hall for us. We worked 'till midnight getting up those _____ feathers. Although Polk had told us earlier to go on to bed, we knew he'd be out with (sportswriters) Waxo and Bibb, so we took off for the Latin Quarter with about six bucks apiece . . . big spenders!

"After sitting through the show, we figure it's time to leave, but we can't find Kardokus, who by this time is in a dime dance parlor with some Latvian hostess. Of course, Kardokus is giving her some big line about being a big basketball star. Then she asks him, *What eez thees game—basket ball?* Well . . . Kardokus was ready to leave then. I think we made it back to the hotel just before Polk."

Traveling in the SEC, however, was not so much fun. "We stayed in some dump in Oxford that had a rope under the bed for a fire escape. At Auburn, you'd be running down the floor, and those seats were so close to the playing area that people would reach out and pull the hair on your legs as you went by," reminisced Finch.

Finch had one more distinction. In the second game of the '52-'53 season, he scored the first point in Vanderbilt's new home, Memorial Gymnasium.

17. Memorial Gym

Stahlman's dream comes true, despite North Carolina thinking

Vanderbilt dedicated its long-awaited Memorial Gymnasium with a 90-83 win over Virginia on December 6, 1952. The souvenir game program included a brief history of the subject development, a standard layman's report on the planning, funding and construction of the facility. Newspapers carried similar pieces over the next few days, presenting a positive, but superficial example of how "teamwork" makes things happen.

I was convinced that Memorial Gymnasium had not come about that easily. Several factors bothered me: 1) The University had three different chancellors during the development of the gym concept. Could all three have possibly agreed on the plans for what would be the University's second-largest building project ever? (The hospital was more expensive.) 2) Why were the balconies, in the original plans, not installed in the building? 3) Why was the gymnasium located in such cramped surroundings—sort of "dropped" onto the campus?

To get some of the answers, I drove up a long private driveway set among the hills of south Nashville. The architect sat behind a table covered with the work of the day; a model of Nashville's Life and Casualty Tower stood in a corner, tribute to one of Edwin Keeble's more visible designs.

I had planned to spend a half hour with Keeble, asking a few main questions, hoping for a possible anecdote or two. Four hours later, I drove away with a head full of Keeble's amazing reflections on the birth of Memorial Gymnasium, and for the rest of the evening wondered how the place was ever eventually built. Edited for the sake of brevity, here is his story:

94

"After finishing Vanderbilt in '24, I went to Paris to study architecture. One summer a friend and I went to Italy, and one of our purposes, besides to have a good time, was to look at some of the great arenas throughout the country, especially the Coliseum.

"So we're sitting in a little cafe in Rome, killing time. We heard a band playing nearby—a procession of some sort—and the music, a Fascist march song, sounded almost exactly like 'Vanderbilt Forever!' Well, we decided to see what was happening and we followed the procession to a great piazza where, we learned, Mussolini was about to speak to about 350,000 Italians. When he finally did show up, the crowd was really excited, stomping and shouting. I stood there thinking—*If only these people had football—they wouldn't need wars!* This has nothing to do with basketball, of course, but it made me realize again how athletic contests could serve to work off tensions.

"Later, back in Paris, I was playing in a Saturday night basketball league just so I could get a shower once a week—there were no facilities in my apartment. In this little place we played, the playing floor ran right up to the wall and fellows were always getting hurt as they ran onto it. The reason we've got so much space around the floor in the Vanderbilt gym is that I had learned what it was like running into that wall in Paris.

"Back to the point. I had always had strong aesthetic convictions about the sort of facility best suited for entertainment—theater, opera, as well as sports events such as basketball. I returned from Navy duty in World War II to my work in Nashville. I knew a new Federal Building was being planned for Nashville, and since it was rumored the architect would be a veteran, I went after that contract. I called Jimmy Stahlman for advice (former Nashville *Banner* publisher, who was then just back from Navy duty as a captain in D.C.) Unfortunately, it was a patronage job, and I couldn't get the necessary "political clearance."

"*Forget that one,* Jimmy said. '*I've got another one for you. We want to build a fine new facility at Vanderbilt—a memorial to those alumni who died in the war—and I want you to design it. Let me know how much it would cost,*' simple as that. When Jimmy gets an idea, he makes it happen.

"I looked at the gymnasium being built at the University of Kentucky; it was costing over four million dollars to seat 11,500 people. It was a handsome structure; however coach Rupp told us *It just wasn't big enough*. This confirmed our research, so we figured Vanderbilt should have a gym at least that spacious. But we knew that UK had spent far more than necessary, due to local politics and the fact that it was an in-house design job. I called Jimmy and told him I thought we would get it built for three million.

"*Hell, no!* he yelled. *You'll build it for two million because that's all we can raise, and I'll be the one who'll have to raise it.* So that's what we designed; the low bid, complete with balconies, was $2,050,000. I was proud of that.

"It came time to present our plans to the Board of Trust, and we had a model. Everyone wants to see a model. And I knew that it helped to have a *gimmick,* too. When discussion began to lag, we removed the roof; they got interested again as we explained what this was and what that would do. Then when that died down, we removed another portion and revealed a pool, complete with underwater lights and a tiny female model on a diving board. It was impressive.

"*This is all fine,* someone said, *but who's going to get the two million dollars?* Well, Stahlman stood up and boomed—*By God, I will!* That did it. They told us that if the money could be raised, we would built it.

"I had studied arenas around Europe and this country and I had some ideas. But there were no perfect examples to follow. The Board appointed a committee—Stahlman from the Board of Trust, Sarratt, University Treasurer A.B. Benedict, Engineering Dean E.E. Lewis, and alumnus Charles S. Ragland as chairman. We set out to look at other facilities, mostly fieldhouses in Michigan and Indiana and Madison Square Garden. What we found was that the fieldhouse concept—a dirt floor with portable basketball playing floor—was a failure. The Purdue officials admitted this, as did the people at Michigan. When you cover over the ground, the worms die from lack of moisture, sun, etc. and thus fail to aerate the dirt, making it as hard as concrete. This makes it impractical to practice football, which is what Vanderbilt originally thought they wanted possible in an indoor facility. So all we had was a hazy, nebulous idea of what the program ought to be.

"We we did want, however, was a gymnasium which would serve a number of University purposes—auditorium, track, theatre, opera and basketball. We wanted the audience to have an intimacy with the actors; this dictated that every seat be within an accepted 110 feet viewing distance from the floor. There was

The Old Gym Annex, home of the Commodores until the Forties, coming down.

no other basketball arena in the country with this intimacy, but we felt it was important.

"We assembled a team of veterans as architects: Bill Briggs, Bill Lincoln, Arnold Nye, Frank Gower, Hank Waechter and Jack Caldwell, and we got started.

"Meanwhile, Vanderbilt was going through three administration changes— Chancellor (O.C.) Carmichael had left, Dr. Sarratt was serving as acting Chancellor and Harvie Branscomb had just arrived. What happened next was what we'll call the intrusion of New York thinking.

"One day I received a call from an administration official asking me what I'd do if I was removed from the gymnasium job. The new Chancellor, I was told, should be able to choose his own architect for the first building constructed under his administration. Well, I told him I felt it was a little late. We had been working on this for over a year; our name had been publicized with the project. This seemed like an unwarranted slap that could

97

cripple us. There was nothing in writing so I couldn't do anything if they did fire me.

"It seemed the new administration wanted *New York thinking* on this project. There are two types of Southerners—the Reconstructed type who thinks everything good comes out of the East, and those who feel you don't have to go to New York to get a job done. I heard that the Administration had asked a New York firm to draw up an alternate design on the quiet. I was incensed—not only because we had put so much work into this, but also because it was a downright unethical and counter-productive procedure according to all professional codes and standards.

"The Chancellor, moreover, had decided that the gymnasium should have a 6,000 maximum seating capacity, the result of more New York thinking. De-emphasis of athletics was a style of the times, understandable, perhaps, from a purely academic viewpoint. A meeting was called to finalize this limit and, not coincidentally, it was to take place with Stahlman and Ragland out of town. I alerted Stahlman to this, and he was able to stop the attempt to subvert our plans.

"After all this, the *New York thinking* was retained—the Administration's architect from New York was working on a master plan for the campus, so he was to serve as special consultant to the gymnasium project. But we kept the job, and that's what we were fighting for.

"Our troubles had just begun, though. We had been ordered to hold the cost to $1.25 million, because that's what had been raised by this time, although we got another $400,000 later. The only way I could prove my conviction that this was no way to run a railroad, I explained that for the good of the project and the university they would have to choose once and for all, one architect. I offered to withdraw and left the room. Some time later, we received instructions as if nothing had happened. Things were moving again.

"So we had to figure out how to retain provision for adding the balconies at a later date. To do that we designed an extra 20 feet in height, which would allow later addition of two balconies. This was accepted as a compromise. We had won.

"Then I saw a chance to provide another four thousand seats by tearing out the end zones. I knew I couldn't get the Administration to agree to this and the additional height, too, so the end zone plan was kept a secret, even from my associates, although I knew it could be done later.

"Dean E. E. Lewis, a project committee member (also head of the Engineering school then) was a constant thorn in our side. He simply hated architects. *We don't need an architect for this,* he told us. *It's just a big old barn anyway. There's no architecture involved.* Later he insisted that the balconies be built with columns extending to the floor for support. Can you imagine what this would do for the people sitting behind them . . . not to mention that they would be just plain ugly?

"Then he wanted to add seven engineers, mostly from the school to the design project. He even designed an alternate building himself—it *was* a barn. We were planning for the basement locker rooms to be especially nice for the varsity teams, and he was strongly opposed to that. *You get the varsity athletes in here and they'll soon be running things,* he said. That prompted a wonderful comment from Stahlman: *I guess you're right—once you get your foot in the door, soon you'll have your ass in the driver's seat.* I'm afraid Dean Lewis didn't think that was very amusing.

"Actually, the gym shouldn't even have been built where it now is. The location just to the north of Dudley Stadium—it's a parking lot now—was better and would have provided an entrance and highly desirable visual impact directly from West End. But Dean Lewis thought it would be too far away for Physical Education students to walk from the campus. Ironically, it's actually farther to walk to the back door of Memorial Gymnasium. Then Professor 'Bull' Harris had a say in all this; he was in charge of the commencement procession and he, too, didn't want to walk so far. That's a strange way to pick a location for a major building but that's how it happened. *New York thinking* then, was to keep everyone buttered up.

"Then came what we'll call the *Philadelphia thinking* concerning the heating and air conditioning. The Administration and the committee wanted to get more East Coast expertise, so they called in a special consultant on this from Philadelphia, at a fee 150% above local costs. His recommendations would cost $350,000 to implement. Later we used local capabilities and found it could be done for $80,000. *Boston thinking*, moreover, caused us to lose an acoustical lining for the roof at a savings of only $1500, believe it or not.

"That brings us to the *North Carolina thinking*. We knew there would have to be toilets in the restrooms, of course. What we hadn't planned is that it would take ten or 15 people—a real committee—to decide what kind. The Administration invited a

Chancellor Harvie Branscomb and
Dean Madison Sarratt.

Rob Roy Purdy, Senior Vice-Chancellor
and Chairman, University Committee
on Athletics.

number of faculty members to sit in on a meeting with five architects to decide what kind of and how many toilets we should use. The group met for seven hours without a decision. Long distance calls were made to officials in Louisville and New York's Madison Square Garden to see how those people like their toilets.

"Finally one of the staff members spoke up. *All you fellows worry about is privacy,* he said. *Now down in Texas where I come from, we like to show off.* So that's why we got troughs in the men's restrooms! The architects and the University spent a thousand dollars or so on this meeting.

"Somehow, it got built. Of course our firm never received another contract from the Administration. We had totally alienated ourselves, but that was the price we knew we had to pay to give Vanderbilt an outstanding gymnasium.

"When I hear from time to time that some people feel its all worked out well enough, it brings a warm feeling. I was somewhat worried in the beginning when Dr. Sarratt pointed out that the only sellouts in the gym were for Billy Graham and Liberace.

"Without question Jimmy Stahlman is the hero in this story. He fought for the building at every point. Without his tenaciousness, they would probably still be playing at East High."

If the original concept of Memorial Gymnasium was the brainchild of Edwin Keeble, the story of its later expansion belongs to Vanderbilt Senior Vice-Chancellor Rob Roy Purdy, who is also the Chairman of the University Committee on Athletics.

Dr. Purdy is the Administration's primary liaison with the Athletic Department and as such is regularly embroiled in the many fiscal crises which face college athletic programs in 1975. In effect, he must coordinate department requests for new construction.

In the Spring of 1964, Purdy faced the University Board of Trust Executive Committee with a modest plan for construction of balconies on the north side of the gymnasium. The previous season had seen a newcomer, Clyde Lee, add new excitement to Vanderbilt optimism for a future SEC championship. Every conference game had been sold out. Purdy's first attempt was

Facilities, 1975.

unsuccessful.

Six months later, he returned to the Committee again, explaining that Edwin Keeble had indicated that the balconies could be built for $450,000. The Committee "expressed indebtedness to the Vice-Chancellor for his continuing efforts," but again expressed doubts about such an expenditure.

"We were told that the balconies would be considered if sufficient interest could be shown through advance sales," recalls Purdy. "A month later we presented our plans for amortizing the 1,754-seat balconies over a 25-year period. But there still was no unqualified approval to proceed."

Athletic department officials then marketed the proposed new seats with considerable success. So in February 1965, Purdy was able to project no difficulty in selling these new seats. The north balconies became reality during the off-season of 1965, at a cost of $631,000. Poor estimates and inflation had driven the price up $181,000 in the nine months the Board of Trust had taken to make the final decision.

"We had a complete sellout the next year," continued Purdy. "So I went back to the Board to point out the need for more seats. By this time Roy Skinner had recruited that fine black player from Pearl High, Perry Wallace, and there was discussion that a new demand for seats would be placed on the program from a source heretofore unexpected, namely the Nashville black community.

"I knew that this next addition would take 18 months, so we had to move quickly."

This time, however, the Board, apparently pleased with the full houses for Clyde Lee's final year, approved the recommendation for South balconies pending approval of the Chancellor, which came shortly thereafter.

"Meanwhile," said Purdy, "the original estimates for the South balconies had gone up $50,000 to $700,000." In December 1967, the Commodores occupied a "new" 11,000-seat gymnasium. These seats, too, were soon sold out.

The following summer, Purdy again approached the Board, this time to ask for authority to study a possible addition of another 4,500 seats. After a three-month deferral, Purdy presented his $2,100,000 plan for construction of the East-West wings. This proposal was quickly approved. Ironically, the final construction cost, which exceeded the entire cost of the original facility, was accepted quickly by the Board of Trust, with few qualifications.

As Vanderbilt opened its 1969-70 season, it possessed an impressive gymnasium which seated 15,581 spectators. Dr. Purdy's five-year effort was completed, 22 years after Jimmy Stahlman first dreamed of this great facility.

18. 1953-57

Bobby, Babe, Little Al, and the Toddle House

For two seasons following their entry into the spacious new Memorial Gymnasium, Vanderbilt was unable to harness its SEC opponents. Although setting new scoring records with 95 and 97 point outbursts in two games, the Commodores were having problems.

Kentucky, suspended for the '52-53 season, returned to win every game in '53-54 but refused an invitation to the NCAA tournament in retaliation for the previous year's suspension. The 'Cats were back on top.

Dan Finch, George Nordhaus, freshman Clarence "Babe" Taylor, Tom MacKenzie, and captain Bob White led the Commodores during '52-53, managing a 10-9 record.

Finch returned to captain the '53-54 squad, which fared little better, winning 12 games against nine losses. Joining Finch this year, were freshmen Al Rochelle and Bobby Thym, from the last class to be eligible for varsity play as freshmen until 1972.

Thym led all scorers as a rookie, and Rochelle played well until academic disqualification at mid-year. This twosome and Taylor teamed with Nordhaus and center Charlie Harrison to lead Vanderbilt back into contention the following year. Harrison, at 6'6", was Vanderbilt's best rebounder of the decade and his records stood until Clyde Lee rewrote the book in the Sixties.

A 16-6 mark in '54-55 with a 9-5 SEC record was sparked by two wins each over Tennessee and Georgia Tech. Rochelle thrilled fans with adroit ball handling in the dying moments of several games as Vanderbilt protected slim leads.

The Commodores routed nationally ranked Alabama, 78-57, to bring talk of a conference title for the first time in four years. Vanderbilt actually rose to 14th in the AP poll after that win.

104

Thym and Rochelle, 1956.

Babe Taylor.

Babe Taylor, finishing his career in '55-56, continued to be a thorn in Adolph Rupp's side, especially in Nashville that year.

The Commodores started Taylor, Thym, Rochelle, Harrison, and Jo "Hobby" Gibbs against the Wildcats, who were tied with Vanderbilt for the Number Four national ranking. Taylor scored consistently in the first half, and Harrison and Gibbs controlled both boards. It was left to "Little Al" to run out the clock with his dribbling show as Vanderbilt won 81-73.

The next week found Vanderbilt in the nation's Number Two spot, its highest ever even to 1975.

Road losses to Alabama and Kentucky cost the Commodores a post-season berth. Having finished with a 19-4 record, 11-3 in the conference, Vanderbilt would have been a natural choice for an NIT bid, but that tournament had been declared taboo by the SEC after the Madison Square Garden gambling scandals four years earlier.

Taylor, in 1975 an Atlanta investment broker, was graduated with second-team All-SEC honors and a 14-point career average. Rochelle was chosen to the second team in '55-56 and to the first team the following year. Thym was also a second-team selection in '56-57.

Rochelle had come to Vanderbilt from Guthrie, Kentucky, where he would return 16 years later as principal of an elementary school.

"I lived to play basketball," he said in his characteristic rural Kentucky accent. "I never thought about college as a kid. My father said I was going and that was that. I didn't even have a say in *where*. In those days you didn't question your elders."

So, as in a marriage of royalty, Bob Polk negotiated with a Guthrie High School coach, who negotiated with Rochelle's father, who finally decided that Al would travel to Nashville to get a college education and maybe play some basketball, too.

"I went there to play. Being a country boy from Guthrie, playing at Vanderbilt was sort of like going to the Emperor's Palace in Tokyo. People have a hard time understanding just how naive I was."

"But you know, I had no trouble adjusting and getting along with people at Vanderbilt. It never dawned on me that a lot of my classmates were rich. I thought everyone was just like me."

Thym and Rochelle led Vanderbilt to another fine season in '56-57. A road trip into Mississippi destroyed SEC title hopes, but the Commodores finished 17-5 and 10-4 in the SEC for second place. Another two wins against Tennessee continued the

Vanderbilt domination over the Vols, but Kentucky was headed toward the conference championship again and won both its games with Vanderbilt.

Now a bank executive in Nashville, Thym was to his teammates the SEC's most underrated player.

"He was the quickest player I ever coached," recalls Polk. "He would consistently out-jump and out-position a bigger or faster opponent."

Thym, Rochelle, and Taylor became legendary through several off-court exploits, too. Although no more risque than their non-athlete classmates, the trio developed a reputation that stands even in 1975. Indeed, when a player is discussed today as a "good timer," invariably a comparison is made with "that Thym-Taylor-Rochelle bunch" nearly 20 years before.

One particular off-season affair remains as the most fre-quently-remembered story about any Vanderbilt athlete, in-volving a complex series of events between the infamous Toddle House (a West End burger parlor), Nashville's downtown over-night rest stop for mischief makers, and an anonymous corpse. Unfortunately, there are too many versions to substantiate, and the tale therefore cannot be told fully here.

"Besides," said Rochelle nearly two decades later, "that *reputation* you mention is entirely unjustifiable. Sure, Babe played better when he'd had a few beers, but *I* had nothing to do with the *incident* you mention."

What would sports be without stories, however exaggerated, such as those inspired by the Thym-Taylor-Rochelle trio?

19. 1958-61

Illness, acting coaches, a playoff

With the graduation of Rochelle and Thym, Polk was faced with a rebuilding effort in his 11th season.

Around high-scoring guard Jim Henry, Polk fielded a team composed of Jimmy French, Bob Gregor, Don Hinton, Hub Houghland, Doug Yates, Ben Rowan, Jack Pirrie, and Martin Holland.

Henry, another Polk prize from Indiana, had shown promising offensive talents the previous season and provided a 21-point average in '57-58 as Vanderbilt struggled to a 14-11 finish. The 6' junior, an accurate lefthander, grew up as a Kentucky fan listening to radio broadcasts of Wildcat games from his home in New Albany.

"But Vanderbilt didn't have to recruit me," he recalls from his 1975 home in St. Louis, where he is an executive of a large plastics company. "I was interested in the academic degree more than anything, and I came as a Navy ROTC scholarship student."

Henry would later finish his senior year with a 19-point average and take his place among Vanderbilt's top ten scorers.

Jack Pirrie (in 1975 a possible candidate for U.S. Senator from Tennessee), was touted as one of Vanderbilt's top recruits ever, but the 6'5" forward was injured his sophomore season and never became the dominant player projected after his first season.

In the fall of 1958, Polk and his young assistant Roy Skinner drove to Paducah, Kentucky, to scout a high school whiz kid, Don Ringstaff. Feeling unusually tired, Polk asked Skinner to drive, and later, after dinner the head coach experienced what he thought were pains of indigestion. Instead, he was floored with a massive heart attack.

Polk spent the next three months in a Paducah hospital and

108

Coaches: Acting and Sidelined

Bill Depp

was then bedridden for three more weeks as the '58-59 season opened without him.

"I could have gone back in January," he recalls, "but the doctors insisted, as they will do in these matters."

Thrust in the top slot for that season was a 28-year-old who only five years earlier had been supervising an athletic program for a Boys' Club in Virginia.

"It wasn't really a problem," remembers Skinner. "Coaching is the same on all levels - high school, college, and so on. You just adjust to what the situation is at the time."

As Vanderbilt faced Kentucky's defending national champions, undefeated and ranked atop the nation's teams in '58-59, it is doubtful that Skinner believed his task to be akin to coaching the Portsmouth Boys' Club.

The Commodores backed up Henry's sensational shooting with solid rebounding (Rowan, Hinton and Bill Depp), and Vanderbilt shocked Adolph Rupp for only the second time since the '51 championship win. The 75-66 victory catapulted Skinner into the national limelight and established him as Polk's heir apparent.

A 14-10 season record, 8-6 in the SEC, was considered a credible performance for Skinner as acting coach. He had dutifully consulted with Polk throughout the season and had avoided the temptation to implement his own preferred brand of fast-breaking, offense-oriented basketball.

"Sure, it was frustrating sometimes," he remembers. "But it all happened so fast we wouldn't have had time to make changes anyway. What hurt most was keeping one of the players off the squad, Hub Houghland, after Polk had ordered Hub off for insubordination before the season. Polk and I just had differing opinions about player relationships. But you've got to remember, I was *acting* coach, and I knew Polk would return."

Depp, at 6'7", 6'4" Rowan and 6'6" Larry Banks had given Vanderbilt legitimate rebounding strength for the first time. When Polk returned for the '59-60 campaign, he had also a pair of sophomore guards, Bill Johnson and Bobby Bland, to run the team.

The '59-60 year (14-9 overall, 7-7 in the SEC) ended without a "big win," which had characterized most Commodore seasons. Depp and Rowan were named to All-SEC teams. Bill Johnson was a second-team selection but was lost for most of the following season with an illness.

Polk fielded an experienced squad in 1960-61. Depp, Banks, Bland, and Clark formed the nucleus surrounded by Polk's best

110

sophomore class in seven years: guards John Russell, Bobby "Lance" Gish, and Sam Hosback; forwards Bob Scott and Don Ringstaff, and center Ron Griffiths.

The completion of the pre-conference schedule found the Commodores undefeated, but not without experiencing minor trauma. At Texas Tech, Vanderbilt was protecting a two point lead late in the game. The Lubbock fans were screaming for a Tech rally when Polk prepared to substitute Lance Gish into the game.

A recounting of Larry Munson's radio broadcast during those final moments tells what happened:

> *This one's going down to the wire, folks. Hang on. We've got Gish coming into the game. It'll be Vandy's ball out of bounds. Wait a minute. What's this? Gish has lost his pants! Bob Polk has pulled off Lance Gish's pants in front of six thousand screaming fans! The place is going crazy!*

In the excitement of the game, Polk was helping Gish remove his warmup pants but inadvertently grabbed his shorts also.

Munson handled his job with enthusiasm, and as in the case of Gish's disrobing in Lubbock, he had no problem injecting color into the broadcast.

Somehow Lance recovered, despite the terrific embarrassment of modeling one's jockstrap for several thousand people, to make two crucial free throws. Vanderbilt won the game, 80-78, and Gish had become a folk hero in that flat Texas town.

The SEC season opened with traditional rivals Tennessee in Knoxville and Kentucky in Nashville. Bland and Ringstaff sparked two-point victories over both, and suddenly Vanderbilt was the team to beat.

Mississippi road trips have always been hostile journeys for every team in the SEC. All road trips are dangerous for even the most powerful teams, but in the days of Ole Miss' classroom-like facility and State's tiny barn, to travel to that state was unusually dreadful.

In '61 the trip was disastrous for Vanderbilt. Losing both games, the Commodores fell out of the national rankings and the SEC lead.

They returned for four consecutive wins, however, before losing at LSU. An easy win over Tennessee in Nashville set up the showdown at Lexington. After building an early lead, Vanderbilt gave way to a Kentucky rush. The Commodores rallied from a 13-point deficit in the closing moments but fell short, 60-59.

Three closing wins left Vanderbilt even with Kentucky in second place with identical 10-4 SEC records.

Mississippi State, taking advantage of the "square round robin," faced the better teams only once that season and finished on top with an 11-3 SEC mark. But Mississippi State officials, feeling intense pressure from the state capital, refused to compete in the NCAA playoffs. There would be "colored boys" playing in the tournament, and the image of the State players competing with them horrified the politicos. This was not necessarily the players', nor coach Babe McCarthy's feeling, but rather the *law of the land.*

So Vanderbilt and Kentucky were faced with a playoff to determine the SEC representative. Playing in Knoxville, the Wildcats handled the Commodores easily, 88-67, and Vanderbilt's chance for postseason play was gone again.

Depp was selected for All-SEC honors for the second year and was later drafted by the NBA champion Boston Celtics. The big center from Edinburg, Indiana, had first become aware of

Bill Johnson and Bobby Bland.

John Russell

Vanderbilt's athletic existence while attending a Kentucky-Vanderbilt football game in 1955 as a 14-year old.

"Vanderbilt beat the stuffings out of Kentucky, and I was impressed. Later, when Polk came to visit my folks, I remembered that game. Also, Polk let it be known that it was his birthday, so my Mom baked a cake and we helped him celebrate while I signed the grant. I wonder if he had a birthday every time he was recruiting someone?"

20. A Passer and a Shooter

Smart guards, great guys, testimonials

The ornament of a house is the friends who frequent it.
    —Ralph Waldo Emerson
    Domestic Life

Through the years Vanderbilt teams have been most noted for the outstanding play of a plethora of excellent guards — combinations such as Heldman-Duvier and Taylor-Rochelle in the Fifties; Miller-Schurig, Miller-Thomas and Hagan-Wyenandt in the Sixties; Ford-Feher in the Seventies. These backcourt specialists consistently kept Commodore teams near the top of the SEC.

None of these were more impressive, however, than the teaming of John Russell and Bobby Bland during 1961 and 1962.

"Individually, they were excellent ballplayers," recalls Polk, "but as a team they were tremendous."

Bland, as a junior, accepted his new sophomore running mate from St. Louis immediately. Together they learned to anticipate each other's every move, even every thought.

"It got to the point," remembers Russell, in 1975 a practicing attorney in St. Louis, "that we always knew what was going on in the other guy's head at any given moment. *That* was teamwork.

"We used to go up to Rand (the campus dining hall) one or two hours before a game and talk about it, the opposing players, patterns, and so on."

"They were so *smart* out there," continued Polk, who glowed with the pride of a successful father when telling of the Bland-Russell years. "They made the fast break a regular play for us."

Bland, at 5'10", was not a prolific scorer, but his speed and mobility allowed him to slip through defenses for easy layups, an especially disheartening move that can quickly demoralize a defense.

Russell, on the other hand, was a shooter. Years later he would say jokingly, "The thing that made Bland and me work so well together is that he liked to pass off, and I liked to shoot. We were both good at those things."

John Russell was perhaps Vanderbilt's best defensive player of all time. Tennessee coach Ray Mears and Kentucky's Rupp are among the first to praise what they termed Russell's "great hands and superb defensive instincts."

"Seriously," Russell recovers, "Bland was a *natural* leader. By that I mean he was totally committed to the game, and that easily spread to his teammates. He was a great guy, too, a *guy's* guy."

After Bland finished in '62, he moved into high school coaching as fluidly as he had executed the fast break with Russell. Later he returned to coach his hometown prep school in Leitchfield, Kentucky. In 1966 Skinner called Bland to join his staff after Don Knodel's departure.

Bland handled scouting and recruiting duties and coached the freshman teams for three years. He successfully maintained that delicate balance between close player friendship and coaching authority that is the trademark of talent in the college profession.

Early during his coaching tenure at Vanderbilt, Bland learned that he was suffering from a serious kidney ailment. He began to undergo dialysis after drug treatments failed to stem the condition, but his condition progressively worsened. Finally, on May 11, 1969, he succumbed to the disease.

Vanderbilt had lost a close friend. Players on the '69-70 squad were crushed. Six years later some reminisced that Bland's death had left them sapped of enthusiasm. Moreover, many felt that they had lost not only a close friend but also a leader with whom they could closely identify.

Bland's life may take on additional qualities as the Sixties grow more remote. But those he touched will have vivid and unexaggerated memories of what teammate Russell called "a wonderful friend to a lot of people."

21. Bob Polk, 1947-61

The Guard Changes

It's futile to talk too much about the past—something like
trying to make birth control retroactive
                    —Charles E. Wilson,
                        Secretary of Defense, 1955

As he prepared for his 14th season, Polk felt that his two-year
recovery from the 1958 heart attack had been successful. In the
summer of 1961, the 47-year-old Polk got the bad news from his
doctors: he would have to give up coaching. "I had no choice,"
said Polk. "I had a family and responsibilities which were more
important to me than coaching, but I hated to quit."

There had also been a confusing and unfortunate episode
involving Polk, football coach and athletic director Art Guepe,
and a job offer at the University of Florida. "There was never
any love lost between Polk and Guepe," states one writer close to
both men. "Football had been on the downslide for five years
since the Gator Bowl in '55. During the same period, basketball
was continuing to grow. Polk's teams were regular contenders for
the SEC championship and had developed a good track record
with ticket sales. It was very simple—Polk was winning and
Guepe was losing."

"I had never gone job hunting during all those years at
Vanderbilt," said Polk. There are several differing accounts of
what happened in '61.

"Polk had been contacted by Ray Graves (Florida athletic
director) to interview for the job there," said the writer. "Polk
then told Guepe he was going to talk to the Florida people.
Guepe felt he was just trying to get a raise, and when he called

Graves to check Polk's story, Graves apparently told an untruth, that he had never contacted Polk."

The situation had become tense for Polk, an additional strain on his physical condition. The misunderstanding was tentatively resolved, and Polk was to stay at Vanderbilt. Soon, however, his health dictated that he retire from basketball. He took a job on the campus as personnel director for the Vanderbilt Hospital and tried to settle into the routine of a life most people would consider to be normal. It's not easy to believe Polk when he says, "I wasn't bored. The new job was a real challenge."

The role of layman and spectator was not an easy one for Polk, and after 18 months of retirement he received another clean bill of health. "But where would I go? Where could I coach?" he thought. Polk worked with a Nashville prep team "to keep my hand in," and when the call finally came from Trinity College in Texas, Polk jumped at the chance for a comeback.

He repeated his Vanderbilt success at Trinity, finishing third in the nation in the "college division" (the smaller schools). In 1967 he moved to St. Louis University, fielding three excellent teams and winning a Missouri Valley Conference championship in his five years there. In 1975 he became head coach at Rice, succeeding former Vanderbilt assistant Don Knodel. Polk's "second career" has been bright.

"Of course, I miss Nashville and Vanderbilt," he says, now slightly graying and several pounds heavier than the 32 year old that assumed command at Vanderbilt in 1947. "You have a wonderful situation there—a great university, outstanding facilities, terrific fans, a super basketball tradition, and the best local press coverage in the country. It's simply a fine place to coach."

Vanderbilt's first *real* coach was now its first real former coach. He brought to the school and to Nashville a new sense of pride in an athletic contest. Football continued to draw its 20,000 fans, but basketball was a winner and the fans loved their new heroes.

Polk had recruited with intensity and success, again and again proving the University's commitment to basketball to be sound and worthwhile. His great players are found in the record books—Adcock; the stars of the amazing '51 team: Southwood, Weiss, Smith, Heldman and Kelley; Dan Finch, the St. Louis goldman; George Nordhaus and the multi-talented, if intemperate, trio: Babe Taylor, Bobby Thym and Al Rochelle; Jim Henry, Bill Depp and the remarkable guard combination of John Russell and Bobby Bland.

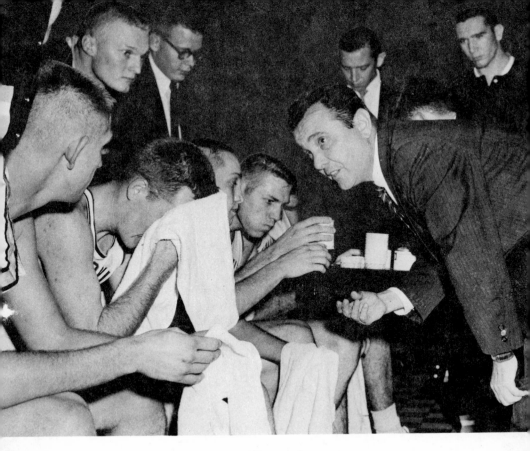

Instructions

Polk had instilled confidence in the less talented teams of the late '40's. For the first time they learned patterns and disciplined offenses and saw game strategy systematically employed to beat opponents. Off the court, their coach was creating rapport with the University faculty and administration, the press, and the community. At the conclusion of Polk's first season, they had seen the coach gather the 16 season-ticket holders to his home for a dinner with the players.

Fourteen years later, nearly 7,000 fans would pack Memorial Gymnasium to watch Polk's teams play basketball on a par with Kentucky.

The Bob Polk era was over. The guard had changed, but unlike previous coaching changes, Polk's successor inherited a stable program, poised for even greater accomplishment.

Part Three
The Roy Skinner Era

22. Skinner's Ballgame

Boy's clubs, reporters' dilemmas, good vibrations

There are two basic routes to becoming a head coach at a major university: utilize a highly publicized career as a college or professional player for instant credibility and a high paying salary; or work your way up through the ranks—high school, junior college, a long assistantship, and finally, with dues fully paid, the top job. Some do make it through the glamorous route, but those who take the tougher path stick around longer.

Roy Skinner grew up in the basketball-crazed state of Kentucky. A slightly built youth, he wasn't attracted to football, but in 'Cat country, who cares about football? As a 5'9" guard, he captained his Tillman High team in Paducah and later enrolled in Paducah Junior College. After two years at Paducah, he transferred to Presbyterian College in South Carolina. While Vanderbilt was busy winning the SEC tournament in 1951, Skinner and his Presbyterian College teammates were capturing the Little Four (Wofford, Erskine, Newberry, and Presbyterian) Conference title.

After graduation Skinner looked about for a start in coaching. What he found was the bottom rung in any coaching ladder—athletic director and coach for the Portsmouth, Virginia Boys Club. A year later he moved to Craddock Junior High in the same city, where an 18-1 record catapulted him to the Craddock High job. His first big break came in 1957 when alma mater Paducah Junior College called.

Junior college basketball was, for many years, the hunting ground of major college recruiters looking for experienced talent. In the Fifties and early Sixties, junior colleges attracted many good high school players who, for many reasons, wanted to stay close to home. This situation still exists in 1975, but the system is more complicated. Now a coach recruits a player and if he cannot successfully be admitted academically, the coach might "refer" the player to a junior college to make acceptable grades. There he can receive valuable playing experience and after a year or two, can enter the major school and take his place on the varsity team. It is the closest thing major schools have to a "farm" system, and it seems to work remarkably well for all concerned.

During the summer of '56 Skinner was sitting in a classroom at George Peabody College, grinding out his work for a Master's Degree in Physical Education. His instructor was Bob Polk. The young Kentuckian introduced himself and asked Polk if the Commodore freshmen would play his Paducah JC team that winter.

Skinner's '56-'57 Paducah JC team won the Kentucky junior college championship; one of PJC's opponents that year was Vanderbilt's biggest and best freshman team in nearly a decade. Skinner's PJC charges handed the Commodore frosh their only defeat that year, 99-90. Former Vanderbilt guard Jack Heldman was completing his third season as a Polk assistant and as freshman coach. In the loss to PJC, Heldman watched Skinner destroy his chance for an undefeated season.

After the loss, Polk asked Heldman what had happened. "We just got outcoached," the assistant replied. The writing was on the wall.

Heldman was dismissed during the summer of 1957. Skinner applied for and received the job as Polk's assistant with responsibilities for scouting, freshman coaching, and some recruiting. "That first year was strange," remembers Skinner. "I didn't help at all with the varsity; I refereed some scrimmages and handled the freshmen mostly. During the following summer I talked with Polk, and he accepted some of my suggestions. Frankly, I was surprised. After that we worked a lot closer."

Polk's heart attack thrust Skinner into the top slot. Although the 14-10 record was unimpressive, he had proved his mettle in the win over top-ranked Kentucky. At 28 years of age, Skinner already had erased any doubt that he was Polk's heir apparent should the time come for Polk to leave Vanderbilt.

As a recruiter, Skinner soon established himself as a master of the "soft-sell." "I enjoyed visiting players and their parents and just getting to know them," said Skinner. "In those days high school players were still hungry, didn't put many demands on

122

you. A scholarship meant a great deal in the late Fifties and early Sixties."

His most famous recruiting prize, Clyde Lee, typifies the high school player's impression of Skinner's technique: "He came into the house and made you feel comfortable with the Vanderbilt program right away; that soft-sell approach left you with a tingle. As a high school player, it was an honor just to have him into your home. The parents loved him. You knew you were talking to an honest man."

As an assistant, Skinner helped recruit such prep stars as Bobby Bland, Ray Clark, Jerry Hall, Bill Johnson, John Russell, Bob Scott, Don Ringstaff, and Roger Schurig. (Note: recruiting is rarely a one-man process. Usually, an assistant will scout a high school player, check grades and report back to the head coach the chances of signing the player. If he is a very important prospect, the head coach then visits the player. Since recruiting is well underway during the playing season, a head coach often delegates most recruiting activities to his assistant.)

When Polk returned in the summer of '59, Skinner stepped back into his less visible role. "Sure there was some letdown," he said, "especially in salary. But I was happy just to be Polk's assistant. You've got to remember that I was only 28 and still had a lot to learn about coaching. Polk was a good teacher, especially of disciplined offensive patterns and game conditions. I've always had a lot of respect for his coaching skills."

Polk's abrupt departure in 1961 left the University without a head coach for the first time in 14 years. "Some of the boys around town wanted us to go up to the Midwest and hire an established 'name' coach," recalls Dean Madison Sarratt, "but we thought this young fella from Paducah could do the job."

"When a coaching job comes open," said then athletic director Art Guepe, "you're always going to have a bunch of names bandied around. There was never any real doubt that Skinner would get the job. He had proved himself as an assistant and had had a good year as acting coach. He was the logical choice."

Skinner assumed command with ease. The players, many of whom had been under Skinner's personal tutelage while he was an assistant, adjusted readily to the new management. For the second-teamers, it was a pleasant change.

"Polk didn't like substituting," remembers one player who played for both coaches as a reserve. "He found five guys to start, and that was it. If you weren't a first-teamer, you never played. It caused a lot of morale problems for the subs.

Coach Skinner wanted everyone to have a chance to play and to develop in game conditions. A lot of guys that were turned off by Polk's favoritism toward starters immediately loved Skinner."

Skinner, like Polk, was not an adamant off-the-court disciplinarian. "I've never thought of—or referred to—our players as *boys*, " he said. "They've always been treated as men and been expected to handle that responsibility."

"I couldn't imagine being treated in any other way," Jan van Breda Kolff would say after he left Vanderbilt in 1974 after a splendid career as one of the Commodores' finest players. "That's got to be the best thing about Coach Skinner. The sort of Mickey Mouse stuff you see at Tennessee—constantly watching guys off the floor—is an insult to a college player."

What all this means is simply that Skinner, while demanding total effort in basketball, allows his players the same freedoms other students enjoy at Vanderbilt, that is, all the frivolities one would expect from 17-22-year-olds. Mischief is not the sole property of non-athletes.

Skinner's new role as head coach did create at least one minor problem. Sportswriters found that Skinner was not especially "good copy," unlike his predecessor Polk. Skinner was frugal with words and seemed even somewhat shy. The writers who were once kept busy with Polk's rambling analyses and gregarious demeanor were now struggling to add color to their coverage. A long question about a particular player's performance would often be answered with a simple "Yes" or "No." What writers would then do would be to turn the question into a quote. For example, if the writer asked Skinner, "Coach, Russell and Bland were awfully sharp out there tonight. Bland shot better than all season, and Russell stole four passes. Was that the key to this game?" Skinner's answer might be, "Absolutely!" Appearing in the paper would be: *Russell and Bland were really sharp. Bland's shooting and Russell's defense were the key to the game,* said Skinner.

All this rarely bothers Skinner, though. In a sports environment controlled by "systems," big business, and media manipulation, Skinner is *real,* and people, especially the demanding sportswriters, are drawn to his open friendliness and candor, if not his "glamour."

As Vanderbilt's second head coach in the New Era, Skinner was eager to begin the '61-'62 campaign. It was now his own ball game.

124

23. 1962-64

Roger shoots, Snake rebounds, McCarthy sneaks the Bulldogs out of Starkville

Bob Polk had given Vanderbilt and Nashville winning basketball; moreover, many of his teams were considered championship contenders. Fortunately for Skinner, the fans had not yet become so demanding, for his first season as permanent head coach was accepted as a rebuilding year. The 10-12 overall mark, with a 6-8 finish in the SEC (6th place), was not a dramatic beginning for the new regime.

Vanderbilt presented Kentucky with problems in Lexington but still lost, 77-68. At least one major upset can help salvage a losing season, and in '61-62, it came as SEC leader Mississippi State journeyed to Nashville. The Commodores romped to a 100-86 win over nationally-ranked State, handing the visitors their only loss of the year.

Mississippi State was then in the middle of a three-year title streak in the SEC. The "square round robin" scheduling allowed State to play Vanderbilt, Tennessee, Georgia Tech and Kentucky only once each season while meeting the less capable teams in the Deep South twice during the season. While sporting such fine players as Jerry Graves, Lealand Mitchell, Joe Dan Gold and W. D. Stroud, Mississippi State, was able to control the conference championship from its tiny Starkville confines.

State's consistent "backdoor" domination was complicated by its two-time refusal to accept its place in the NCAA tournaments, a move to prevent competition with black players elsewhere in the country. Mississippi had not yet opened its eyes to what was happening in college athletics and society.

This official statement of racism came after, Babe McCarthy's most frustrating period as State's head coach. One of the game's most skilled strategists until his death in early 1975, McCarthy had developed three consecutive SEC championships, only to see the rewarding post-season competition withheld from his deserving players.

Later, after the '63 championship season, he devised a plan to circumvent the legislature. Bo Carter, a Vanderbilt graduate and, in 1975, the assistant sports information director at Mississippi State, relates McCarthy's scheme:

"The Legislature had voted to prohibit the team from going on to the NCAA, since blacks would be playing in the tournament. Local sherrifs and state troopers were even instructed to serve subpoenas on McCarthy to prevent his departure for the tournament.

"Coach McCarthy sent all the players to private homes around Starkville to keep them under wraps until time to leave. Then McCarthy and his assistant coach drove to Nashville and hid out in a hotel. At an appointed time, all the players met at the Columbus (Mississippi) airport and flew to Nashville to meet McCarthy, who then loaded everyone on a charter flight to East Lansing, Michigan for the Mideast Regionals.

"They lost to Loyola (eventual NCAA champion that year) in the first round, but they were the attraction of the tournament—everyone congratulated them on their escape from Starkville. It was like a spy movie."

"It should certainly be noted that the Mississippi State President then, D. W. Colvard (now President of the University of North Carolina-Charlotte), was one of the prime sponsors of McCarthy's plan. He really wanted the team to be able to play in the tournament."

McCarthy's struggle to draw Mississippi State teams out of embarrassing local politics was a courageous effort. It also signaled the beginning of the end to racism in Southern athletics.

Now, back to 1962—

Vanderbilt junior guard John Russell led the team scoring with a 15-point average, followed by captain Bobby Bland's 12 points; both were second-team All-SEC selections. The losing season was a sad affair especially for Bland, who ended his playing career as one of Vanderbilt's most skilled playmakers and most respected individuals.

Russell returned to captain the '62-63 unit and was billed as a possible All-American. Also back for another year were forwards

126

Bob Scott and Jerry Hall and an outstanding group of sopho-mores: Bob "Snake" Grace, Roger Schurig, John Ed Miller, Mike Gambill and Wayne Taylor.

Schurig became one of Vanderbilt's most controversial players. As Vanderbilt's top recruit from St. Louis since Dan Finch, Roger began a stormy college career by suffering a detached retina as a freshman, then experiencing academic difficulties resulting in ineligibility his sophomore year. His classroom problems ("I simply didn't go much," he said.) became a public issue when the daily sports pages began carrying a progress report of Schurig's grades and exam readiness.

"That stuff really wasn't fair. The sportswriters put a lot of pressure on me off the court. What other student has headlines like—'*Schurig In Exam Trouble!*'? After I finally did flunk out in '65, it was actually a relief." Schurig would later return to Vanderbilt for his degree; he is now an executive with a St. Louis travel agency.

While Schurig faced problems with his studies, he was enjoying a remarkable reputation as a "clutch" player, capable of scoring five or six consecutive baskets in a matter of moments. "Roger refused to get beat," recalls Skinner of the 6'2" guard. "He played so hard and was just a fantastic streak shooter."

During the '63-64 campaign, Schurig sealed his reputation as a dangerous opponent. As the Commodores were recording a 16-7 mark, Roger was winning five of these contests with extra-ordinary, off-balance, last-second shots. First there was Clemson (60-58) in the opening round of the Christmas Poinsetta Tournament, then Furman (69-68) in the finals of that same event. After similar heroics against Alabama (74-73), he brought Tennessee to its knees for the second time that season, 74-72. Appropriately, the season ended with Schurig scoring at the buzzer to beat Georgia Tech, 75-74. To add to these perform-ances, Schurig scored 32 points against Duke, the country's No. 2 team, and had 20-point-plus nights against Tennessee in Knox-ville and in the 69-67 win over Kentucky in Nashville.

"That sort of thing was unconscious," Schurig remembers. "In that first game of the Poinsetta tournament (Clemson), I stole a pass and scored to win the game. Then for the next few games everything just went in. I could have kicked it in, I think. It was quite a thrill."

When Roger was not playing well, however, he exhibited an outward frustration that fans soon came to believe was "hot-dogging" at its worst. He appeared difficult and moody,

127

sometimes unwilling to play defense. On especially unsuccessful shooting nights, Schurig received much criticism for "gunning" instead of passing to teammates.

"There's a lot of tension out there," he said. "Some guys hold it in, but I guess I just got caught up in it. I got mad at myself."

Schurig was one of Vanderbilt's most popular players both with fans and teammates. Schurig and "Snake" Grace were favorites with the press, who seemed to be living in Memorial Gymnasium. Cocky and light-hearted, Schurig and Grace added a needed comic relief during practice sessions. These players could often be bantering with the press from the floor, while writers Bibb and Green shouted "instructions" and gave cheers from courtside seats. It was one big, carefree family, and Skinner was enjoying being at its head.

Schurig ended a sensational sophomore year with a 17-point average, a team-leading average for field goal and free throw accuracy. Forwards Bob Scott and Jerry Hall graduated after making important contributions. Russell repeated as an All-SEC second-team selection with a 12-point average, although he failed to attain the national recognition predicted before the season. A painful hip bruise sidelined Russell, and Skinner inserted sophomore John Ed Miller into the starting lineup for the last five games. Miller sparked a new life into the Commodores – they won all five contests to finish the SEC season 9-5.

As the '63-64 season began, Skinner was faced with a dilemma any coach would covet: Grace, the SEC's top rebounder as a sophomore center, would have to be moved to forward to make room for varsity newcomer Clyde Lee. That combination would ultimately prove to be magic, giving Vanderbilt its best front line ever.

"Snake" had been an All-State center at Christian County High in Hopkinsville, Kentucky. He had watched Vanderbilt play games on television and had liked the Commodores' "run-and-gun style," as he remembers it. Grace was heavily recruited by all the SEC teams, but was unimpressed with the aura of the University of Kentucky basketball.

"I wanted to help beat Rupp more than I wanted to play for him," recalls the lanky 6'7" Grace, now an executive with a steel supplier in Nashville. "And, too, I wanted to go to a school close to home so my parents could see me play. I signed with Vanderbilt without seeing the campus."

Snake soon became a campus institution. He moved easily from the competitive atmosphere of basketball to a rigorous

John Ed and Snake, post-game
celebration

Shurig moves on Kentucky.

classroom regimen to a somewhat elite social environment, but was unabsorbed by any element during those years at Vanderbilt. Snake became his "own man." Like Schurig, his grade problems soon became public record as he vacillated between the Engineering School and the College of Liberal Arts, hoping to find the right combination of courses.

"The difference between 'Snake' and Roger," remembers one student manager close to both, "is that Snake usually went to class. And the professors loved Snake. He was entertaining company and they liked the way he played basketball. He got a lot of breaks with the professors—nothing any other student wouldn't get—but breaks nevertheless. I guess they liked his *attitude*."

With Super-Soph Lee at the pivot, Snake now played with abandon and soon developed a reputation as a "hatchet-man," even. "That's not nice," he smiles. "I'd like to think I was just sometimes *ungentlemanly*. I always had a good time out there. I always got along with the officials and chatted with them as much as possible. You could sometimes get a break that way; those guys are human just like everyone else."

Grace started every game while at Vanderbilt, all 76 of them. His "ungentlemanly" play came to a head in the 85-83 win over Kentucky his sophomore year. The Wildcat's Mickey Gibson had "crawled all over me all night and the officials missed every foul. So one time I figured I'd had enough. He jumped on me again, and I just gave him an elbow in a very sensitive area—he was out the rest of the game. The officials missed that one, too."

After the game, Wildcat star Cotton Nash tabbed Snake "the dirtiest player in the SEC." As with everything else about Kentucky, Grace was unimpressed.

Snake, John Ed, Schurig, Taylor and sophomores Keith Thomas, Wayne Calvert, Ron Green and, of course, Lee started the season with ten consecutive wins. The wire services took notice and shoved the Commodores into the top six teams in the nation, the highest ranking Vanderbilt had ever enjoyed.

The winning streak included a 97-92 overtime win over Duke, who came to Nashville ranked No. 2 in the country. It was an electric affair from the opening tipoff as the 7,000 fans were treated to Nashville's finest-played college basketball game to that date. Nearing the end of the second half, the two teams swapped baskets. Miller scored again and again from nifty layups and 20-footers from the top of the circle. John Ed seemingly had won the game in regulation time with a long jump shot, but

Miller's last-second shot beats
Kentucky.

Duke's Jeff Mullins responded with a goal at the buzzer to tie the
game.

Miller picked up the pace again in overtime as the Commodores finally defeated Duke. Miller finished with 39 points, a
career high. Lee scored 21 points and grabbed 26 rebounds (a
second record), and Snake added 16 rebounds to cap what Grace
later called "the greatest game we ever played during those
years."

After the ten non-conference wins, however, Vanderbilt
dropped the SEC opener to Tennessee in Knoxville, 57-55, as
several last-minute Commodore shots fell short. Lee dominated
Kentucky's Nash, and Vanderbilt won an important contest with
Kentucky the following Monday, Miller again scoring on a
last-second jump shot to win the game. Two more SEC wins and

The student section, 1964.

Vanderbilt re-entered the national rankings, but Auburn chilled the title hopes with an 81-63 upset in the little Auburn gym. Vanderbilt rebounded with another three conference wins, including a 111-73 smashing of a weak Alabama squad.

Georgia Tech won a controversial overtime game with Vanderbilt in Atlanta; the loss started a three-game slide that dropped the Commodores out of the championship picture. Tech withdrew from the conference the following year to seek greener financial pastures in football as an independent. Ten years later they would beg for re-entry into the SEC, unsuccessfully.

A 104-73 humiliation by Kentucky in Lexington was soothed only slightly by a closing 103-89 win over Georgia Tech, but the year had been one of optimism for the future. Impressive as sophomores and juniors, the group would return intact for the next season. Its 19-6 record included all six losses in conference play. The team had inaugurated the new Vanderbilt Invitational Tournament over the holidays and became its first winner.

Lee had been a first-team All-SEC performer and received honorable mention All-American honors, while averaging 19 points and 16 rebounds. Moreover, he had instantly erased any doubts by critics that he would be a formidable player by SEC standards.

Miller earned second team All-SEC honors and was the team's second leading scorer with a 17-point average. Grace had accepted a lesser role with Lee on the scene but still managed 11 rebounds per game.

Kentucky's national domination had been gradually eroded, and they proved a poor conference representative, losing early in post-season play. The Wildcats were no longer a sure bet to win SEC titles. Mississippi State had proved that over a three-year period, and now Vanderbilt was taking its spot as the No. 1 challenge to Kentucky's traditional prowess.

The Commodore basketballers had generated new support and fan interest. The *Commodore* prophetically stated that then freshman Clyde Lee, "the Nashville skyscraper," would someday build balconies in Memorial Gymnasium. SEC coaches were picking Vanderbilt as a pre-season favorite in '64-65 and the 6'8" Lee was a sure All-American.

All this was happening as Vanderbilt football was skidding to an all-time low; Guepe's last three teams won only six games while losing 24. He was replaced in 1963 by Jack Green, who then produced 1-7-2, 3-6-1, 2-7-1, and 1-8-1 seasons. Green, who like Guepe was also athletic director, enjoyed basketball and was a constant booster of the program. His gruff, militaristic West Point exterior belied a keen sense of humor and personal concern for athletes as young men.

"It really hurt to field such consistently losing teams," he once told a writer, "and I suppose the winning basketball program made us look that much worse. But I really loved those basketball guys and was just as excited as everyone else when they won."

As football seasons became less interesting each November, the rumbling chant—"I can't wait 'till basketball gets here!" grew louder. Before the '64-65 season opened, it was a roar.

24. 1965

Panty raids, Clyde's record, That Championship Season IV

Here I am at the end of the road and at the top of the heap.
—John XXIII, upon succeeding the late Pius XII
Time, 1958

"Before the season began, we set some goals for ourselves," recalls Miller, who was to captain the '64-65 squad. "We knew we had talent, good coaching and scouting, and most of all, we were very, very close personally."

Team "unity" is a mark of all great athletic teams, especially in basketball. Dissension will wreck a title contender quicker than any mechanical problem. The '64-65 Commodores were *close,* a sort of fraternity of winners. If a small personality clash threatened to become full-blown, it somehow disappeared in the course of a game and was never to be heard of again.

"It was kind of an unspoken understanding," said Miller, "that what counted most was winning basketball games and eventually the SEC."

Easy wins over Rice, SMU and Western Kentucky at home poised Vanderbilt for the top ranking in the nation after weekend losses by Michigan and Duke. The ever important top spot was not to fall to the Commodores, however, as they experienced a disastrous road trip, dropping close games to unheralded VPI and tough North Carolina. The guard play of Schurig, Miller, Thomas, and Calvert, so impressive late in the previous season and in early '64-65 games, simply disintegrated into incompetence.

"We were awful," remembers Thomas. "There we were with the Number One ranking in our pocket and we lose to VPI of all teams. I think our guards were about five-for-50 from the field during those two games."

A word about ratings: the Associated Press and the United Press International wire services poll coaches (AP) and sportswriters (UPI) to determine the order of merit for the week. This national recognition for those ranked high is important for several reasons. It gives the players some reinforcement if they are playing well, especially before crucial conference schedules begin; conversely, it provides added incentive to opponents who can "knock off" a top-ranked team. For coaches, ratings give their programs added visibility, and for independent schools it provides a better chance to be selected to one of the at-large spots in post-season competition. High school prospects become aware of the smaller colleges through ratings, and recruiters use this awareness to their advantage.

After the VPI-North Carolina debacle, Vanderbilt dropped out of the national rankings altogether, and the players agonized.

"But it helped us regroup and realize we'd have to play each game as it came along. We still felt like we were a pretty good team," said Miller.

Lee and Grace had played well on the raod and Snake's 26 points and 17 rebounds against North Carolina furthered the prediction that Vanderbilt's front line would be unbeatable.

The Commodores then won the VIT title again, beating Baylor and Oklahoma State. Miami of Ohio threatened to embarrass Vanderbilt in Nashville, leading by 14 points late in the opening half, but Schurig came off the bench to score 12 straight points, and the Commodores finally won, 74-68.

In the Sugar Bowl in New Orleans, Vanderbilt stopped Texas Tech 83-73 and then destroyed a supposedly strong Louisville team 80-47 for the title. Rewarded with a night on the town, the players scattered to the French Quarter to celebrate, returning to the Jung Hotel just in time to make a bumpy, four-hour, five-stop, hangover-ridden flight back to Nashville the following morning.

At 6 a.m. any unusual behavior attracts attention, but New Orleans airport workers were more than a little perplexed to see Roger Schurig take a long pass (with the Sugar Bowl title game ball) from Snake Grace, dribble a hundred feet or so down the lobby corridor, perform a beautiful "hook-slide" into a corner cuspidor, with manager John Tarpley calling him "Safe!" All this was done "under the influence," as they say. It was great to be a winner.

Celebration, 1965.

Wayne Calvert, the big "sixth-man."

Ray Mears brought his Vols to Nashville with a 7-1 mark, primed for victory in his second season at Tennessee. He had quickly become the SEC's most controversial coach. Running onto the floor to argue with officials, flamboyant gestures to his players and regular "walks" along the sidelines—these were, to Mears, just additional coaching tools.

"We have always done those crowd-inciting things with a purpose," he admitted in 1975. "It helps us get mentally ready for a game, especially in Nashville."

It didn't work for Mears that first game in '64-65, though. Tennessee built a nine-point lead midway in the second half, and their slow, deliberate play presented a catch-up problem for the Commodores. Suddenly, Lee and Thomas made quick baskets and Vanderbilt was back in the game, tied with four minutes to play.

To counter Mear's nagging ball-control tactics, Skinner installed a full-court press by the guards for the entire game. Incredibly, those guards—Miller, Schurig, Thomas and Calvert—did not commit a single foul in the execution of the press. Moreover, the team had only eight turnovers in the entire game (a "turnover" takes place when a team loses the ball without getting a shot).

Clyde scored 30 points, 12 of those during the four-minute second-half stretch in which Vanderbilt rallied to take the lead. For Lee it was an important game. Experiencing two losses to Tennessee his sophomore year, he yearned to beat the Big Orange.

"I can remember a particular moment in that game, vividly," said Clyde, reminiscing a decade later. "I took a pass on the base line with Red Robbins (UT center) guarding me. I started to pass the ball back out to the guards, but Schurig yelled—*Dammit, Clyde, take him!* I wheeled on Robbins and dunked the ball. It was a great feeling, and I think that really got me started. I beat Robbins every time after that."

Mears was upset, as he always was after a loss. F. M. Williams, the *Tennessean's* "UT man," reported Mears' displeasure the following morning:

"I find it hard to believe a team can press the entire game and make only 14 fouls, said the Vol mentor. It's a great defense if you can get away with it."

Kentucky was in the midst of one of its worst seasons that year, yet Vanderbilt traveled to Lexington after the Tennessee game ready for a difficult contest.

"Playing Tennessee is nice," Snake would say, "but Kentucky, that's *special.*"

The Commodores held a slim four-point lead at the half, but then something happened to Clyde and he ran amok, breaking Kentucky's defense to score 41 points, a new school record. That performance paced a 97-79 Vanderbilt assault, the most decisive victory ever over a Wildcat team in Lexington. Overshadowed was a splendid effort by forward Wayne Taylor, whose 14 points and seven rebounds kept Vanderbilt on top in the opening half when the rest of the squad was slumping.

Rupp was calm, praising the Commodores and Lee's spectacular individual effort. He was in the midst of one of his worst seasons at Kentucky, and Rupp, by 1965 slightly mellowed, recognized early that the '65 season was to be Vanderbilt's turn.

"They were a wonderfully talented team," he said. "And that Lee was just terrific. But then you've got to remember we were terrible all year."

These consecutive wins moved the Commodores back into the national rankings, as high as fifth in the nation when Vanderbilt then reeled off five straight SEC wins. Tennessee had had nine straight conference wins since dropping the earlier game to Vanderbilt. The Vols, with their best talent in a decade in Ron Widby, A. W. David and Red Robbins, hosted the Commodores in a critical SEC game in Knoxville.

Tennessee had prepared for weeks for this game; Mears had plastered numerous "psyche" posters throughout the areas where UT players moved. The stimulus was effective, for Tennessee caught Vanderbilt on a poor shooting night and won the contest, 79-66.

"Of course, we hated to lose that game," recalls Grace. "But it was like (Don) Knodel (Skinner's assistant coach) said in the locker room—*For Tennessee, that was their season. They will fold. We won't.*" Knodel was right. Vanderbilt did not lose another contest. Tennessee soon collapsed.

"It would have been easy to let up against Kentucky that next game," said Miller, "and that's what a lot of people thought we'd do."

Kentucky came to Nashville that season hoping to salvage some prestige and even possibly to shoot themselves back into a possible title race. They came out like Kentucky teams of old, streaking to a 14 point lead after only ten minutes. Vanderbilt was sluggish.

Kentucky-Vanderbilt games are as close to the pace of

Instructions, 1965.

professional basketball as can be found in the SEC. Both have traditionally been fast-breaking, shooting teams. With players in '64 like Miller, Thomas, and Lee for Vanderbilt and Kentucky's fine sophomores Louie Dampier and Pat Riley, a 14-point lead was good enough to win only if the game were over.

Again, it was John Ed who saved the Commodores. His two free throws with ten seconds to play climaxed a 91-90 win; Miller finished the night with 30 points and Lee added 33. Meanwhile, Tennessee was losing to Alabama.

Four games later, Vanderbilt wrapped up its first SEC season championship at Auburn with a 15-point win. As the team left the floor, word came that Tennessee had lost to Florida that night, thus sealing the SEC title for the Commodores. No hysterics, tossing of coaches in showers, etc.; Vanderbilt had simply done what it had set out to do earlier in the campaign.

Listening together to Larry Munson's radio broadcast that evening were four members of the '51 SEC tournament champions: Dave Kardokus, Bob Dudley Smith, Jack Heldman and

Gene Southwood.   They reveled in the win. Several thousand students swarmed Metro airport to await the team's return, traveling just like the '51 team—on a roof-hopping DC-3 aircraft. These overstimulated students also destroyed some property, raised hell with bewildered passengers waiting to *get out* of Nashville, and generally made life miserable for those Nashvillians not interested in such foolishness that crisp March evening. Earlier, these rowdies had even conducted a partly successful panty raid on the new women's dormitory. An assistant basketball manager, who had stayed in Nashville to monitor events, tried for weeks to find the owner of the flimsy material marked "Tana."

Five final SEC games were won with ease, and Vanderbilt finished the regular season 23-3, the most wins ever for a Commodore team. Moreover, the SEC schedule had been toughened by requiring that each team play every other SEC team, providing a true "round-robin" affair. Vanderbilt's 15-1 conference mark was the most decisive winning margin in 12 years.

To those accomplishments the '64-65 Commodores added a long list of additional records: Clyde's 41 points against Kentucky and 27 rebounds against Georgia, Thomas' field goal and free throw accuracy marks. In addition, *every* other individual season record fell.

"You never look at that stuff until years later, anyway," said Thomas. "Besides, by that time someone will have broken those records."

Winning seems to inspire a gracious attitude toward lesser statistical contributors. "It was a team effort," might be a coach's response, although his star scored 71 points, grabbed 33 rebounds and blocked ten shots. Have you ever heard a winning coach state that *Bronowski won that game. The rest were dogs.* Of course not. In Vanderbilt's case, however, the '64-65 season *had* been a "team" venture. Indeed, earlier in the year, the squad's depth prompted one reporter to observe that "if basketball were a nine-man game, Vanderbilt would never lose."

The '64-65 team had one "full-blown star," Clyde Lee; two "semi-stars" in John Ed Miller and Snake Grace; a "could-be-star" in Keith Thomas; a "fifth-man" in Wayne Taylor; "subs-that-could-start-anywhere-else," Wayne Calvert and Ron Green; and two others, Kenny Gibbs and the scholarly Garner Petrie. (Roger Schurig and Jerry Southwood left school after the first semester near the beginning of the SEC season).

140

After the first four, few remember the contributions made by the other six players that year. Taylor, as a regular starter, was an emotional, aggressive rebounder who had once scored 52 points in a high school game. "Mallard," as he was known, was the third man in the SEC's best front line.

"Pops" Calvert was Skinner's reserve ace. "He made the biggest sacrifice," says Miller. "He swung between guard and forward and had a lot of pressure as the only substitute guard after Schurig and Southwood left. He got so little recognition and deserves so much."

Green, the quick forward from Miami, was Taylor's backup and insurance against foul trouble for the other two big men. Gibbs was just beginning to mature as a player; his best season would come two years later. Petrie, at 6'9", lacked the basketball skills required for SEC play. He was instead the team "philosopher," more capable of wry commentary on the relevance of the game in modern society than of execution of the full court press.

The team left for the NCAA Mideast Regional tournament in Lexington as the nation's sixth-ranked team. Representing the Big Ten Conference was Michigan, national leader and bully-extraordinaire.

While waiting to play DePaul University the first night, Vanderbilt watched Michigan humiliate Dayton, as Cazzie Russell, Oliver Darden and Bill Buntin out-muscled their highly regarded opponents.

"I'm sure we were thinking about Michigan all through the DePaul game," recalls Miller. DePaul forced the game into overtime, but missed late free throws, and Vanderbilt finally won, 83-78. It was only the second time an SEC representative other than Kentucky had gotten this far in NCAA post-season competition. Vanderbilt's big chance had come.

141

25. Michigan

K. T. stops Cazzie, Munson almost loses control, down to the wire

We're eye-ball to eye-ball and the other fellow just blinked.
—Dean Rusk, during crisis with Cuba
Saturday Evening Post, 1962

Michigan was, in 1965, college basketball's most impressive team physically, outweighing the Commodores nearly 20 pounds per man. In their win over Dayton, Michigan had intimidated the losers with dunk shots and bruising rebounding.

Vanderbilt was, for sure, the underdog. A *Sports Illustrated* article the previous week had predicted little trouble for Michigan. Midwest writers saw the game as another easy win. As Vanderbilt players ate steak and eggs that afternoon, fans came to their tables to offer pre-game consolations.

To relieve some of the tension, Knodel chalked the Michigan players' names and statistics on a blackboard in the Commodore dressing room for the last minute strategy session. He knew that the most critical psychological problem facing the Commodores would be Cazzie Russell's 6'5", 230-pound frame against a much lighter, shorter Keith Thomas. As he came to Russell's name on the board, he marked in: *Russell—5'10", 125-pounds.*

That's just what I needed," recalls Thomas. "We were charged up, but you couldn't help but worry about Russell, this monster All-American I had to guard."

Thomas then turned in the game of his life and one of the most inspired performances ever for a Vanderbilt player. During the first half he continually fooled Russell defensively, taking the ball away from the Wolverine guard three times and causing

142

Tears in Lexington, March, 1965.

Russell to commit two charging fouls.

Halftime: Vanderbilt 38, Michigan 37.

Lee picked up four early fouls in the first half, and the Commodores appeared in trouble. Somehow Lee managed to avoid the disqualifying foul in the second half, while rebounding against a rugged Michigan front line.

Clyde's 28 points and 20 rebounds, Thomas' 21 points and Miller's 17 were *almost* enough. Vanderbilt had led most of the second half until Thomas picked up his fifth foul. Russell then blistered the Commodore defenses; Thomas' exit might have been the deciding factor.

With a minute remaining, Michigan had taken a one-point lead on Cazzie's jump shot. Then came the most controversial call in Vanderbilt basketball history. Miller found an opening in the foul lane and drove for the go-ahead basket. The crowd roared, thinking Vanderbilt was ahead with less than a minute to play. But then came that sickening motion—a rolling of the hands signifying a "walking" violation and nullifying Miller's basket. Michigan's ball. And the ball game.

The Commodres fouled in desperation. Michigan missed three straight free throws, but the balls bounced over Clyde and Snake and into the hands of Michigan players. Finally, Darden was fouled and made two free throws to put the game out of reach. Wayne Calvert made a long shot at the buzzer as Vanderbilt's final point, however impotent, of the season.

Final score: Michigan 87, Vanderbilt 85.

The 1965 Commodores, Southeastern Conference Champions.

(seated) John Ed Miller, Coach Roy Skinner, Coach Don Knodel, Kenny Campbell. (standing) Trainer Joe Worden, Garner Petrie, Bob Grace, Ron Green, Wayne Calvert, Keith Thomas, Wayne Taylor, Kenny Gibbs, Clyde Lee, Manager John Tarpley.

Skinner would not blame the loss on officiating. A look at the game film the following week seemed to vindicate John Ed. Another look in 1975 did, too. Miller had an unusual habit as he was about to cut in another direction or shift the ball to another hand—his feet moved quickly and, at least to one official, appeared to violate the "walking" rule.

After Michigan went on ultimately to lose to a quicker, sharper-shooting UCLA team in the NCAA finals, more than one writer observed that Vanderbilt would have been more equally matched with the Bruins, who were about to start their ninth-year title string. But talk is cheap . . .

That game remains one of Vanderbilt basketball's most exciting. Larry Munson's television and radio broadcasts gave Nashville fans a memorable evening as he almost lost control toward the game's end. Nashville sports pages would be dominated for days with "sidebars," various details about the contest.

For Miller, Grace, and Taylor, Vanderbilt basketball was now a memory. Taylor later finished Vanderbilt Law School and is, in 1975, a practicing attorney in Ohio. Miller joined the telephone company and is a personnel official with that utility in Birmingham. Snake Grace is now an executive with a Nashville steel supplier. The team's 11th man, Garner Petrie, later sought advanced degrees in theology and in visual sciences communications.

A championship makes for demanding fans. As the '65-66 season approached, everyone figured Vanderbilt's success would be repeated. Everyone except Kentucky.

26. 1966

Kentucky beats the zone, stops a repeat

I do not think that winning is the most important thing. I think winning is the only thing.
—Bill Veek,
President, Chicago White Sox, 1963

The 24-4 record of Vanderbilt's SEC champions had brought a season-long sellout crowd to Memorial Gymnasium, and the 7,000-plus seats were simply not sufficient to accomodate the growing numbers that would want tickets in '65-66.

The Balconies that Clyde Built were hurriedly finished in the off-season, a construction feat. The additional 2,000 seats were sold out almost immediately. Everyone came to see Clyde lead another title chase.

Lee was now an All-American on every selection that counted. Keith Thomas, chosen to the all-tournament team the previous season, was now charged with providing outside shooting strength. His "double-clutch" hesitation jump shot was uncanny.

Joining Thomas and Lee in the '65-66 starting lineup were guard Jerry Southwood, forward center Kenny Gibbs, and a sophomore forward, Bo Wyenandt. Immediately before the season, regular starter Ron Green had been bitten on the hand by Wayne Calvert in practice, accidentally, of course, and both were subjected to medication, although Green was lost for the opener. It might have been an omen.

An early win over Tennessee sent the Commodores into a nine-game winning streak, the last game a bone-wearying 113-98 shooting duel with Dave Bing's Syracuse team in the prestigious Los Angeles Classic Christmas tournament. Southern Cal stopped

Clowning in Disneyland: Thomas, Lee, Southwood, Green, Wyenandt.

the Commodores' winning streak, 74-72.

Meanwhile, Clyde and Thomas had been impressive. Southwood showed new maturity and was directing the game with growing authority. The sophomore Wyenandt was showing signs of becoming, like Roger Schurig before, one of Vanderbilt's most dangerous streak shooters. As the SEC season began, Vanderbilt was still the "team to beat" for the title.

The Commodores reeled off four SEC wins, the last coming over Tennessee in Nashville to sweep that series with the Vols. They then went to Lexington to meet a surprising, undefeated Wildcat team. The game was of national import, with Kentucky ranked first nationally and Vanderbilt among the top ten teams.

Kentucky had responded to the previous year's disastrous 15-10 mark as only the Wildcats were wont to do. "Rupp's Runts" lacked height (no starter over 6'5") but nothing else. Junior Pat Riley and Louis Dampier, later to become All-Americans and professional stars, gave Kentucky remarkable outside shooting prowess; and against Vanderbilt that first game in Lexington, they were unstoppable, winning 96-83.

While it was only one loss for Vanderbilt, the Wildcats were definitely in control from that point on. Later in the season Kentucky came to Nashville, and Dampier broke all Memorial Gymnasium scoring marks, the Wildcats winning with ease, 105-90. The game struck an odd note with the players and assistant coach Knodel, who explained:

"We worked hard the previous week preparing a man-to-man defense for Kentucky's great outside shooters. We felt we had the personnel to handle them that way. Well, just before the tipoff, Roy informed me that we would open with a zone defense. Well,

148

I could have gone through the floor. It just didn't make sense."

Southwood agreed. "We were fired up. We knew just what Kentucky's offense would be and thought we could stop it. When Coach Skinner told us we'd open in a zone defense, K.T. (Thomas) and I looked at each other and couldn't believe it."

"We did this often," rebutted Skinner, years later. "In the case of that game, I wanted to see how Kentucky would react to a defense they weren't expecting. No one could expect they'd come out and score about 20 straight points. Besides, I've never heard of anyone second-guessing a decision in a game where you got your brains beat that bad."

"You can always find excuses. I can't really fault Skinner, though," says Southwood. "After all, 22 wins weren't bad."

Yet the loss to Kentucky proved fatal to Vanderbilt's chances to repeat as SEC champions. The streaking Wildcats continued undefeated until Tennessee derailed them in Knoxville for their only loss of the season, the same day Mississippi State was putting a damper on "Clyde Lee Day" on regional television in Nashville. Kentucky ultimately advanced to the NCAA finals before losing to Texas Western.

The Commodores finished 22-4 that season and broke many of the records set the year before. Clyde was predictably named to every All-American squad, and Thomas was chosen to the Associated Press All-SEC team.

For Thomas, it had been a dream career. As a "borderline prospect" at Louisville Waggoner High, he was offered only a one-year scholarship from Vanderbilt and almost nothing anywhere else, for most recruiters were interested in a teammate, Paul Long. After Long turned Vanderbilt down, Skinner offered Thomas a full grant. He turned out to be Skinner's best "find" among unheralded high school players.

As a player, K.T. "shunned the limelight," but was an intense worker, overcoming a mediocre start his freshman and sophomore years to become one of Vanderbilt's best offensive players. His work in the '65 Michigan game won him pre-season accolades the following season as one of the SEC's two best guards (along with Dampier).

Thomas later was graduated with a Law degree from Vanderbilt and became an attorney with the U.S. Customs offices in Washington, D.C.

Wayne Calvert, another Kentucky native, also finished his four years at Vanderbilt. He had been the most important "sixth man" ever at Vanderbilt. He is, in 1975, a bank officer in

The bench, 1965. (Author is at far left.)

Nashville.

Ron Green, who blossomed into a regular player, was to travel to Israel as a member of the U.S. team for the Maccabia Games and later to play professionally in Israel. He is now an Atlanta businessman.

Assistant coach Knodel, credited by many players with personally supervising their development, was now ready for a head coaching position after five years under Skinner. Before the start of the '65-66 campaign, Skinner was offered the head job at Purdue, and Knodel had been tentatively informed that he was to be Skinner's successor. The University made Skinner's position at Vanderbilt more attractive financially, and Skinner sent Purdue his regrets. Knodel stayed on as an assistant for '65-66 but was now restless. Too, Knodel was disturbed with Skinner's change of plans in the Kentucky loss in Nashville, and that sealed his decision to leave.

The two coaches had worked well as a team, Knodel's effervescence and close identification as almost "one of the

150

guys" was a superb complement to Skinner's quieter, yet masterful, overall supervision.

One player who knew both coaches well described the relationship: "Knodel was everybody's buddy. And he was a hell of a scout. He'd go to a game and could come back and tell you how many times a player scratched his crotch; he was that thorough. But Skinner ran the show. Besides, Knodel had little success recruiting, an area Skinner was a master at."

Knodel took the head position at Rice, but after only sporadic success over nine years at this primarily football school in a strong football conference, Knodel quit the game in early 1975.

"I loved Nashville," he stated from his job with a Houston building contractor. "I guess Rice was a letdown after Vanderbilt. You can't make chicken salad out of chicken crap."

Gone, too, was Clyde Lee.

K.T. doing what he did best.

27. The Big Fish

Records, more records, Clyde Lee Day, and a place alongside Nate Thurmond

All animals are equal, but some animals are more equal than others.
—George Orwell
Animal Farm

Nine years and four months after he had been honored as no other Vanderbilt athlete had been, Clyde Lee flew into Nashville to look for a home. Not a house, but a *home*. It was a quiet return for the 31-year old alumnus who had made the Commodores a national power a decade earlier.

Clyde left school in 1966, without a degree, after a firm professor had found him a couple of points shy of a "C" somewhere. "That's the way it should have been," he remembered, recalling, too, that he had returned a year later to finish the work for his degree. "I was like a lot of athletes. I didn't realize what I had available to me from an academic standpoint. Too many movies during the week, cramming before exams, you know."

Clyde's "commencement" came earlier, in another way. Before the final college game against Mississippi State, he was the object of "Clyde Lee Day," a special moment in Vanderbilt athletic history. Although the Commodores lost the game, 92-90, on a sloppy play in the closing moments, an aura of sweet nostalgia fell over Memorial Gymnasium as the many accolades were read before the regionally televised contest. Trophies were presented, dignitaries summoned praise for Vanderbilt's all time best player.

Unaware that all this was to happen, Clyde prepared for the afternoon game just as he had for all the others. As he dressed, he saw what 12,000 others would find as they came to watch their hero in his final appearance. The *Banner* had dedicated its entire front page as a tribute to Clyde. The paper became a souvenir piece immediately.

Afterwards, Clyde accepted congratulations from dozens of admirers in the locker room and signed autographs for 4'-tall eight-year old future Clydes for the last time.

"It was a great feeling, a sense of relief that all that pressure had finally come to an end." he recalls. "I could have done more while I was at Vanderbilt, but I was pretty well satisfied. Most of all, I was ready for something new."

What Clyde had *done* was break every individual scoring and rebounding record at Vanderbilt, lead the team to an SEC title one season and national rankings all three seasons, earn All-American honors twice, and generally dominate play in the conference as few had ever done before.

Eight solid seasons followed as a professional with the San Francisco (later "Golden State") Warriors, culminating in an annual salary rumored to be near six-figures. During the '74-75 season, Clyde was traded to the Atlanta Hawks and then almost immediately to the Philadelphia 76ers. In 1977 he plans to retire to his new Nashville home, near his family and the close associations of his first 22 years.

"I never really thought much about going anywhere else," he remembers about his decision to attend Vanderbilt. "My parents and I really liked coach Skinner, and it was just a thrill to be recruited by Vanderbilt."

"I wish I'd known that," smiled Skinner, when reminded that Lee had resolved his decision so early after his high school senior year. "I went to a Lipscomb (High) game to see one of Clyde's teammates and wasn't impressed, but I liked Clyde and thought he was a real prospect, although most people didn't think he was.

"Clyde became the most unselfish player I ever had—he could have scored a lot more and gotten a lot more personal publicity, but he fit into our team situation perfectly."

"He was a real coach's player," recalls Tennessee's Ray Mears. "He always hurt us, and I was glad to see him go."

Clyde's teammates showered compliments on their friend and former leader. He was one of those individual performers that make sports wholesome and its heros important.

During his sophomore season at Vanderbilt, a news article

A classic combination.

reported that Clyde had once been confronted by a Lipscomb College coach, who encouraged him to stay at Lipscomb for his college playing days, instead of entering the larger, more pressurized Vanderbilt program.

"Clyde," said the coach, "if you go to Vanderbilt, you'll just be a little fish in a big pond. If you stay with us, you'll be a big fish in our little pond." The story's veracity is questionable, but it caught on with Clyde's teammates. He was "Big Fish" from that point on.

Vanderbilt's "railbirds" (local fans who regularly even attended practices) have always held that Clyde's quick development as a college rebounder and defensive ace could be attributed to Snake Grace's presence on those teams. Neither player completely agrees.

"The first time I saw Clyde," recalls Grace, "was when our freshman team played Clyde's high school team. I had a pretty good hook shot, you'll remember, and I tried two early hooks against Clyde. He blocked both of them."

"It was more of a case of Snake and I complementing each other," said Clyde, "a lot like Nate Thurmond (Warrior center) and I were at San Francisco. Teams couldn't afford to double team me, because Snake was so good he'd get everything off the boards.

"Schurig was more of an inspiration to me, always yelling at me to get off my butt and do something. Knodel worked with me individually and could really get everyone psyched up for a game. He had you thinking every team could potentially eat you up."

Clyde is close to Skinner, in whose summer camps he has worked since graduation. "He did what I don't think any other coach could have done," said Clyde. "He brought together a great bunch of guys that became close and played well together. His forte is making players feel good about playing basketball at Vanderbilt. Most guys would tell you that his easy-going way made it *fun.*"

There are no ribald Clyde Lee stories, as he was not the typical wild-eyed collegian. For most of his years at Vanderbilt, he lived at home with his parents and was deeply involved with his church; indeed, he was a lay minister and even performed wedding ceremonies.

"I was just a naive, innocent kid with a limited life experience," he said. "I certainly wasn't ready for San Francisco."

Eight years in the Bay City created a new Clyde, more

155

self-assured and worldly and, for certain, a more aggressive basketball player.

"I learned right away that I'd have to get tough if I was going to make it. My rookie season was a real initiation." Clyde did get tough and even developed a reputation as a "hatchet man" in his later seasons with the Warriors. One of the National Basketball Association's top offensive rebounders, Clyde now pushes, elbows, and knocks heads with the roughest of the NBA's forwards.

"It gets harder physically each year, though," he notes. "At 28 the aches came quicker and stayed longer. Now, at 31, it's even more so. And the young players coming up are much better in every phase of the game. I'll give it two more years."

Like most other former professional athletes ending high-paying, "glamorous" careers, Clyde faces a difficult adjustment when he does return to Nashville. Coaching is an appealing dream for Clyde, but how does one go from over $80,000-a-year to a $700-a-month job in the Nashville public school system?

"I'm not worried about the big bucks," Clyde remarked as he left for pre-season practice with the 76ers. "The main thing is to have a nice home and be productive in some way. My outlook and personal philosophies have broadened, and I think I can offer more than just basketball skills. Something will come along."

Vanderbilt would have other fine players, but the great athletes of the Seventies are of a different breed, more self-aware and streetwise to the ways of big time college basketball. The "innocent" 18-year old would become an animal of the past. Out of Vietnam, Kent State, Timothy Leary, Richard Nixon, the "Generation Gap," The "Credibility Gap," and the "Morality Gap" would come a new sort of college student, and consequently, a new kind of athlete.

Unquestionably, they don't make 'em like Clyde Lee anymore.

Blocking a shot.

The *Banner's* front page:

"Clyde Lee Day"

28. 1967-68

Bobby, Bo, and an unexpected run at the title

The only hope now, I felt, was the possibility that we'd gone to such excess with our gig, that nobody in a position to bring the hammer down on us could possibly believe it.
—Dr. Hunter S. Thompson
Fear and Loathing in Las Vegas

As the chartered bus made its way up U.S. 41 toward Bowling Green, the Boys on the Bus—the writers—played a game of their own: figure out how many games this short, untested group of 1966-67 Vanderbilt basketballers could possibly win. The consensus was 13 wins and 13 losses.

"The two earlier years were great, with Clyde and all those guys," recalls Southwood, then senior captain. "But for just getting the most out of only average players, you couldn't beat that bunch my senior year."

That bunch was Southwood, senior center Gibbs, junior forwards Bob Warren and Bo Wyenandt, a sophomore newcomer, Tom Hagan, and leading reserve guard Kenny Campbell. Reserves Gene Lockyear, Bob Bundy, Dave Boswell and Ronnie Knox completed a team that no one felt could finish among the SEC's first division at season's end.

Instead, the Commodores opened with a startling upset of national power Western Kentucky in Bowling Green, 76-70. That same evening a 17-year old freshman, Perry Wallace, became the first black athlete to play basketball in the Southeastern Conference. Perry's freshman team had also upset the Western freshmen, and as a worried Skinner prepared to put his Commodores on the floor, Wallace looked the coach in the eye and assured him the varsity would do *okay*. They both smiled.

Three wins, a loss to Duke, and another V.I.T. title preceded the SEC slate. Florida, boasting a front line that averaged 6'8" and figured to be a title contender, was upset in Nashville before Auburn topped the Commodores on the Road.

After an easy win over Alabama, Vanderbilt topped Kentucky, 91-89, in Lexington and returned home to beat Tennessee, 65-59. Four more conference wins put the Commodores on top of the SEC, but Florida won in Gainesville and Vanderbilt fell into a tie with the Vols. Two more wins and the Commodores made the trip to Knoxville and the year's most important game.

This was Tennessee's best team ever, with forward Ron Widby, 7' gargantuan center Tom Boerwinkle, and guard Bill Justus. They handled Vanderbilt easily that evening, 70-53.

Mississippi State destroyed Vanderbilt's last chance for a Cinderella finish, beating the Commodores in Starkville. Kentucky, suffering through a 13-13 season that year, caught the Commodores frustration in Nashville for their final game. The 16-point, 110-94 margin was the worst beating a Rupp team had ever experienced.

It had been a year for the fans. Winning in two overtimes and two double overtimes, the Commodores had been a pleasant surprise for Skinner, who had expected to agonize through a rebuilding year. Instead, Vanderbilt finished second in the SEC with a 14-4 mark and 21-5 overall. Most of their shooting accuracy records set that year still stand in 1975.

Southwood graduated and later became an accounting specialist for a Nashville steel supplier. He remains as one of Vanderbilt's "gutsier" competitors. ("My kind of player," said Ray Mears.)

The team's two junior starters, Bob Warren and Bo Wyenandt, gave Skinner a fascinating pair of scrappy, high-scoring forwards. With Hagan, centers Bob Bundy, at 6'9", and Wallace, at 6'5", and returning guard Kenny Campbell, the '67-68 team opened with four straight victories, including wins over nationally ranked North Carolina, Davidson and Duke.

As the Number Three ranked team in the nation, the Commodores won a road game in Gainesville to dampen Vanderbilt's national prominence.

A fourth straight V.I.T. title and another Sugar Bowl crown (over Michigan State and Davidson) poised Vanderbilt for the SEC race. Kentucky, the eventual title winner, beat Vanderbilt soundly in Nashville, followed by another Commodore loss to

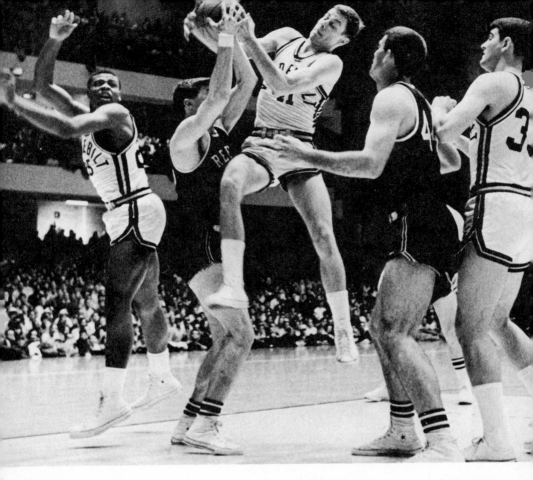

Wyenandt rebounding, Wallace (left) and Bob Bundy (right), 1968.

Tennessee in Knoxville. Four wins, another loss to Florida, and the Commodore's SEC championship hopes were gone for another year. Vanderbilt's win over the Vols in Nashville destroyed Tennessee's chances for a run at Kentucky.

Warren and Wyenandt graduated: Wyenandt finishing a disappointing senior year. Wyenandt had been, like Schurig four years before, an uncanny pressure player, winning several games on last-second, spinning baseline shots. He had perhaps more potential for greatness than any player before him at Vanderbilt. After a brief attempt at professional basketball, Bo entered his father's business in Cincinnati.

Bob Warren, on the baseline.

Warren, however, made the American Basketball Association, the NBA's rival (if not equal) league, his home for the next eight years. After playing on six different teams—in Los Angeles, Memphis, North Carolina, Utah, San Antonio, and in 1975, San Diego—Warren is a veteran substitute guard. What he'd like most, though, is to return to his hometown Hardin, Kentucky, and his farm.

"Professional ball is a game of breaks; you get in the right situation and you can play forever," remarked Warren from his motel room home in San Diego. Like so many constantly touring pro athletes, Warren's personal life went sour. It's no fun for a country boy who'd like to settle down.

"You do this three, four years and it becomes real work. And the ABA is so unstable, although it looks alright now. It's simply not as much fun as college ball. The crowds are so cynical. Everyone knows that loyalty is bought and paid for in this league."

Warren waxes nostalgic about his days at Vanderbilt. It is a normal "in the good old days" feeling that is shared by most former collegians, athletes or otherwise. Unfortunately, you can't freeze those carefree years and bring them back for those days of depression and frustration with the bitter moments of adulthood.

29. 1969

Peru and "sixth-man" Tommy-Gun

If you achieve success, you will get applause, and if you get
applause, you will hear it. My advice to you concerning applause is this: Enjoy it but never quite believe it.
> —Robert Mongomery to his daughter upon
> entrance into an acting career
> *Woman's Home Companion,* 1955

Skinner had taken the team to South America during the
summer of 1966. The trip was the first of three such overseas
jaunts Vanderbilt would enjoy over the next nine years. Several
years earlier, the coach had toured Taiwan, teaching and
lecturing through a special U.S. State Department exchange
program. The Chinese were impressed with Skinner's patience
and friendliness and referred him to a dynamic San Francisco
sports tour organizer, Chuck Taylor.

Taylor later arranged two trips for Vanderbilt, to South
America and in 1970 to the West Indies. These team junkets,
terrific recruiting incentives, are closely scrutinized by the
NCAA, which limits such trips to once every four years. Taylor
was working on an around-the-world journey for Vanderbilt in
1979 at the time of his death in 1975.

"Of course, you've got to have enough money to make the
plane fares," said Skinner, "and Vanderbilt has been awfully
good to us in that respect." Ironically, athletic departments are
well-known for curbing trivial expenses, such as extra socks or
towels, but fifteen coach seats to Hong Kong, no sweat.

The Making of a Star can take place in weird surroundings. In
the case of Tommy Hagan, as a sophomore in 1966, it was
somewhere in the Peruvian Andes Mountains. Skinner had hired

162

Tom Hagan: The pass.

two new assistants, Homer Garr and Bobby Bland, after Knodel's departure. Bland, the exceptional guard-captain in 1962, was to become a great favorite with players, but Garr was not so successful.

"We were sitting around down there in Peru that summer," remembers Hagan, "and coach Garr took me aside for a *pep talk.* He said, *Tom, if you work hard, you can be a great sixth man for Vanderbilt.* If I'd thought he was just trying to get me fired up for the year, that would have been one thing, but he was serious! What a thing to tell a player! I didn't come to Vanderbilt to be a *sixth* man."

Indeed he didn't. Hagan was a first team All-SEC player for all of his three years, a feat not even Clyde Lee had equaled. Hagan's 20-point career average was second only to that of Lee.

Like so many Vanderbilt players who contributed so much to the winning years, Tom Hagan was not a head-turning recruit. Not especially fast, Hagan made up for shortcomings with a deadly outside shot and what coaches like to call "quickness."

"Quickness," as opposed to "fastness," means not that a player might be able to run from point A to point B faster than others, but rather that his body movements are so responsive that he can fool an opponent with sudden spurts of motion. "Quickness" is just one of hundreds of vague tidbits of jargon known only to coaches, players, fans, and sportswriters, and not to the general public. And even these "insiders" don't always understand what they are saying.

For instance, a coach might brief a writer on a prospective recruit: He's got good hands and *quickness* and can go to the boards with the best of 'em. He's smart and coachable, too. A real competitor, he'll take it to you and beat you a lot of ways. He's a real player. We like him."

The writer *might* understand all that stuff, and when it comes out in the paper, the fan *thinks* he understands it.

During a disapointing 15-11 season in '68-69 (a seventh-place SEC finish), Hagan continued his scoring binges. He broke Lee's single-game record with a 44-point outburst against Mississippi State in the year's final game.

"We looked to Tommy for scoring," said earlier teammate Bob Warren. "He was a leader in his own way. Tommy didn't say a great deal, but he knew what he could do with the ball - he could shoot the eyes out of it!"

The year had been topsy-turvy with the usual assortment of high-scoring, ulcerating finishes. Against Kentucky in Nashville,

164

the Commodores led that year's SEC Champions by nine points with two minutes to play. The Wildcats pressed Vanderbilt's in-bound play so effectively that Kentucky stole four straight passes and scored on each to nearly pull out a win. The final score was 101-99 in Vanderbilt's favor, but the officiating was subjected to a terrific blast by Skinner and Hagan.

"Butch Lambert (one of the officials that night) was determined not to let me run up and down the baseline looking for an open man after they had scored each time. Well, of course, that's legal; and the next day Lambert apologized for making a mistake. It shows you how bad officiating can cost you a game. We won, but we almost didn't," remembers Hagan.

"Officiating in the SEC," says Tennessee's Mears, "is about as good as anywhere else."

Realistically, however, the game has simply become so fast and physically rough that most officials are simply unable to keep up with the pace. Moreover, there are so many requirements on officials to count time (the five-second ball-holding rule, the three-second lane violation, the ten-second back-court violation, etc.), that they are actually unable to officiate the more important points, such as slugging, elbowing, biting, pushing, and so on. College basketball officials are just as good as ever. That, however, is just not good enough.

Back to Hagan. He later joined the Texas Chaparrals in the American Basketball Association and then was traded to the Louisville Colonels. Although financially rewarding, Hagan's professional experience has given him few warm memories.

"I don't think I ever quite adjusted to the letdown of not playing every game as I did at Vanderbilt. Pro ball is sort of political - if you know the coach and the club is on your side, you'll do all right." Hagan remembers that the Chaps "tried about everything to win - platooning, using all black players, flipping a coin to see who'd make road trips, stuff like that. Not much consistency."

After an injury-ridden three seasons, Hagan left the ABA and returned to Nashville slightly bitter about the experience. Sadly, his private life had suffered from the unwholesome routine of travel in the ABA. Four nights, four cities, four games; home for a couple of days and on the road again. It was a broken record for Hagan and hundreds of others competing in what the American male thinks is the top of the world.

30. Perry Wallace

Fear and loathing in Oxford

Sometimes, it's like a hair across your cheek. You can't see it,
you can't find it with your fingers, but you keep brushing at
it because the feel of it is irritating.

> —Marian Anderson, on racial prejudice
> *Ladies Home Journal,* 1960

If a guy's got it, let him give it. I'm selling music, not
prejudice.

> —Benny Goodman, first conductor to
> integrate Negroes into a big-time band
> *Saturday Evening Post,* 1954

In the spring of 1962, Vanderbilt's undergraduate student
body held an unusual referendum. The issue: should the school
be racially integrated. At other southern colleges, there was no
need for students to vote; racial prejudice was a fact of life. At
least at Vanderbilt it could be openly debated.

Across West End in a modest home near Pearl High School, a
thirteen-year old black youth was reading the morning sports
page with pride. His idol, Wilt Chamberlain, had just scored 100
points in an NBA contest. "Man, that is all right," he thought.

Perry Wallace turned then to his trumpet practice, retaining
the glow of fantasy, thinking about big Wilt . . . *wouldn't it be
terrific to play basketball like that?* He had already taken up the
game as an awkward adolescent, but to even dream of big time
stardom—that was something else.

Three years passed and he spent more time with basketball and
less with his music. His coach, Cornelius Ridley, had been one of
the state's—even the country's—most successful black high school
coaches and had produced such aces as Vic Rouse and Les

Jumping.

Hunter, stars on the 1963 NCAA Championship Loyola (Chicago) team. Ridley soon began to appreciate Perry's quick intelligence and extraordinary jumping ability.

By his senior year at Pearl, Wallace had moved into the starting center slot. For Perry, the timing of this season was important. After the previous season, the Tennessee State Athletic Association voted to integrate its tournament for the upcoming school year. Prior to that, the state's all-black high schools had played among themselves, culminating in a state and even a Southern tournament.

Perry's senior season, 1965-66, produced the most powerful high school basketball team in the state's history. After playing mostly all-black regular season opponents, Wallace, Theodore (Hound) McClain, James Douglas and Walt Fisher awed white opponents and fans as they marched unbeaten—and almost uncontested—through a 32-game season, culminating in the state championship. They were so much better than their tournament opponents that rumblings were heard to the effect that the TSSAA had acted too quickly and embarrassed the other schools. But the barrier had fallen and Tennessee Prep basketball would be better off for it. The accomplishments of that Pearl team would not be repeated. Indeed, when full integration came several years later, the reservoir of great black basketball talent at the high school level would be spread among all schools.

Meanwhile, the Southeastern Conference had remained all-white, not surprising considering the following events in the Deep South:

In the summer of 1962, Mississippi Governor Ross Barnett blocked the entry of James Meridith as the young black man attempted to enroll in Ole Miss. Meridith, later in 1966 as an Ole Miss graduate, was seriously wounded by a gunman as he was leading a march on Jackson.

In 1963, Alabama Governor George Wallace repeated Barnett's act, this time at the University of Alabama. Again federal troops were called in to insure that a black student be enrolled in the public institution.

Three civil rights workers were murdered in 1964 by Klu Klux Klan members in Philadelphia, Mississippi.

In the spring of 1965, President Johnson dispatched 4,000 troops to guard 25,000 civil rights marchers on their Selma-to-Montgomery walk.

In short, racism was everywhere.

According to Skinner, Mears and Rupp, racial considerations had not prevented their schools from recruiting black athletes. They simply hadn't found the right ones. While the three northern members of the conference had always been more progressive socially, the coaches' statements were only partly true. Perhaps *they* wanted black players, but for the most part, black players didn't want them.

For Skinner, Perry Wallace presented the first real opportunity to break the color barrier. The time was right, too. Skinner had been assured—indeed was encouraged—by the administration that he could recruit black players.

Skill-wise, Wallace was a good prospect, if not a great one. The dunk shot was legal, and Perry could execute this move with such ease that opponents were humiliated with his jumping ability and strength. Moreover, with the graduation of Clyde Lee, Vanderbilt was sorely in need of additional rebounding strength and Wallace could provide that.

Skinner made his recruiting objective clear immediately and the race was on to recruit the 6'5", 225 pound articulate seventeen-year-old. His scholastic skills were sound, removing a factor which had often shut Skinner out of recruiting contests for both black and white players.

"I was primarily interested in Purdue and Northwestern," said Wallace from the Mayor's office in Washington, D.C., where he is a legislative aide, a Columbia Law School graduate heavily involved in urban youth affairs. "They had fine basketball at Purdue and a good engineering school, which attracted me. But an unpleasant thing happened while I was there which ultimately kept me from going to Purdue. Several of us were visiting the campus and played a pickup game in the gymnasium, just shooting around. Well, there were nasty accusations to the effect that Purdue had conducted a tryout for us (against NCAA regulations) and that put my trip in a very bad light."

"Besides, Vanderbilt was in Nashville, and that was home. My parents were certainly interested in that and, sure, there was a lot of community pressure to go to Vanderbilt and, you know, be the *first*."

Toward the end of the spring of 1966, with recruiting nearly completed, Skinner and the community waited anxiously for word from Wallace. The anxiety caused a local reporter to write a lead story to the effect that Wallace would sign a grant with the Commodores the following day, although the writer had not been informed that, in fact, Wallace had even made a decision. He sent the story "up," as they say in the business, and then sweated it out for a day as Wallace made his way back from Northwestern and his last visit. The reporter, and Vanderbilt, won out.

"I liked the small campus, the competitive academic curriculum, and Skinner—all those things, I guess, that attract most high school athletes to Vanderbilt," he said. "I didn't want to be just a number." There was little chance of that, for he immediately became a campus celebrity, of sorts.

"He worked hard as a freshman," said Skinner. "He had a long way to go offensively, especially with the outlawing of the dunk the following year, but he was a solid, intelligent player and I always felt he could contribute to our program." Skinner recalls limited negative pressure when he announced his intention to sign Wallace, a few petitions and phone calls, but little more. "His color just wasn't a consideration."

Through a remarkable freshman year, Wallace managed 20 rebounds and 17 points. He gave Memorial Gym fans their last look at the magnificently-executed dunk and began to adjust to the initiation process as the first black varsity player in the SEC. Trips to Starkville and Knoxville were marred with jeers—the redneck battle call of "nigger" piercing the playing atmosphere with constant regularity.

Perry recalls that at Tennessee, a group of orange-coated men in a section under the goal constantly baited him with threats of lynching and castration. "We gonna hang you up, boy!" came the cries. It was a low point for basketball in the state.

The actual rites of maturity were administered in Oxford the following season as Wallace, now a sophomore, met a hostile, racist Ole Miss crowd for the first time. "There were lots of things going on in my head during that game," he remembers. "First, I had been in a slump and had lost my starting position, then I took an elbow and got hurt during the first half. At the half I sat in the locker room bleeding, thinking about that crowd out there; I simply didn't want to go back out on the floor. The coaches and the team weren't much help; I suppose they really didn't know how to react."

"As I stood there in the doorway, everyone else ran out on the floor for the second half, and I knew that if I was going to make all this work, now was the time. I would have to make a comeback and I would have to do it myself."

Perry finished the Ole Miss game with 14 points and 11 rebounds as Vanderbilt disposed of the Rebels 90-72. It could have been a perfect "all's well that ends well" pivot for Wallace and Vanderbilt, but there were two more seasons and more road trips to places like Oxford. And it wasn't 1975, but 1968; times were different.

"There were various pressures that no doubt affected my performance," he continued. "From some whites there was a hope that I would fail, to prove whatever point they felt they could make. And in the black community it was expected that I would be a superstar, to prove their point that blacks could make it. I was always on the chopping block."

Skinner and Perry's teammates remember that Perry fit in well with the system, his quiet demeanor seemingly an internal fortitude to be drawn upon in difficult times. But in fact, he was turbulent inside. "They tried as much as they could, considering that there was no way they could really identify with what I was going through. It was insensitivity more than anything, and I can't really blame anyone for that."

He finished his sophomore year with a rush and a credible ten point and ten rebound average for the 20-6 Commodores. Wallace followed that with eleven points and eleven rebounds per game his junior season. He was not setting the SEC on fire, but neither was he a failure. Bob Warren roomed with Wallace on road trips and gradually grew close to his sensitive friend.

"I suppose we identified with each other's problems. I came from a small town background and felt alienated in many ways

170

Clowning.

from the Vanderbilt student body; and although this wasn't nearly as bad as what Perry had to face, we were attracted to each other by our problems." Wallace credits this close friendship with Warren as one of the bright aspects of his college career.

"He was simply a super guy," continued Warren, "and there was, I think, even some reverse discrimination among students and players. We probably bent over too far backward to make him feel like part of everything. It made him feel self-conscious when he really *did* just want to be treated like everyone else."

Wallace's senior year brought honors—second-team All SEC after an 18-point average and 14 rebounds per game, third best in the conference. On the campus he was chosen Bachelor of Ugliness, the students' highest recognition of achievement in all aspects of university life. Earlier players had won the title—John Ed Miller, Clyde Lee and Tom Hagan—but Perry was special. He was black.

To most community followers of the program and to University officials, it seemed ironic that the man who had reaped so many rewards from his years at Vanderbilt with never a public word to indicate unhappiness, would now speak up. To Perry, it was a natural, constructive emotion. "I had bottled up a lot of feeling through those years and felt that if things were going to get better at Vanderbilt for blacks, I should say something."

He met with *Tennessean* reporter Frank Sutherland shortly after his final varsity game and talked freely of his experiences. He had been lonely and had had little social life, and, although things had improved for blacks during those years, Vanderbilt—

171

and other schools—still had a long way to go in making the black athlete a real part of university life.

"Yes," recalls Wallace, "that's what I felt and I can't really regret saying those things. I suppose it closed some doors for me, and that's unfortunate, but sometimes you just have to speak out. Most of all, I just thought it would be good for everyone if I talked openly."

Sutherland, an aggressive interviewer, was surprised at the reaction his story would bring. "I figured it would make University officials mad, but they needed to wake up to reality. I did not, however, anticipate the community hostility. You must remember that during that period, from '66 to '70, things were different. People were more paranoid." Neither Wallace nor Sutherland regret the story's appearance, although Perry has expressed sorrow that his comments were taken as vicious stabs at his coaches, teammates and the town.

"Vanderbilt and Nashville were an important part of my life and I'm very grateful for the opportunity to experience those things—both good and bad. But you've got to be truthful. Don't all students—black and white—go through bad times and criticize what they consider to need change!"

If vindication is necessary, Wallace's critics must look at his active role in the subsequent recruiting of future black Commodore cager Bill Ligon and football defensive ace Doug Nettles. He was then, and still is, sincerely interested in the welfare of the University and its athletic programs. His personal sacrifice has helped smooth the paths of many later black athletes not only at Vanderbilt but also at all Southern schools.

Wallace, the school and town, and basketball have changed. Blacks populate all SEC schools in increasing numbers. With the overnight entry of black players at such Deep South schools as Alabama, Auburn, LSU, Georgia, and even Ole Miss and Mississippi State, the barriers (at least those related to athletics) have finally fallen.

It was a long time coming.

31. 1970-71

Immaturity, misunderstandings, The Thorpe Weber Years

Be careful that victories do not carry the seeds of future defeats.

> —Ralph W. Sockman
> Sermon of March, 1961

> ... *Sought by over 100 colleges after rating All-American his senior year ... Active in Methodist church work ... Likes steak and pizza ... Favorite sports star Rick Barry ... favorite TV personality John Wayne ... ATO fraternity ... Plays clarinet skillfully.*
>
> —Personal background description of Thorpe Weber in 1969-70 Vanderbilt basketball brochure

The 1969-70 season sent Vanderbilt's record to the losing side for only the second time in 21 years with only 12 wins against 14 losses. Perry Wallace, the team's only starting senior, finished a creditable career with an 18-point and 14-rebounds per-game average and second-team All-SEC honors.

In beating Kentucky, 89-91, for the No. 2-ranked Wildcat's only regular-season loss, Vanderbilt looked more like earlier teams but followed that win with five straight losses.

The year had begun on a note of sadness with the death of assistant coach Bobby Bland.

"Bland and Skin (Skinner) made a wonderful team," recalls John Russell, who had been one half of the great Bland-Russell guard combination in the early Sixties, and who later served as a freshman coach while he was in law school. "Bland was

Thorpe Weber hooks.

all-basketball, and that enthusiasm rubbed off on everyone. He would have been a great head coach someday."

Wallace, beset with many inner problems, was unable as team captain to provide the senior leadership to prevent the self-interests that would soon become a nightmare inside Vanderbilt basketball. The '69-70 and '70-71 seasons would later become known sardonically as the Thorpe Weber Years.

Weber came to Vanderbilt from Joplin, Missouri, as an extraordinary prize for Skinner. Weber had, in his estimation, 205 offers to play at schools across the country, including UCLA, Kentucky and Duke, top teams of the late Sixties.

"All those UK guys wanted to do was fix me up with wild women at beer parties," Weber would remember from his home in Little Rock, Arkansas, in 1975. "When I visited Vanderbilt, I asked to stay in the dorm to see what all the other students see. I liked the honesty of Vanderbilt."

After a four-year career marred by public criticism of his, and some of his teammates', immaturity and selfishness, Weber left Vanderbilt bitter and disillusioned, unsure of his own abilities

174

and character.

Indeed, almost five years after the graduation of the class of '71, Vanderbilt followers still place considerable blame for the 12-14 and 13-13 seasons from '69-70 on the shoulders of Thorpe Weber.

A prima donna? A self-centered troublemaker? A corrupting influence on his teammates?

Weber nearly refused to be interviewed in 1975, not because of any personal arrogance, but because the pain of recalling those years is not easy to bear. Amateur athletics is meant to leave one with a sense of competition, fellowship, and personal growth. With Weber, there is mostly sadness when he opens his senior *Commodore* and sees headlines attached to the dubious achievements of his 1970-71 team: "Mediocrity. Waste. Sickness."

Weber cannot rewrite his school yearbook to make it less disturbing for his grandchildren; moreover, he accepts much of the criticism as being correct. A successful businessman in Little Rock, Weber has long felt there was more to the Thorpe Weber Story than has ever been written.

Part of that story, told in late 1975:

"When you finally face the reality of having *really blown it,* you want to know why. I think it goes deeper—I mean the problems our team had—than just team dissension and misunderstandings with the coaches.

"During the first year I was at Vanderbilt, that would have been '67-'68, there was still a lot of support on the campus for athletics. After a game, you'd go to a fraternity house and everyone would be sitting around having a beer and talking about the game. It was very prestigious to be a varsity athlete.

"Later on a sort of negativism set in with the drug culture, protests against Vietnam, Nixon, and so on. Next thing you know, you're back at those same fraternity houses, and everyone is smoking dope and putting everything down.

"Most athletes were caught in the middle, wanting to be disciplined jocks on the one side and a part of the regular students on the other. It was awfully frustrating. The coach, for instance, wanted relatively short hair, which was all right with me, but the rest of the University had shoulder length hair. I know that's a small thing, but it represents what was happening then. The athletes were being set apart as *different* from the other students, and when the frustration set in, the players took it out on the coaches and their teammates. And the coaches just weren't able to relate to the players.

Tension in the locker room.

"All this was complicated by the fact that at Vanderbilt you can't just slide through like at some state schools, where athletes can put playing first and studies last.

"Early that senior year, we drew up a questionnaire for the players to speak their minds about the situation. We opened them with the coaches, and the personal despair that was shown was incredible. Things just got out of hand. We were simply too many chiefs and not enough Indians. I'll give you an example: earlier another player had come up to me and said, *Thorpe, you feed me and I'll feed you and we'll both become All-Americans.*

It's sad, but that was the kind of problem we had.

"I think I became controversial personally because I didn't play the *games* everyone expected—I mean the off-court stuff. When everyone was getting psyched up for a game, I'd be sitting five or six rows back during a freshman game eating a hot dog. That didn't look good to the fans, I guess.

"Also, I didn't give sportswriters the typical interview, saying the same old stuff that was good to print. Actually, I just figured that you played a game, you won or lost, and that was it. All this super-serious crying about a loss is baloney. There's more to life than that. I always gave it everything I had as a player. I *never* played without enthusiasm. The problem was that, once we had lost four or five games in a row, everyone began to play for themselves.

"I was a very conservative person, perhaps the most conservative on the squad—your basic, crew-cut, true-blue jock. We had a wonderful freshman year, a lot of comaraderie and fun. And we were good, too. Coach Bland's death was a terrible blow to all of us. He had done a great job of instilling a winning spirit in us. Where did it all go? Coach Garr and Coach (Ray) Estes were pretty poor replacements after Bland.

"We were immature and we were selfish. I think the coaches might not have done the best job in bringing us together, but I've got a lot of respect for Coach Skinner. He hasn't always had it so easy, and we didn't help."

Watching the varsity debacle that year was a different breed of freshman players: team players, possibly no more talented than Weber and his classmates, but determined not to let the mistakes of the past be repeated.

32. 1972-73

False hopes, a new set of winners

It is not only fine feathers that make fine birds.
      —Aesop
      Aesop's Fables, 4th century, B.C.

In the spring of 1968, a former Vanderbilt basketball manager was swatting flies in a Vietnamese guonset hut with his copy of Stars & Stripes. Although he resented the paper's "party line," he anxiously awaited its sports page each day. It had become his only link with sports in the U.S.

On the back page he saw an article which explained that Vanderbilt University had signed the tallest high school player in the country, seven-foot-four Steve Turner. It went on to say that this would probably make Vanderbilt a contender for the National title several years hence. Three years later the former manager returned from the Orient wondering why the Commodores were not winning the SEC with this superstar, much less the NCAA.

"Steve just wasn't the great prospect everyone made him out to be," Skinner would say in 1975. "We were pleased to get him, but he had a long way to go and people expected him to be an All-American right away. He worked hard with his game, but he had many problems in school. I really believe he was pushed into basketball at an early age because of his height."

After three frustrating years, Turner failed to meet scholastic requirements and was dropped from school. He moved home to Memphis, a construction job, and a chance to sort out his difficulties in adjusting to college life and basketball.

"He was going through tremendous changes," recalls Tom Arnholt, Turner's roommate for three years and one of the "Big

Five" freshman class of '68-69 that was supposed to give Vanderbilt another SEC title. The other three were Glenn Butler, Chris Schweer, and Jimmy Conn.

"Steve had had a football coach for a high school basketball coach and wasn't skilled in the fundamentals. He had come to Vanderbilt hoping to be successful, like we all had. But he was a very sensitive person; trying to beat something into him just wouldn't work. He was close to Bobby Bland, and after his death, Steve just didn't seem to develop.

"Besides, he was going through a 'love' stage and traveling back and forth from Jackson (Tennessee) to see his girl. All that didn't help, either."

That heralded freshman class never did live up to its "press." Arnholt, a superb shooter and ball handler, had only limited success after a sparkling freshman season in which he scored 51 points in one game. Butler finally left the team during his senior season after a mild training-rule infraction. Conn, a star infielder for Coach Larry Schmittou's perennially successful Vanderbilt baseball teams, signed a professional contract with the Los Angeles Dodgers after his junior year.

A note about High School All-Americans: In 1965, Lew Alcindor (later Kareem Abdul-Jabbar of professional fame) was recruited by UCLA after a highly publicized high school career in New York. He was the first such prep star subjected to a media blitz nationwide. Soon after that, the high school player became a marketable commodity, and everyone—magazines, soft drink companies, department stores, and many others—published and promoted a High School All-American Team for various purposes. By 1975, there were at least 12 such lists, each considered the *real thing,* "honoring" anywhere from five to 100 "All-Americans."

Realistically, it is impossible to compare the basketball skills of a player in, for instance, Georgia with one in California or Chicago. In short, these lists do not necessarily reflect player superiority but rather simply the statistical strength of a player in his own immediate area. Nothing more, nothing less.

Arnholt, Butler, Schweer, Conn, and Turner were high school All-Americans. So were several hundred others. When the "Big Five" were successfully recruited but later did not produce a title for Skinner, the coach came under considerable criticism.

A typical comment was "If Skinner could win with unrecognized players like Keith Thomas, Bob Grace, and John Ed Miller, then why can't he win with high school All-Americans?" Fans

Steve Turner dominating.

rarely actually look for answers; they just ask questions. It's an easy game that doesn't require much thinking.

The fact is this: Had the media been as attuned to the prep game before the mid-Sixties, then Thomas, Grace, and Miller certainly would have been "All-Americans." As it was, they were just normal players without the pressure of all that early publicity.

"We were pretty much spoiled by everything when we got to Vanderbilt," said Arnholt, in 1975 a commercial art director in Nashville, "a lot of superstars going through the culture shock of college and basketball competition with bigger and stronger players."

The 1971-72 Commodores set all that aside. Injected into the program was a new wave of sophomores who brought about immediate change. Led by Jan van Breda Kolff, this group took control immediately. Terry Compton, Lee Fowler and Bill Ligon joined van Breda Kolff as second year players, bolstered by the tough juniors, Rod Freeman and Ray Maddux.

During the previous years, Skinner had begun to feel the pressure of losing. Although there had been no overtones from the Administration about a possible dismissal, students, especially the campus publications, the *Hustler* and the *Commodore*, had been particularly rough on the coach. Students have short memories.

"There was a lot of pressure from within," Skinner recalls. "I always felt a real obligation to field a team that Vanderbilt would be proud of year after year."

Although the '71-72 squad was not a major success, (16-10), it represented exceptional progress in the rise out of the depths of the two previous years. There were four losses to Tennessee and Kentucky, but the squad had at least returned the VIT title to Vanderbilt after two losses the past two years. Also, they had scored over 100 points in six different games. The fans were back in the fold.

"Coach Skinner had segregated us as freshmen from the varsity while it was having all its problems," remembers Lee Fowler, a Columbia, Tennessee, native who had become Skinner's first signee for that team two years earlier. "I think he took us under his wing; we were winners and we were cocky, and I don't think he wanted to ruin that feeling. We even practiced apart from the varsity."

Compton, the "Long Rifle" from Horse Cave, Kentucky; Ligon, from Gallatin and the second black varsity player, (Godfrey Dillard had come to Vanderbilt from Detroit but never played varsity ball); and Fowler had accepted van Breda Kolff as their leader "from the first day of practice."

The 6'7" guard had "all the tools" to be a successful collegian, plus the right name. His father, Bill van Breda Kolff, had been basketball coach at Princeton, where he developed one of the game's best players of all time, Bill Bradley. He later became a professional coach in the NBA.

Skinner added Doug Bates, John Cattelino, Bob Chess, Hayworth Parks and Alex Thompson to the Fowler, Ligon, Compton, and van Breda Kolff combination, one of his best recruiting efforts.

The '71-72 squad gave Arnholt a pleasant farewell as a winner and as a scorer. As they warmed up for the final game against Mississippi State, van Breda Kolff instructed (a leader *instructs*, not asks) his teammates to feed Arnholt as much as possible, to make it his big game.

Arnholt responded, unaware of the conspiracy, with 33 points, his varsity career high. "That was the way I should have played all along," he said several years later.

The season was a frustrating affair for Rod Freeman, a tough 6'7" forward from Anderson, Indiana. Despite a painful ankle inury the previous season, Freeman had been a leading player, and he started the '72-73 season with healthy expectations.

The nagging ankle problem became a tragedy in mid-season however, and Freeman only saw action in half the games. His loss

181

was a terrific blow to Vanderbilt's otherwise excellent chances for a conference title.

The year had a warm tone, however, with the return of a much-matured Steve Turner. The young giant had left school the previous year and played for a sandlot team in Memphis. After an appearance with that team against the Vanderbilt B-team in Nashville, Turner sent the crowd an uncomplimentary sign amid much jeering. When he prepared to re-enter Vanderbilt the following year, Skinner was forced to seriously evaluate Turner's possible contribution—positive or negative.

"He had changed a great deal during the off-season," recalls Skinner. "We talked about everything and I decided that Steve could indeed help us. His attitude was very good."

Turner played out his senior year in an environment of winners—van Breda Kolff and his classmates—and graduated on a high note. Steve Turner, a creative, sensitive intelligent 24-year-old, is now a furniture craftsman in Jackson, Tennessee.

The '72-73 schedule opened with genuine optimism for the first time in four years. With the now junior-studded team and seniors Freeman and Maddux, Skinner produced another 20-win season. Their 13-5 SEC mark was only a game away from title-winner Kentucky, whom they had defeated, 76-75 and 83-76, in their two meetings.

Disappointing losses to Alabama at home and Auburn and Florida on the road prevented a possible championship. Alabama and Florida, however, had given notice to the SEC that year. C. M. Newton was developing, with the help of seven black players, an awesome lineup at Alabama. Florida, with the advantage of its tiny gymnasium, was becoming the league's most formidable "spoiler."

An impressive 86-74 televised win over Tennessee capped a satisfying comeback for Skinner and the youthful squad that was headed toward even more success before they would be graduated.

182

33. 1974

Getting one's mind on the game,
That Championship Season V

Success is that old ABC—ability, breaks and courage.
    —Charles Luckman
    New York Mirror, 1955

The '64-65 squad had established a precedent with their SEC title and for nearly a decade they were the example to be met, their feat a mark to be duplicated. Those balconies were the ones "that Clyde had built," and those scoring records were *his.* Subsequent teams lived in the shadow of the '65 champions.

"It was almost uncanny," remembers John Bibb, *Tennesseean* sports editor. "I was having coffee with the manager of the Springs Motel in Lexington where the Vanderbilt teams have always stayed when playing Kentucky. When that '73-74 team walked into the restaurant for lunch, I was overcome with the strange feeling that but for nine years this could have been Clyde's bunch."

After an early loss to Auburn the previous year, van Breda Kolff called his teammates together for a meeting, to discuss what was wrong.

"It's important to get your mind on the game," stated Jan, "especially on the road. Everyone is studying or something and unable to concentrate on the *opponent.* These meetings were important."

"They gave us a chance to build confidence and talk about the things we would have to do to beat the team we were playing," said Compton. "We simply weren't getting properly prepared before we started having the meetings. It wasn't a slap at the

The 1974 Commodores, Southeastern Conference Co-Champions.

(kneeling) Warren McSwain, Bob Chess, Lee Fowler, Jan van Breda Kolff, Mike Moore, Jeff Fosnes, Spence Young. (standing) Haworth Parks, Joe Ford, Butch Feher, Bill Ligon, Terry Compton, John Norton, Neil DeCourcy.

coaches - they were involved in strategy and so on, and we weren't meeting to gripe about anything like that. It was just that sometimes the coaches tended to forget some small things that players would remember."

"The fact is," recalls Fowler, "that we wouldn't have won the conference if it hadn't been for the team meetings."

The team opened with a flurry of December victories - Rice, Texas Tech, Nebraska, and cross town Tennessee State in the VIT, a squeaker over tiny Samford, Kansas, and Vermont.

While undefeated, the Commodores had not *slaughtered* any of these opponents, none of which were considered strong teams. Alabama came to Nashville early in January to truly test Vanderbilt for the first time.

The Crimson Tide had, over the past three years, grown into a conference contender - even a power - for the first time in 20 years. Ranked sixth nationally and undefeated, Alabama brought an impressive group to play also undefeated and 10th ranked Vanderbilt.

Sports Illustrated dispatched a writer to spend several days in Nashville before the game, billed as the most significant matchup in the country for that week.

His account began:

> There was a novel, thumping beat in Music City last Saturday night, but this particular Nashville Sound was neither nasal country & Western nor raucous strobe-light rock. The cacaphony was strictly of college basketball-Vanderbilt going against Alabama, a game played at a whirling rpm on the turntable of Memorial Gymnasium.
>
> By a critic's standards, the performance had everything—a surfeit of Southeastern Conference drama, big plays, rallies and enough action to tie slip knots in the tongue of the glibbest disk jockey. Vandy made more comebacks than Sinatra. Often the Commodores were moribund; their breath would not have fogged a mirror. But at each seeming demise they rallied, just as they had predicted they would.

The Commodores trailed the entire evening until sophomore Butch Feher made a layup with seconds to play, pushing Vanderbilt on top, 73-72. The finish had been frenzied, with Alabama's Ray Odoms missing a sure layup a minute earlier that could have cliched a 'Bama win. Feher then had missed the second shot of a one-and-one situation and Alabama rebounded, but Compton slapped the ball away and Feher finally made the game-deciding basket.

186

It was fitting that the SEC championship race would ultimately be decided by two extremely close games between Vanderbilt and Alabama. The Commodores had won at home, but that is an absolute necessity for a title run. Beating Alabama on the road would be the real test.

After another close win over Mississippi State, Vanderbilt traveled to LSU and suffered its first loss of the season, a fight-marred 84-81 decision.

Van Breda Kolff remembers the evening vividly. "I was trying to draw LSU into a charging foul after Wade Evans (LSU player) had gotten a rebound late in the game. It was the only way we could get back into it. Well, this guy ran over me, and the referee didn't see it. I got up and he ran over me again. Then Evans pushed me to the floor, and Collins Temple ran off the LSU bench and kicked me in the back. An LSU player sat on me as the fight really broke out. I'm grateful to him, he was trying to protect me.

"Actually, Temple had had problems like that before. During his freshman year he came off the bench and slugged a Tennessee player who was shooting a free throw, and that was in Knoxville!"

After the game, LSU coach Dale Brown denied any wrongdoing on the part of his players, even accusing van Breda Kolff of hitting Evans. No LSU apology was ever tendered. Baton Rouge was still football territory, so why couldn't their good ol' boys play basketball the same way?

The fracas had nostalgic overtones. Bob Dudley Smith, a member of the Vanderbilt tournament championship team in '51, had come to the game without a ticket from business in New Orleans. He managed to get WSM broadcaster Paul Eells to vouch for his credibility and accompanied Eells to the courtside press table to watch the game.

"I got so excited I just couldn't keep quiet," recalls Smith two years later, "Well, Waxo (Green, the *Banner* reporter) told me I would have to be quiet if I was going to stay on press row, since I was a *guest* there.

"What happened was actually Jimmy Davy's (*Tennesseean* reporter) fault, 'cause he was yelling at the officials, who were just awful. Hell, I figured, if he can do it, so can I.

"Then when van Breda Kolff got attacked by Temple, I sort of had a flashback to my high school days, when I remember Billy Joe (Adcock, Smith's teammate at West High in Nashville) getting hit by some opponent and just about beaten up.

"I just couldn't stand it. Something possessed me to jump over the table and help Jan. I always thought they just ejected you from the gym for that sort of thing. Hell, they put me in *jail!*"

Bob Dudley's misbehavior rejuvenated concern over crowd control in SEC gymnasiums. The fact that he had come not from the stands, but from the press table, made matters worse. Players fighting is a serious matter, but when over-excited fans get involved, an unfortunate incident can turn into tragedy.

Smith is an otherwise orderly, intelligent Vanderbilt alumnus. *What would happen if a bonafide maniac were to come onto the floor?"* The tension in a gymnasium during an important basketball game is one thing that makes the contest so exciting. That same crowd dynamism will also always pose a difficult security problem for college officials.

Vanderbilt bounced back with two easy wins, over Georgia and Auburn, the latter being a 96-51 destruction of the team that had been a thorn in Vanderbilt's side for years.

Then came the first of two incredible road victories over Tennessee and Kentucky. In Knoxville, the Commodores took an early lead, van Breda Kolff surprised Mears with excellent outside shooting, and Vanderbilt left Knoxville with an 82-65 win. It was the second worse drubbing Mears had ever experienced at home, the worst an 18-point Vanderbilt win in 1963. Mears and his players, obviously shocked by the Commodores' amazing performance in Big Orange Country, heaped praises on the winners.

After a home victory over Ole Miss, Vanderbilt moved to Lexington for a game against faltering Kentucky. The Wildcats had lost only seven times in 11 years in their Memorial Coliseum, the worst, again by a Clyde Lee-led team in '65, by 18 points.

The '74 squad was rapidly generating comparisons with the shadowy '65 champions, and at Kentucky the similarities became uncanny. After an unbelievable second half shooting percentage of 82%, Vanderbilt coasted to another 82-65 win. Van Breda Kolff had established himself as the SEC's most talented player, scoring 22 points, grabbing 12 rebounds and blocking 10 shots.

"In all my life," he told reporters after the game, "I have never played a better half of baskeball."

Florida was defeated in Nashville before Vanderbilt bussed to Tuscaloosa for its showdown with Alabama.

With one SEC loss apiece, Vanderbilt, now the nation's fifth-ranked team, and Alabama were playing, in effect, for the title.

In the final minute, free throws by Compton and Fosnes put Vanderbilt in front, and with 17 seconds remaining, Fowler had

188

Lee Fowler shoots in a crowd.

an opportunity to clinch the win at the foul line. He missed the first shot of the one-and-one, but seconds later forced a charging foul by Alabama's T. R. Dunn and made the free-throw to win the critical contest for Vanderbilt, 67-65.

"That team had poise," recalls Dudley Green. "They always seemed to be behind with about two minutes to play, but then always had just enough to win. They won a lot of games that way."

Vanderbilt managed to get by Mississippi State in Starkville, 60-59, and returned home to avenge the season's only loss to LSU. The problems Vanderbilt had had in Baton Rouge gave new

189

meaning to the return match in Nashville, and several Memorial Gymnasium rowdies heaped abuse on Temple, the first black to play at LSU. This was expected and tolerated by LSU's coach Brown, but a crank caller from off-campus put the second half in a different light with a threat to shoot Brown if he played Temple the second half.

Vanderbilt won the game, 91-88, even though both van Breda Kolff and Ford were unable to play at full speed due to illness. Van Breda Kolff was recovering from a collapsed lung, possibly caused during the fight at LSU weeks before. There were no incidences arising from the threatening call. Perhaps the security force had overreacted to the caller, but it was still a frightening moment for Vanderbilt officials. Brown, Skinner, and the game officials were informed of the call by security guards, but they were alone in this knowledge that somewhere in the stands there might be a demented gunman.

Basketball had traveled a long, not altogether healthy road since Naismith concocted the pleasant game 80 years ago.

Wins over Georgia at home and Auburn on the road made the Tennessee game in Nashville even more important than the usual intense rivalry.

Tennessee, with seven-foot center Len Kosmalski leading a specially-designed zone defense, won, 59-53, to regain some of the prestige lost after the trashing Vanderbilt had dealt the Vols in Knoxville. It was the only home court loss for the Commodores that year.

A win over Ole Miss, and Vanderbilt hosted Kentucky. During the contest, word was received from Gainsville that Florida had upset Alabama; all that was needed for at least a share of the SEC title was a win over Kentucky. Sophomores Fosnes and Feher catapulted the Commodores to a narrow, 71-69 win and a guaranteed trip to NCAA post-season competition for the first time in nine years.

A subsequent loss to the streaking Florida at Gainesville stifled the Commodores' claim to an outright SEC championship. The race ended in identical 15-3 records for Vanderbilt and Alabama, but the Commodores represented the SEC in the tournament since they had beaten the Crimson Tide twice that year.

But it *was* a title, and it had been a long time coming.

34. Marquette

Bad calls, no muscle, and the Horse Cave celebrity

The NCAA Mideast Regional appearance for Vanderbilt had all the makings for success and further advancement to the finals in Greensboro, North Carolina, the following week.

Notre Dame, the Mideast favorite, had been upset by Michigan in the opening game, and all the Commodores had to do was beat an equal opponent, Marquette, to face a weaker Michigan team.

Al McGuire's Marquette team was big and rough but not unbeatable. After trailing by ten points at the half, 40-30, the Commodores whittled away at the margin and actually tied Marquette twice, late in the game. Two controversial calls, or non-calls, by the officials seemed to destroy Vanderbilt's rally.

With Vanderbilt down by four points, Fosnes lofted a shot that appeared headed for two points, but a Marquette player knocked the ball away. It appeared, at least to the Vanderbilt partisans, to be a blatant example of goal tending, which should have given the Commodores the two points.

Then Marquette came down and scored on an obvious illegal dunk shot to put the game out of reach.

"I didn't *mean* to dunk it!" Bo Ellis would be quoted after the game, which Marquette finally won, 69-61.

The consolation game with powerful Notre Dame was a nightmare for the Commodores as they were unable to handle the Irish's muscle. Notre Dame ended Vanderbilt's remarkable season on a sour note, 118-88.

The accomplishments of the '73-74 Commodores were duly recorded and filed away. A second SEC championship and NCAA representation climaxed a long climb from the turmoil of the 69-72 seasons.

Terry Compton: the steal, 1974.

The sophomore combination of Fosnes, Ford, and Feher had proved to be so effective that all three were starters at season's end. Fosnes was named to NCAA Mideast Regional first-team tournament honors and was the team's leading scorer for the season.

The sophomore combination of Fosnes, Ford, and Feher had proved to be so effective that all three were starters at season's end. Fosnes was named to NCAA Mideast Regional first-team tournament honors and was the team's leading scorer for the season.

Dubbed the "F Troop" by the Banner's Green, they would return to lead two more Vanderbilt teams.

Fowler and Ligon became key players, not as starters, but in a reserve role. In several occasions, they consistently rejuvenated the Commodore offense with quick baskets or crucial rebounds, becoming a two man team of sorts.

"It was tough not to start," recalls Fowler, now an insurance salesman in Nashville. "Bill and I both wanted to play more, but we developed confidence in coming off the bench and winning games. 'Waxo' (Green) got behind us in the press and built an unusual sort of pride in our reserve status.

Ligon's playing years had not been completely pleasant. Bothered by his substitute role, he sometimes felt he was not treated entirely fairly. One of Vanderbilt's finest outside shooters, he considered a blast at the school and the basketball program. The frustrations of being a black man in a nearly all-white school rose to the surface, just as they had with Perry Wallace four years earlier. Ligon reconsidered, according to a close friend, realizing that a true perspective would come only after several years.

Ligon, after a year with the Detroit Pistons in the NBA, returned to Nashville in 1975 to seek entry into law school.

"He is closer to the basketball program than ever," commented one coach, who noted also that Ligon will assist the staff for the upcoming season.

With the departure of assistant coach Ray Estes in 1971, Skinner added Wayne Dobbs to his staff. Ron Bargatze had joined Skinner the previous season and, along with Dobbs, gave Skinner the type of complementing personalities and skills that had not been at Vanderbilt since Don Knodel had left in 1967.

Dobbs had once coached Nashville's Belmont College to a conference championship, even defeating powerful Western Kentucky in 1965. After four years at George Washington University, where Dobbs would learn just how de-emphasized sports can actually become, he returned to Nashville at Skinner's request.

"I was a GW two years before we could even get the department to wash our socks and give us a key to the equipment room," laughs Dobbs, once considered controversial in the conservative Belmont atmosphere. At Vanderbilt he blends well with the more liberal campus mood.

Bargatze had once played on a Dobbs-coached Belmont team and later became a high school coach in East Tennessee. Following a stint as an assistant at Tennessee Tech, Bargatze joined Skinner's staff.

Dobbs and Bargatze manage recruiting and scouting assignments which carry them across the country several times each year. Moreover, they must establish rapport with players.

"College players require a lot of time," stated Dobbs. "If you don't establish a personal relationship, you'll have problems."

Training rules have never been a major problem at Vanderbilt. The liberal policies of personal responsibility, as opposed to rigid off-court rules, has worked well with few exceptions. Additionally, new personal freedoms enjoyed by collegians as young as 18 years old required that coaches adjust more to the independent thinking of their players.

"I can't imagine a player putting up with a lot of silly rules like you find at some places," remarked Fowler. "It's an insult to order a guy into bed at a certain time and always watch him for infractions. It won't work, at least not at Vanderbilt."

The SEC championship in '74 had been a "dream come true" for Terry Compton, the senior forward who had once fantasized about one day playing for Kentucky. As a high school senior Compton had chosen Vanderbilt but was worried about his poor academic background. A high school teacher had told him he simply couldn't make passing grades at Vanderbilt.

"Coach Bargatze and I were sitting in a car outside my home in Horse Cave, and I told him I was worried. He assured me I *could* make it and help out the basketball program, too. I hate for someone to tell me I can't do something! Bargatze was a big influence on me."

Compton did make his grades, on court and off. Chosen as a second-team All-SEC player his sophomore year, he followed with first team honors his junior and senior seasons. He graduated with a degree in civil engineering and is, in 1975, working with a Nashville consulting firm.

"I wasn't much of a player when I came to Vanderbilt, " he remembers. "I couldn't jump, play defense, or handle the ball, and I was afraid to shoot."

Somehow those fears were assuaged; and Compton grew into a deadly shooter, with inside moves resembling the unorthodox styles of former Vanderbilt stars, Bo Wyenandt and Keith Thomas. His defensive skills improved to the point that he regularly made important game-winning steals.

"He was very clever," recalls the analytical van Breda Kolff. "He was not great 'straight-up' against a player, but he'd watch a guy, the way a guard passes to the forward, for instance, and then be able to judge precisely when he could make the steal."

Compton, Ligon, Fowler, Feher, Ford, Fosnes, and their leader, Jan the Man.

35. King of the Assist

Braces, Bill Bradley, leadership, and lots of money

The leader must know, must know that he knows, and must be able to make it abundantly clear to those about him that he knows.

> —Clarence Randall
> *Making Good in Management,* 1964.

"Mostly," recalls Jan van Breda Kolff, "I wanted a school where basketball was a more important sport than football. Of course, it would have to be a good school academically and have a fine basketball program. I felt that left me with Vanderbilt and Princeton, where my Dad had coached.

"There at Vanderbilt, there was terrific support, about 13,000 a game even when they were losing. That was impressive."

Vanderbilt probably devoted more money in air fare recruiting van Breda Kolff than any other player.

"I read about Jan in the Los Angeles Times and flew out there to see him play," recalls Bargatze. "After the game I met Jan. He was wearing braces and talked fast, an unusual kid. I asked him if he would visit Vanderbilt, and he sort of shocked me when he said *If it was good enough for Bill Bradley, it's good enough for me.* Bradley, who had played under Jan's father at Princeton, had been Jan's idol, and Jan knew Bradley had almost chosen Vanderbilt several years earlier.

"Lee Fowler had already signed with us, and when Jan visited, he and Lee hit it off right away. I remember him looking through Lee's high school scrapbook and saying *Wouldn't it be something to have two 6'6" guards playing together at Vanderbilt?"*

Bargatze would later return to Los Angeles, blow a few hundred athletic department dollars in the California sun, and

Jan the Man.

come home with van Breda Kolff's signature on a grant. They would prove to be dollars well spent.

"There was never a question as to who was the team leader from the first day Jan stepped on the court," remembers Bargatze. "He made the others feel bad about forcing shots, not passing to the open man. His leadership ability was incredible. Other than Clyde, he was the most important player Vanderbilt ever had."

After three years as a guard, van Breda Kolff was moved to center in the absence of a "big man."

"He never presented much of a problem at guard," recalls Alabama coach C. M. Newton, "but when Roy (Skinner) moved him into the pivot, he gave us real match-up dilemmas. When I heard early in the season that this had happened, I felt Vanderbilt would be tough."

"He was a typical great Vanderbilt player," said Kentucky's

Joe Hall, who was victimized four times with van Breda Kolff-led Commodore victories. "He was so versatile - he had a lot of freedom with his plays."

"I would have bet he'd never make it in college ball. He didn't even start for his high school team until he was a senior," said Dobbs. "He was one of those players that come to you on the ascent, sort of like Clyde, I guess."

Bargatze recalls that van Breda Kolff refused to lose at anything. "He and Compton were never beaten at Hearts (a card game) while we were on the road."

Fowler continued the testimonial. "He loved to make the assist; that was his way of becoming the very best, and he wanted to be recognized for it."

"Nothing he ever did surprised me," recalls Compton. "His understanding of the game was simply incredible. Jan would make suggestions about small parts of your game, like the way you were turning your wrist on a shot, or a matter of timing. He had that great family basketball background, and you could tell he had seen the best."

The tributes go on and on for the Leader. Chosen by the coaches as the SEC Player of the Year, van Breda Kolff was later drafted by the Denver Rockets in the ABA for a reported $500,000 over a five-year period. With that salary, he became the highest paid former Vanderbilt player.

After an injury-plagued year in Denver, van Breda Kolff was traded to the Virginia Squires, with whom he began preparations for the '75-76 season as a starting guard. Like Clyde Lee, Bob Warren, and Tom Hagan - other Commodores who have been a part of the professional game - van Breda Kolff yearns for at least one aspect of the college game.

"The crowds just aren't the same, not only in numbers, but they're not as vocal and enthusiastic. At Vanderbilt the students would pack in there two hours before a game. Now *that* is enthusiasm!"

The appearance of Jan van breda Kolff upon the Vanderbilt scene has given fans one positive controversy to resolve over the coming years - Who was better and/or more important to Vanderbilt teams, Jan van Breda Kolff or Clyde Lee?

Statistics cannot solve this sort of problem. Lee was certainly the more impressive player in the record books, yet van Breda Kolff's equally valuable contributions were simply more intangible.

What do you think?

36. 1975

The F-Troop and Skinner on the future of the game

In the winter of 1975, Vanderbilt sorely felt the loss of van Breda Kolff, Comton, Fowler and Ligon from the championship squad. Skinner faced a much stronger slate of conference opponents. In addition to Kentucky, Tennessee and Alabama, coaches at Florida, Georgia, and Auburn had been successfully recruiting and posed new problems for the perennial leaders.

Fosnes, Feher, and Ford were established "quality" players, and junior 6'7" forward-center Mike Moore had progressed rapidly the previous season. To these Skinner added four promising freshmen: guard Dickie Keffer, 6'5" forward Tom Schultz, and centers John Sneed (6'9") and Neil Bemenderfer (6'10"). The team's only senior, 6'8" center Bob Chess, provided experienced reserve strength. Chess was a quiet favorite among players and coaches; after graduation he would enter Vanderbilt medical school.

The key to possible success was quick maturity of the freshmen. While each rookie would have periods of excellence, that maturity never came. Vanderbilt sagged to a 15-11 season, 10-8 in the SEC for a fifth-place finish.

The year opened with four early wins over St. John's, VPI, Southern Illinois, and Texas Tech - all played in the warm atmosphere of Memorial Gymnasium. Frustratingly close losses to Southern California and Jacksonville in the Trojan Classic in Los Angeles followed, the latter loss of 107-104 double-overtime affair. Nebraska stopped the Commodores to complete a disastrous road trip.

After a home win to Middle Tennessee State, Vanderbilt began its 43rd Southeastern Conference schedule at Alabama. Eleven

Fosnes, Ford, Feher.

months earlier Tuscaloosa had provided a stage for one of Vanderbilt's greatest wins, which ultimately led to a Commodore share of the title. That loss had ruined Alabama's season, and they were determined not to allow a repeat in '75. Vanderbilt was crushed, 104-77. While it was only the first loss in the opening SEC game, the defeat was ominous.

A road victory at Mississippi State was followed by a pair of wins in Nashville over LSU and Georgia. A 3-1 SEC mark was soon leveled at 3-3, as Auburn and Tennessee each handed the Commodores four-point losses.

Vanderbilt went back on the road to defeat Ole Miss before watching its remote hopes for the title dissolve in Nashville as Kentucky edged the Commodores, 91-90. Gainesville continued to be rugged for Vanderbilt as the Commodores lost to Florida.

Hoping to serve at least as a spoiler during the final half of the conference season, Vanderbilt hosted powerful, nationally-ranked Alabama. The taller, more rugged Tide left Nashville atop an 86-72 win that could have been much worse for the Commodores.

Wins over Mississippi State and Auburn in Nashville and LSU and Georgia on the road kept vague hopes alive for a possible NIT bid should Vanderbilt upset Kentucky and Tennessee. But Vanderbilt lost both games - narrowly (75-71) to Tennessee and devastatingly (109-84) to Kentucky. It was against Vanderbilt in Lexington that Kentucky came of age in 1975. The Wildcats had been winning inconsistently through the year. In the opening half against the Commodores, Kentucky executed its offense with incredible ease and harrassed Vanderbilt incessantly with a pressing defense.

The win propelled Kentucky into an eventual tie with Alabama for the SEC crown; but because they had won both their games with Alabama, the Wildcats represented the Conference as champions. Kentucky eventually muscled its way to the NCAA finals against UCLA before losing to Johnny Wooden's last team.

It was the second consecutive season that Alabama had finished 23-4, shared the title, but lost the top berth to its co-champion. In 1975, however, Alabama received an "at-large" invitation under new NCAA tournament-broadening rules. Playing without enthusiasm, Alabama fell quickly to Arizona State in the Western Regionals.

The Commodores closed their season with a crowd-pleasing 102-83 win over Florida. Unable to defeat Alabama, Kentucky and Tennessee in any of its six games with the leaders, Vanderbilt was never in contention. The freshmen were forced into the fray against bigger, stronger opponents and gained valuable experience for later seasons. The F-Troop, with Fosnes and Feher as offensive leaders and Ford as the team 'quarterback,' gave Skinner a nucleus for rebuilding in 1975-76.

Fosnes moved into the following season in position to break several Clyde Lee scoring records and reap many post-season honors.

"Smooth." as he is called by teammates, is one of Vanderbilt's best outside shooters of all time. At 6'6", with exceptional jumping skills, Fosnes averaged over 22 points per game in '74, and was especially effective against zone defenses.

"His only weakness is concentration on defense," states assistant coach Bargatze. "He is a super offensive rebounder. If he played with intensity on both ends of the floor, he would be unbelievable.

"Feher is my favorite subject," says Bargatze. "He's *the* inspirational player, everything you'd ask for in a player. He's the perfect competitor. By that I mean he's a guy who wants the ball when you've got one second left. He's not afraid to miss. Butch simply plays himself out physically."

Fosnes, from Lakewood, Colorado, where he was heavily recruited for both football and basketball, and Feher, from Alpena, Michigan, were two unusual prizes for Vanderbilt.

"Jeff's father felt that he should attend a conservative, smaller school not on either coast," explained Bargatze. "We found Butch (Feher) through Jan van Breda Kolff, who had seen him play in a summer camp in Michigan. We sent him our standard recruiting form and later watched him play."

"After two minutes of warming up, I knew he would be a great player," recalls Wayne Dobbs.

Skinner is convinced that Fosnes and Feher are superior professional prospects. Fosnes, a serious student, might pass up the pro game for medical school. Bargatze compares Feher to Jerry West, one of the NBA's finest guards for many years.

Statistically, the '74-75 team was unimpressive, especially as rebounders. That factor may hold the key to success in '75-76.

"And we'll have to be a real *smart* team," states Skinner. "It's obvious we'll not be a strong rebounding team, so every player will have to realize his strengths and weaknesses and carry his load. Our offense is sound and it will take care of itself."

Maturity in '75-76 players John Sneed (6'9") and Carl Crain

(6'10"), both products of Nashville's Father Ryan High, may give Vanderbilt that edge at center. It must come soon, for with the graduation in '76 of Ford, Feher, Fosnes, and Mike Moore, the Commodore coaches will face the toughest rebuilding job in many years.

Roy Skinner has been there before, and he has learned to deal with the problems created by only average material. He has been through personal crises and a pair of traumatic seasons that tested his inner strength. Ordinary players, good ones, and even a few extraordinary performers have worn Vanderbilt uniforms under Skinner. A few have even been publicly critical of his technique, although most admit that his smooth handling of the program is its strongest point. Students have called at least once for his dismissal, as short-sighted youth is sometimes wont to do. Eager fans, some influential, question his every move during a mediocre season.

After fifteen seasons, he is basically the same person who replaced Bob Polk. "Skindo" remains open, candid, and friendly with all who enter his office, announced or otherwise.

He plays golf and tennis, drinks beer with a small group of close friends, and attends to the needs of his family.

With the '76 season opener only three weeks away, Skinner sat through a final series of questions for this book. For nearly a decade the writer has wondered about Skinner's seemingly shy demeanor toward people. Not an easy person to get close to, but impossible not to like, Skinner's smile is contagious. He *listens,* preoccupied only with the subject at hand.

He discusses the future of basketball at Vanderbilt.

Recruiting: "There *has* been a change. I saw it coming about ten years ago, when some high school players all of a sudden weren't happy with just a scholarship. They began to want to know what else you had to offer.

"There are other factors, too. The top players get so much publicity these days, it's very seldom that you'll go to a small town, say in Kentucky, and recruit a good player no one has heard of.

"The players are so much better. The good high school coaching and all the summer basketball schools have developed players faster. It used to be that a boy would learn to shoot at a rim in his backyard and get his coaching on YMCA or church teams. Now they are learning fundamentals the right way.

"Recruiting is such a big business—so many thousands of dollars are being spent on recruiting at the college level. You're

202

Feher over the Wildcats.

going to have flaws in anything that big.

"Violations sometimes happen when a coach gets his back to the wall after a couple of losing years and thinks the only way out is to have an instant winner. Then he tries to get top players at any price."

Rules: "It's incredible that there are no officials on the NCAA Rules Committee. The Committee is just not well informed as to the officials' view of the game. If it was, you'd see some of these counting (5-second ball handling, 10-second backcourt) violations removed.

"I'd like to see the dunk put back in. It's an exciting part of the game. And I'd like to see more experimentation with the 11-foot basket. Of course, a 30-second clock would help."

Growth: "I don't see any downhill slide in popularity. Even when we've had bad years, we've nearly sold out the gym. The fans feel a closeness to the players, feel like they know the players. They can read their lips even, and see the facial expressions. They feel a part of what's happening.

"There's no limit to how much players can continue to improve. Coaching will get better, there will be much more exposure. It's a great game."

203

37. The Administration

I find that the three major administrative problems on a campus are sex for the students, athletics for the alumni and parking for the faculty.

—Clark Kerr,
President, University of California
Time, 1958

If former Vanderbilt Chancellor Harvey Branscomb was a "conservative" regarding athletic growth, then present Chancellor Alexander Heard can best be described as a moderate-progressive.

A university administrator completely opposed to successful athletic programs is rare. Most simply do not want the intellectual stigma of being termed an "athletic president."

Chancellor Branscomb did not *oppose* sports; he simply felt that big-time competition, football especially, belonged at other schools, not Vanderbilt. In 1975, he is one of the most enthusiastic spectators from his lifetime box at Dudley Stadium and his seats in Memorial Gym.

After a distinguished tenure as Dean of the Divinity School at Duke University, Branscomb came to Vanderbilt in 1946, as the post-war boom was just beginning. He was a Reformer, and he began planning for change.

One early plan, although only conceptual, proposed that the entire Vanderbilt campus be moved 10-15 miles from the town. He was concerned about the role of fraternities and eventually managed to have all off-campus fraternities build smaller, new houses on the campus. He soon became known to students as the "De-emphasizer."

One of Branscomb's most intriguing plans came in the early Sixties, when his concern for Vanderbilt's future in the burgeoning economics of college football had become increasingly frustrating. To Branscomb the only answer, or at least one that was possible, was to leave the Southeastern Conference and form a new conference with schools of similar academic objectives.

"I contacted presidents, or their representatives, at several universities—Southern Methodist, Rice, Duke, Georgia Tech, North Carolina and Washington University (St. Louis). Each agreed to discuss the possibility of a new conference that would limit athletic scholarships and retain academic standards. We decided to meet in Atlanta." (A university official recalled years later that Tulane had soured on this idea to such a degree that they not only pulled out of the meeting, which was originally scheduled for New Orleans, but even petitioned Branscomb not to have the meeting in New Orleans for fear that Tulane would become identified with the attempt to leave the SEC.)

"Well," continued Branscomb, recalling the plan, "we each flew to Atlanta and registered in a hotel under pseudonyms for the secret meeting. Unfortunately, it was unsuccessful, because everyone had special worries about losing a natural rival, losses in attendance, and so on. It's too bad, I think it would have been a good conference."

Six years later, Chancellor Heard would address his Vanderbilt Trustees with alternatives for new directions in the athletic program. Some excerpts from that address in November 1967 are remarkable:

"There is a recurring ambiguity in the position of Vanderbilt—like that in the position of universities and colleges like Vanderbilt across the country. The ambiguity at Vanderbilt is between loyalty to the University's academic goals and standards, and the desire to win in the Southeastern Conference.

"This ambiguity runs through much the University does in this area. The alumni urge the same thing: win, but don't lower our academic standards or institutional reputation. Chancellors are accustomed to being caught in the middle, being asked to satisfy all aspirations simultaneously, whether compatible or not. When I see a chance of getting some clarity, I grasp for it. I hope we can work toward clarifying our ultimate objectives, toward getting a consensus among us as to what we ought and want to do.

"The result of all this is that the University—and, most personally, its Chancellors—have been caught in the conflict of purposes described earlier.

"I believe we have reached the point where we should openly acknowledge that issue and the fact that creates it. The fact is

Vanderbilt Chancellor Alexander Heard

that Vanderbilt is in the public entertainment business." A university has three traditional functions, oft cited: teaching, research, and service—i.e., as concerned with knowledge: transmitting knowledge, discovering knowledge, applying knowledge. Like many other colleges and universities, Vanderbilt has in fact added a fourth function to the conventional three rendered by a university. This "fourth function" is especially present with us because of Vanderbilt's place in the Nashville community, because of the popular interest in influential circles that certain of its intercollegiate athletic programs have commanded over the years, and because sports are the primary or only interest in the University many such persons have. If the University will openly acknowledge this "fourth function" and accept it for what I think in reality it is, an explicit function of a university, then Vanderbilt can better consider the alternatives that are open to it. These include, but are not confined to, the following:

(1) Vanderbilt can continue in its present ambiguous position without reconciling its conflicting objectives; if so, it will have much company. Vanderbilt is unique in the Southeastern Conference; it is the only private university and the only member of the Association of American Universities in the conference; all the other institutions are academically unlike Vanderbilt.

(2) Another alternative is to change the Conference itself, upgrade its standards.

(3) Vanderbilt could go independent—get out of the Conference. All who have dropped out—except the more recent ones, Georgia Tech and Tulane—have either joined another conference or wish to do so. The independent schools have encountered

206

scheduling difficulties, particularly in basketball. They have suffered from lack of player and student interest. The incentive to get out of a conference is usually financial. Vanderbilt does not have that problem. It has had increasing receipts. In the last 20 years the net operating football gate has nearly doubled; the net basketball earnings are ten times greater.

There is always the argument that Vanderbilt might lose alumni support by going independent. There is no real evidence either way—no clear-cut case. The ability of institutions to find outside financial support is infinitely more dependent on the quality of those institutions and on their trustee, faculty, and administrative leadership than on the presence or absence of intercollegiate athletics.

(4) The formation of a new conference. The difficulties are several. A major one is that of timing, getting simultaneous interest and availability. Another problem is loss of traditional rivalries.

(5) There might be support on campus for the next alternative: to abolish all grants-in-aid, putting intercollegiate sports on a purely amateur basis.

The University must consider radical and unfamiliar alternatives, too, if it wishes to get away from the ambiguous situation in which it finds itself. Two illustrations:

(6) It could propose in the Conference creation of an intercollegiate athletics degree, a BIA for example, (later the Chancellor said he preferred B.Ath.—Bachelor of Athletics) to make it possible to enroll "student-athletes" on an equal basis in all institutions.

(7) It also might abolish student teams and rent its facilities and name—the Commodores or Vanderbilt Commodores—to professional teams. Close identity with the institution could be achieved, better sports witnessed, and possibly some money might be made.

"The University must examine every conceivable alternative. I want the University in the future to agree on a course of action that is acceptable to itself and is publicly defensible."

Chancellor Heard's comments and recommendations were made in 1967. In the succeeding eight years, numerous advances would be made in the athletic program: two major gymnasium additions, the construction of McGugin Athletic Center, and numerous lesser expenditures.

It could be argued that these improvements have brought success: another SEC basketball championship, two conference titles in baseball, and a Peach Bowl football appearance. The Chancellor's statements are rendered obsolete; or are they?

The Vanderbilt athletic program is now a multi-million dollar effort each year—nearly $1.7 million for football and another $700,000 for basketball. The program showed an overall profit in 1975.

"We have at Vanderbilt the only semblance of the free enterprise system on the American campus," states athletic director Clay Stapleton, who candidly expresses some anxiety about the future of athletic economics not only at Vanderbilt but everywhere.

"Our dollars just don't go as far as before. At Vanderbilt we spend more on football than certain state schools; and, too, we must pay the University $645,000 each year for scholarships, an expense not so great at the state universities.

"Basketball at Vanderbilt is a delight to an administrator, but I can't help being worried about the possibility of lost revenues in basketball. We've gotten used to living off this, since the revenues from football have been about the same for a long time. If our basketball teams were to start losing, and the seats went un-filled, we could literally be thrown into a fiscal crisis."

Add all this to the primary problem of fielding a successful basketball team for the coming season, and Roy Skinner has *pressure*.

38. The Media

Poker, cigarettes, nostalgia

I like to get where the cabbage is cooking and catch the scents.
>   —Red Smith
>   *Newsweek,* 1958

The *working* press.

Bob Polk called them "an extension of our teams, as important to our success as any player."

Roy Skinner says Vanderbilt is lucky, for the press "has bent over backwards to help us. Without their cooperation we'd have had big trouble during the bad years. You should hear what some coaches around the country have to say about *their* papers."

Whatever they are, the men who have covered Vanderbilt basketball through the years are certainly well known, almost celebrities in their own right. Energetic, partisan, often highly subjective and critical, Nashville's sportswriters and broadcasters are a story by themselves.

The Vanderbilt press corps has enjoyed continuity. In nearly 30 years since Bob Polk "sold" them his plans for a competitive program, only three reporters and two broadcasters have had the Vanderbilt basketball "beat": John Bibb, until his promotion to sports editor of the *Tennessean* in 1970, followed by Jimmy Davy from that paper; Dudley "Waxo" Green of the Banner; Larry Munson of WKDA and WSM Radio stations, followed by WSM's Paul Eells in 1967. *Banner* sports editor Edgar Allen and, more recently, reporter Greg Thompson have also covered the Commodores sporadically, while Jeff Hanna of the *Tennessean* is an occasional contributor of Vanderbilt material.

Earlier in the century, the major games were usually covered in the sports pages. Besides the legendary Ralph McGill's articles, mentioned earlier in this book, other pieces appeared by the *Tennessean's* Blinkey Horn, another prominent sportswriter of the Twenties and Thirties.

Banner sports director Fred Russell succeeded McGill and produced basketball columns from several SEC tournament sites, as did the *Tennessean's* sports editor until 1970, Raymond Johnson.

With no known exceptions, none of these scribes ever played college basketball. Possibly the closest example of player-turned-reporter is that of Grantland Rice, who captained his junior class team to the Vanderbilt University championship in 1899, when no varsity existed.

Eells, dressed in a dapper, flowered shirt and a leisure suit for his evening broadcast, receives visitors in the tiny, noisy cubbyhole that serves as his office in the WSM studio.

"When I came in '67, the football program at Vanderbilt was in a state of total apathy, so I had a hard time believing what people told me about basketball," recalls Eells, whose "Holy Smokes!" exclamation has become a trademark for the University of Iowa graduate.

"I was shocked at that first basketball game, 12,000 people in there screaming, the press box going wild. It was incredible, and it was the best basketball I'd ever seen."

Eells' broadcasts are beamed to 15 stations "down the line," to an estimated audience of 60,000. A former Keokuk, Iowa disk jockey, Eells benefits from sophisticated technology on road trips, eliminating some of the mechanical problems that broadcasters once encountered. Sending the show back to Nashville and subsequently to listeners is as simple as dialing a phone call.

The *Tennessean's* Davy notes another change in coverage. "Players today are much more sophisticated about dealing with the press. Most of them have had a lot of publicity in high school, so it's not a new thing. It used to be that you had to protect a player from making a statement he'd regret. Now you have to protect yourself."

"Coverage is so much more personal, especially in basketball. I don't pay much attention to the implications of what I write about football, but basketball—everyone knows every player, it seems."

For over 20 years, Bibb and Green were synonymous with basketball at Vanderbilt. Traveling to every game, attending every practice, the two became a fixture; indeed, as Polk noted, a part of the team.

"Things were pretty rugged on the road in those early days," remembers Green, now in his fourth decade with the *Banner*. "and Polk didn't trust anyone, anywhere. Bibb and I had *assignments:* I kept the scorebook to make sure the officials were correct in counting fouls and so on, and it was Bibb's duty to watch the clock to see that the timer didn't lose a few seconds if his team was ahead."

Bibb and Green, both Vanderbilt alumni, grew close to Polk, sharing food, drink and entertainment on road trips. An early routine found the three gobbling 50 or 60 Krystal hamburgers after a game, recounting the event until the wee hours.

The intimacy of basketball travel became a relief from the rigors of covering football, especially during losing gridiron seasons.

"It was pretty loose then," recalls Green. "You'd finish a football season and there'd be two or three weeks before they'd start basketball. You had a chance to *recover.* Now (1975) they're playing football in late January and practicing basketball in early October. It doesn't make much sense."

As they became closely identified with the program, Bibb and Green presented a new dimension of camaraderie for Vanderbilt players. The "Bibb & Waxo" stories are endless.

"Polk didn't exactly like to see us with cigarettes," remembers Dan Finch, a star guard of the mid-Sixties, "so we'd have to bum them from Bibb and Waxo before practice. And then the doublecross came. We lost a game to somebody we should have beaten. I can't remember which team. So what do these guys write the next day? *Team Loses: Poor Conditioning to Blame* And we'd gotten all those cigarettes from them!"

"Hell, if we hadn't given them the cigarettes," laughs Green, seeking vindication, "they'd have thrown us down and *stolen* them! What were we to do?"

Bobby Thym, a forward of the same era, recalls nearly missing a team bus while trying to resolve a sticky poker problem with Green.

"I was sitting there with a full house, and Waxo raised me a quarter. I sat over that hand for 20 minutes trying to figure out whether to call him or not. *He was going to let me miss the bus!*" More than one player confesses to learning the rules of such games from Green and Bibb.

It was truly a remarkable example of friendship between

John Bibb at work, 1975.

Waxo Green at work; Singapore, 1969.

reporters on competing papers. In 1968, when Green was honored with a spectacular testimonial dinner at Belle Meade Country Club, Bibb served as master of ceremonies. Prominent figures from the golf world—Nicklaus, Palmer, etc.—were in attendance, for Green had established a national reputation as a golf writer. Bibb related one tale after another, and devoted a column in the *Tennessean* to his friend from "across the hall."

Later, after Bibb assumed the top sports position on his paper, the two would see less and less of each other. Bibb's horizons expanded, and a morning radio show now features his comments.

Bibb's quick witted, subtle sarcasm is a natural talent for radio. Each morning, thousands of Nashvillians are treated to the same sort of knee-slapping humor that Vanderbilt basketballers and coaches enjoyed with the Bibb-Waxo travelling show for years.

As he grew older and players seemed to become more serious about the game, and after Bibb's departure from the daily beat, Green became less like "one of the boys."

"Back then we (the reporters), were just about their age," he notes. "We were with them all the time. I've grown older, and they're still 19 to 20. Back then it was always *Waxo,* now it's *Mr. Green.* I'm not so sure we have as much fun as we used to."

Moreover, Green isn't sure if the "beat" method is the means for a newspaper to offer the best coverage.

"When you're around a beat so long, you don't always *interrogate* as you should. You tend to become more of a promoter and less of a reporter. Maybe you get *too* close, can't see the forest for the trees.

"Fans are more knowledgeable about the game. They want features, they want to know more about players personally. Statistics have become incidental."

As colorful as the Bibb-Green relationship, if not as long-lived, was the work of Larry Munson. He came to Nashville in the early Forties from Wyoming, with a remarkable voice that drew the listener into the game.

"I got a call one time from a guy who was sponsoring a new radio program in Nashville—a broadcast of Vanderbilt basketball," recalls Norm Cooper of the first broadcast Munson performed for Vanderbilt. Cooper was, in 1947, serving in his last season as an assistant to football head coach Red Sanders. "He told me to listen to this guy and let him know if he was any good. Damn! He put me right at courtside! I told my friend that I didn't know who he was, but he'd sure as hell better hire him."

Munson broadcast all home games for WKDA Radio and, for road games, utilized a bit of old-time media trickery to "bring the game back home for the fans."

Sitting behind a Western Union wire machine, in Nashville, Munson would read the score-by-score reports and translate these into "live" action for his listeners, turning up a "crowd noise" control to simulate the ambience of the arena.

"Of course, I'd fake a lot of it," he remembers. "I had no idea what sort of defense the other team would be playing, or the circumstances for a stolen ball or whatever. But I think that probably only about a third of the listeners ever knew we were doing it that way."

After three years of that sort of acting, Munson did go on the road, using a telephone hookup to send the game. His rousing technique and tendency to grow excited during the course of a game created a controversial following for Munson.

"I know I got involved," says Munson, "You wanted this team to win. I can remember many times feeling as if I was about to start referring from the press table; I'd give a description with a certain inflection, however unintended, and it would come out as a criticism of the official. And it was!" More than one otherwise-unaffiliated fan has been won over to Vanderbilt basketball through Munson's stirring accounts.

Munson, left WSM after a stormy history with management and became the announcer for University of Georgia football broadcasts and several professional basketball teams. He also has a fishing show for Nashville public television.

"I don't know how many times I've been flying back to Nashville after doing a late night pro ball broadcast in some Midwest town, and I'd be the only one on the plane at 4 a.m., snowing outside. I'd sit there thinking how great it was years before to be on the road with Vanderbilt. I can tell you, I *miss* it."

An empty scotch bottle sits on Munson's hearth. Inside it is a faded, yellow note, which reads:

> *Waxo Green, John Bibb, and Larry Munson killed this bottle on the occasion of Vanderbilt's first major college championship. Vanderbilt 79, Auburn, 64, March 1, 1965.*

For the working press, sentimentality runs deep.

214

The Author's All-Time Teams

1900-1947

Tommie Zerfoss
1916, 19 – 20

One of Vanderbilt's greatest all-round athletes; All-Southern end in football and an All-SIAA forward for the 1920 basketball champions. Though ruled ineligible during his senior year, the 5'10" Zerfoss was an accomplished ball handler and shooter even in 1920, when the game was only three decades old.

John McCall
1925 – 27

The floor leader, at 6'3", in the '27 drive for the Southern title, McCall was Vanderbilt's top rebounder and started the fast break. The All-Southern guard was also an intimidating defensive player who blocked numerous shots.

Jim Stuart
1925 – 27

Vanderbilt's first exceptional "big man", at 6'4", Stuart was an All-Southern center and high scorer for the 1927 tournament champions. Stuart was the cornerstone of Josh Cody's best team.

Willie Geny
1934 – 36

A 6'4" forward from Nashville, Geny was an All-Tournament team selection in 1934 and returned to lead Josh Cody's final three teams at Vanderbilt to 5-4-2 finishes in the SEC. Also an All-SEC football end.

Brant "Pinky" Lipscomb
1939 – 41

Vanderbilt's finest player of the pre-scholarship era. A two-time All-SEC tournament selection, Pinky set all tournament and school scoring records. Adolph Rupp calls Lipscomb one of the ten best players to ever face his teams, no small tribute for the 6'2" forward who made the jump shot a fixture at Vanderbilt.

1948-1975

Billy Joe Adcock
1947 – 50

Vanderbilt's first scholarship player was a good investment, indeed. Chosen to the coaches All-SEC two seasons and to at least one All-American team, the 6'2" forward was a prolific scorer, finishing a four-year career with a 14 point average. His 1,190 points still rank among Vanderbilt's top ten scorers.

Al Rochelle
1954 – 57

Possibly Vanderbilt's best ball handler ever, "Little Al" was an All-SEC guard for Vanderbilt's fine teams of the mid-Fifties. Averaging 16 points for four years, Rochelle still holds several free throw records.

Clyde Lee
1964 – 66

Vanderbilt's top player of all time. All-American, All-SEC and holder of two-thirds of all scoring and rebounding records, Clyde led his '65 team to the school's only unqualified title and a near win in the NCAA tournament. His 21-point and 16-rebound career averages will stand for years. The 6'9" center later became a respected professional player.

Tommy Hagan
1967 – 69

Three-time All-SEC guard, Tommy "Gun" Hagan became Vanderbilt's second highest scorer, with a 20 point career average, holding all the records Clyde doesn't. Freak injuries and unstable team management cut short Hagan's promising ABA professional career.

Jan van Breda Kolff
1972 – 74

SEC's Most Valuable Player during '73-74 championship season, van Breda Kolff had an exceptional understanding of fundamentals; a confident, inspiring leader on a team of diverse personalities. The professionals recognized all this, for van Breda Kolff later joined the ABA for a reported half-million dollars. That's a little over $1,000 per assist during his Vanderbilt years.

40. The Last Chapter of This Book

The real war will never get in the books.
            —Walt Whitman
            Specimen Days

How does one end all this?

As the last word falls on the page, it becomes dated, for Vanderbilt basketball did not die with the '74-75 season. But how alive is it?

Opinions vary among those supposedly in the know. Sportswriters generally cite the absence of a punishing 6'8" or 6'10" pivotman as the element Vanderbilt must produce to compete with Alabama, Tennessee, and Kentucky, each of which have become known as "physical" teams.

Others claim that Vanderbilt is having difficulty recruiting prominent black players, who seem to dominate conference play more and more with each passing season. Tennessee went to New York to lure its impressive sophomore center, Bernard King. Alabama has stayed at home to sign the top black prep players in that state.

At 44 years old, Roy Skinner has won 262 games for Vanderbilt, while losing 124, a record placing him among national leaders. He produced two Southeastern Conference championsips and a dozen contenders.

The basketball program generates nearly $750,000 in annual revenues. Memorial Gymnasium has been sold out through season tickets for eight of the past 11 years. The $300,000 annual "surplus" created beyond operating expenses will retire the debt on gymnasium improvements by 1981. Basketball not only carries its load at Vanderbilt, it shoulders an extra measure.

Dr. Dudley would have been shocked. Dr. Naismith would

have rejoiced. Somewhere in the misty afterlife of university officials and athletic coaches, the two are perhaps arguing the relative merits of football and basketball - Dudley never wavering in his defense of the "great outdoor contests;" Naismith promoting the speed and intensity of basketball. Old fans never die, they just move to a different grandstand.

The development of basketball has been phenomenal, more pronounced than any other sport over such a short time. Millions of youngsters will bounce a basketball for organized teams this winter. Many more will dominate their own fantasy world of the backyard game - each a Rick Barry, Jabbar, or even a Jeff Fosnes.

Faking a pass, you dribble to your right, now behind your back and to the left, completely fooling the imaginary defender. Burned you, you turkey! A jumper from the baseline - good!

Now a steal at midcourt, you drive to the basket with everyone screaming...you make the layup! You've singlehandedly beaten Kentucky!

Dyn-O-Mite!

Mister Basket...BALL!

Gimme the ball! I'm hot!

Cheerleaders, 1974.

Bibliographical Note

Instrumental in the research for this book were the following publications: *All the Moves, A History of College Basketball,* by Neil D. Issacs (Lippincott, 1975); *The Rupp Years,* by Tev Laudeman (Louisville Courier-Journal & Times, 1972); *A Brief History of Vanderbilt University,* by Robert A. McGaw (Vanderbilt University, 1973); and *Basketball's Hall of Fame,* by Sandy Pawde (Prentiss-Hall in cooperation with the College Hall of Fame, 1970).

Invaluable were past issues of the Vanderbilt *Hustler* and University yearbooks, the *Comet* and the *Commodore;* and past issues of the Nashville *Banner* and *Tennessean.*

Vanderbilt athletic department basketball brochures produced through the years by sports information directors Elmore "Scoop" Hudgins, Bill Stewart, Boo Odem, Ron Barnes, and Lew Harris were constant reference sources.

Photographs

Vanderbilt Archives 20, 32, 34, 42 (2), 47, 52 (2), 58 (2), 61, 176, 189, 192, 196, 206, 219; Vanderbilt Athletic Department 65, 70 (2), 80, 83, 86, 93, 105 (2), 112, 113, 144-5, 148, 163, 180, 184-5, 203; *Commodore* 38, 39 (8); *Comet* 23, College Basketball Hall of Fame 3; John Bibb 109; Bill Goodman 129; J. T. Phillips 131, 167; Frank Empson 132; George Tapscott 77; Roy Neel 100, 102, 212; Joe Rudis 174; Dale Ernsberger 171; Eldred Reaney 73, 139; Bill Preston 78; Robert Johnson 161, 199; Gerald Holly 118, 154; Jimmy Ellis 160; Jack Gunter 143, 150; Durward White 100; Bob Ray 90, 129, 136, 157; Charles Warren 136, 151.

Part Four
Records, etc.

The Players

The following is a list of Vanderbilt players through the years. The 1900-1951 names were derived from the Commodore; *those since that date from sports information brochures. We apologize for ommisions, especially the managers.*

Abernathy, Dick, "Ab", '30
Adams, A.G., Jr., '08
Adams, Alf, "Shug", '19,20
Adcock, Billy Joe, '48,49,50
Akin, Lewis E., '57
Arnhold, Tom, '70,71,72

Bailey, J.M., '18
Baird, Sonny, '42
Baker, Dave, '27,28
Ballenger, Ryan, '42
Ball, J.A., '46
Banks, Larry E., '59,60,61
Bartch, Hal, '68,69
Bates, Don, '57
Bates, Doug, '71,72,73
Bell, Alvin, "Pep", '21,22,23,24
Bennett, Erskin, '75,76
Bemenderfer, Neil, '75,76
Biles, Shelton, '44
Blair, Frank, '14,15,16
Blair, Frank, '46
Blake, C.B., '04
Blake, B., '07
Blake, D., '07
Blake, J.V., '08
Blake, R.E., '04
Bland, Robert R., '60,61,62
Bomar, Lynn, '22,23,24
Boswell, Dave, '66,67
Bridges, Frank, '26,27,28
Brock, Jack, '45
Brooks, Dan, '26,27,28
Brown, Enoch, "Nuck", '12,13,14
Brown, Manning, '22
Brown, Robert, '09,10,11
Brown, Tom, '12,13,14
Brubaker, Robert, '37

Brumbach, Charles F., '09
Bryngelson, Bill, '44,45
Buchi, Harold, '35
Buechlein, Charles A., '55,56
Bundy, Bob, '67,68,69
Burton, Robert E., '60,62
Butler, Glen, '70,71,72

Caldwell, W.H. Gerald, Jr., '55
Calvert, Roy Wayne, '64,65,66
Cammarata, Rick, '69
Campbell, Kenny, '65,66,67,68
Carloss, Matt, '34,35,36
Cattelino, John, '72,73
Chalfant, Bertram, '30,31
Chess, Bob, '72,73,74,75
Childs, Ralph A., '56
Clark, Jimmy, '51
Clark, Ray, '60,61,62
Clary, Ben, '02,03
Clary, J., '02
Clary, Lawson, '02,03,04
Cody, Joshuway, '15,16,20
Coffee, Shelby, '29,30,31
Coleman, Dave, '35,36,37
Compton, Terry, '72,73,74
Conn, Jimmy, '70,71
Cook, Charlie, '27,28
Corcoran, Tony, '42
Corman, George, '18
Coverdale, Jonas, '24,25
Covington, Connie, '18
Cowan, Gerald, '21,22
Craig, Mike, '48,49
Crain, Carl, '76
Cram, Donald, '28,29,30
Crook, Senter, '18,19
Cummings, Jim, '53

*(NFNA—no first name available.)

Cummings, John, '29
Cuninggim, Merrimon, '29,30
Curley, Pete, '34,35,36
Curtis, Bucky, '49

Dalton, John, '46
Davidson, Robert '13,14,15,16
Davis, George H., '54
Davis, H.W., '01,02,03
Davis, Joe, "Sticky", '41
Davis, Douglas P., '29
DeCourcy, Neil, '74,75,76
Dehoney, Homer, '43
Depp, William B., '59,60,61
Diffie, Jimmy, '45
Disharoon, '30
Dixon, Rand, '34
Doninger, John A., '60,61
Doyne, (NFNA)*, '31
Drace, C.G., '18
Due, Dan, '68,69
Duvier, Hank, '48,49,50

Elbert, (NFNA)*, '26
Embry, Slim, '22,23
Erwin, Roy V., '08
Evers, Bill, '45,46
Ewing, William M., '31

Feher, Ray, "Butch", '73,74,75,76
Feix, Bill, '52,53
Fields, Charley, '36,37
Finch, Dan, '52,53,54
Fiser, Warren S., '59,60,61
Floyd, Johnny, '20
Ford, Joe, '73,74,75,76
Ford, Turney, '38,39
Fortune, Chuggy, '33
Fosnes, Jeff, '73,74,75,76
Foster, Julian, "Jule", '31,32,33
Foster, Raymond, '23,24
Fowler, Lee, '72,73,74

Franklin, Adolph, '29
Franklin, Tom, '30
Freeland, E.Y., '10,11,12
Freeman, Rod, '72,73
French, James E., '56,57,58
Fridrich, Gerald, '53,54,55

Gambill, John M., '63,64
Gannaway, Herbert, '01
Gee, Billie Frank, '53,54,55,56
Geny, Willie, '34,35,36
Gibbs, Jo Malcolm, '54,55,56,57
Gibbs, Kenny, '65,66,67
Gibson, Roy M., '28
Gilbert, Mack, '29
Gilmore, W.L., '10
Gish, Bobby Lance, '62,63
Gleaves, Dick, '20,21
Godchaux, Frank A., '21
Godwin, Alex E., '31
Gore, Charles, '31
Govedarica, Ted, '75,76
Grace, Robert W., '63,64,65
Graham, Alvin, '33
Graham, Dick, '11
Graham, Ed, '42
Graves, Joe, '45
Graves, L.M., '16,17,18,19,20
Graves, White, '29,30,31
Greenbaum, Ralph M., '58
Green, Robert E., '64,65,66
Gregor, Robert M., '56,57,58
Griffiths, Ronald S., '61,62
Grossman, Thomas R., '53

Hackett, Walter, '37,38
Hagan, Tom, '67,68,69
Hale, John W., '59
Haller, Alex, '45
Hall, Glen, '07
Hall, Jerry Don, '60,62,63
Hambrick, David, '43,44

Hamilton, E.J., '03,04
Hanna, Ross, '38,39,40
Hardage, L.W., '12
Harlan, Bill, '38,39
Harrison, Charles E., '53,54,55,56
Heistand, Ed, '39
Heldman, Jack, '50,51,52
Henderson, Tommy, '31,32,33
Hendricks, Harvey, '18
Henry, Douglas, '11
Henry, James E., '57,58,59
Herring, Bucky, '51
Hines, Charles R., '63,64
Hinkle, Carl, '36
Hinton, Don R., '57,58,59
Holdgraf, Maurice, '40,41
Holland, Martin W., '58
Holman, Whit, '46
Horowitz, Arthur, '38
Hosbach, John S., '62,63
Houghland, Hubbard, '57,58
Howell, Joe T., '02
Howington, Jim, '07
Hudson, L.D., '03
Huggins, F., "Skinny", '32,33,34
Hughes, Russell, '13
Hunter, Ed, '37,38,39
Hutcheson, W.G., '13
Hyden, John, '40,41

Irby, Jack, '39,40
Ireland, Charles, '38
Ireland, Francis J., '30
Izard, George D., '11
Izzaguerre, Carlos, '44

Jarrett, J.H., '15
Jenkins, Jack, '41,42
Jennings, William R., '56
Johnson, John H., '63
Johnson, W.S., Jr., '60,61,62
Jones, Bob, '49

Jones, Grinnell, '01,02,03,04
Jones, Herbert, '11

Kardokus, Dave, '50,51,52
Keene, Jess, '26
Keene, Pete, '34,35
Keeton, James, '37
Keffer, Dicky, '75,76
Keller, William F., '54,55,56,57
Kelly, George, '49,50,51
Kilzer, Walter, '43
King, Red, '31,32
Kirkes, Leonard, '24,25
Kirwan, Patrick, '30,31,32
Klein, Louis, '62
Klyce, W. Henry, '12
Knox, Ron, '66,67
Kraft, Joe, '43,46
Kramb, Tom, '75,76
Kuhn, "Doc", '22,23
Kyle, Frank, '03

LaFevor, Bill, '68
Laks, Henry, '41,42,43
Lane, Bill, '49
Lanier, Sartain, '31
Lassiter, R.L., '18
Laurent, John W., '59,60
Lawrence, Bobby, '44,49
Lawson, Douglas, '44,45
Lee, Clyde W., '64,65,66
Ligon, Bill, '72,73,74
Lipscomb, B., "Pinky", '39,40,41
Little, Joe, '38,39,40
Lockhart, Eugene, '07
Lockyear, Gene, '65,66,67,68
Lowenstein, Louis, '28,29
Lowenthal, Jay, '76
Luck, J.M., '13

Maddux, Ed, '43
Maddux, Ray, '71,72,73
Malone, Charles, '46
Malone, William, '33
Manning, Ray, '37,38
Marsh, Earl, '30,31,32
Martin, Carl, "Zeke", '09,10,11,12
Martin, Willie, '26,27
Mason, James, '46
Mayes, Ralph, '60,70,71
Mayfield, George, '45
McBee, Dalton, '35
McCall, John, '25,26,27
McChesney, George, '50,51
McGehee, R.B., '09,10
McGuire, Bobby, '48
McKenzie, Tom, '52,53,54
McKibbon, Fred, '25
McSwain, Warren, '73,74
Meiers, Freddie, '23
Metz, (NFNA)*, '41
Mifford, J.A., '15
Miller, Cleo Maurice, '21
Miller, John Ed, '63,64,65
Miller, Marvin, '33
Milliken, John, '38,39,40
Mills, Chuck, '43
Moore, Mike, '73,74
Morgan, Walter, '12,13,14
Morrow, Garland, '18,19,20,21,23
Moss, Malcolm, '25,26,27
Motlow, Thomas, '01
Munday, Irvin, '48

Neely, W.D., '08.09.10
Nelson, Oscar G., '10,11,12,13,14
Newland, Bruce, '43
Nordhaus, George, '52,53,54,55
North, John, '43
Norton, John, '73,74,75,76
Norton, Roland, "Rolly", '19,20

O'Callaghan, Harry N., '26
Oliver, Bobby, '34,35
Oliver, Van, '69,70,71
Olsen, Julian, '41,42,43
Overly, Ken '34,35,36,37
Owen, Tommy, '42,43

Page, Keith, '76
Pardue, Howard, '34
Pardue, Tom, '43
Parker, L., '15,16
Parks, Hayworth, '48,49
Parks, Hayworth, '72,74
Paschall, A.B., '09
Patterson, R.M., '08,09
Patton, W., '03
Peebles, Mac, '40
Pentecost, Clement, '09,10
Perry, Alexander, '01
Petrie, Garner, '65
Pickens, D.R., '03,04
Pirrie, Jack Allen, '58,60
Pinson, T.W., '12
Pinson, William, '08,09
Plasman, Dick, '35,36
Porter, Slim, '24,26
Procter, J.B., '08

Ray, Felix, "Rope", '43
Ray, H., '16
Reese, Ernest, '01
Reese, Gil, "Gibby", '24,25
Reeves, Bobby, '48,49
Reeves, E.E., '23
Reyer, George W., '13,15,16
Rice, Lee, '44
Rice, Lee, '44
Richardson, Dave, '69,70,71
Richter, Harry, '41
Riley, William Joe, '53,54,55,56
Ringstaff, Don E., '61
Roberts, H.H., '16

Weber, Thorpe, '69,70,71
Webster, J.B., '07
Weiner, (NFNA)*, '31
Weise, Al, '51,52
Welhoelter, Art, '68,69,70
White, Bob, '52,53
Whitnell, W.M., '13
Williams, Dick, '48
Windes, Ken, '26
Woodard, F.C., '15,16
Woolf, E.L., '01
Wyenandt, Bob, '66,67,68

Yates, Douglas J., '57,58,59
Yates, Les, '69,70,71
Young, B., '31
Young, Spence, '74,75,76

Zerfoss, Tommie, '16,19,20

Individual Records

POINTS SCORED

Game: 130 vs Ole Miss, 12-22-70 at Nashville
Season: 2359 (28 games) in 1964-65 for 84.3 average
2,258 (26 games) in 1971-72 for 86.8 average

FIELD GOAL ATTEMPTS

Game: 120 vs Lipscomb, 12-8-52 at Nashville
Season: 2246 in 1951-52

FIELD GOALS SCORED

Game: 52 vs Ole Miss, 12-22-70 at Nashville
Season: 916 (28 games) in 1964-65

FREE THROW ATTEMPTS

Game: 59 vs Yale, 1-1-53 at Nashville
Season: 785 (28 games) in 1964-65

FREE THROWS SCORED

Game: 40 vs Texas, 12-20-54 at Nashville
Season: 594 in 1971-72

HIGHEST FIELD GOAL PERCENTAGE

Game: .657 (44-67) vs Cornell, 1-18-72 at Nashville
Season: .504 (834-1654) in 1966-67

HIGHEST FREE THROW PERCENTAGE

Game: 1.000 (16-16) vs Tennessee, 1-21-74 at Knoxville, (12-12) vs Kentucky, 1-28-74 at Lexington, (9-9) vs Tennessee, 2-23-74 at Nashville
Season: .802 (477-595) in 1973-74

REBOUNDS

Game: 90 vs Sewanee, 12-4-54 at Nashville
Season: 1466 (25 games) in 1963-64

AVERAGE REBOUNDS PER GAME

Season: 58.6 (27 games) in 1950-51
58.6 (25 games) in 1963-64

FOULS COMMITTED

Game: 30 vs Miss. State at Nashville, 1-13-62
Season: 582 in 1964-65

FOULS COMMITTED
(Both Teams)

Game: 60 Vanderbilt (30), vs Miss. State (30) at Nashville 1-13-62

AVERAGE FOULS PER GAME

Season: 22.0 (22 games) in 1953-54

MOST CONFERENCE GAMES WON

1964-65—Vanderbilt: Won 15, Lost 1

FEWEST POINTS SCORED
(Both Teams)

1938—37, Vanderbilt 16, Tennessee Tech 21 at Cookeville

Team Records

POINTS SCORED

Game: 44 by Tom Hagan (vs Mississippi State) 3-8-69, at Starkville, Miss.
Season: 631 by Clyde Lee, 1964-65
Career: 1,691 by Clyde Lee, 1964-65

FIELD GOAL ATTEMPTS

Game: 34 by Tom Hagan (vs Mississippi State), 3-8-69, at Starkville, Miss.
34 by Bo Wyenandt (vs Alabama), 2-20-69, at Nashville
Season: 516 by Clyde Lee, 1964-65
Career: 1,383 by Clyde Lee, 1964-65

FIELD GOALS SCORED

Game: 21 by Tom Hagan (vs Mississippi State), 3-8-69, at Starkville, Miss.
Season: 246 by Tom Hagan, 1968-69
Career: 633 by Clyde Lee, 1964-66

FREE THROW ATTEMPTS

Game: 19 by Al Rochelle (vs Georgia Tech), 1-9-56, at Atlanta
19 by Clyde Lee (vs Kentucky), 1-5-65, at Nashville
Season: 228 by Clyde Lee, 1964-65
Career: 610 by Clyde Lee, 1964-65

FREE THROWS SCORED

Game: 16 by Al Rochelle (vs Kentucky), 1-28-56, at Lexington; 16 by Butch Feher (vs Florida) 3-8-75 at Nashville
Season: 153 by Al Rochelle, 1955-56
Career: 425 by Clyde Lee, 1964-66

HIGHEST FIELD GOAL PERCENTAGE

Game: .909 (10-12) by Bill Ligon (vs Rice) 12-1-73
Season: .631 (108-171) by Bob Bundy, 1967-68

HIGHEST FREE THROW PERCENTAGE

Game: 1,000 (14-14) by Al Rochelle (vs Washington & Lee), 12-6-54; 1,000 (10-10) by Joe Ford (vs Kentucky) 1-27-75 at Nashville
Season: .918 (56-61) by Rudy Thacker, 1970-71

REBOUNDS

Game: 28 by Clyde Lee (vs Mississippi), 1-10-66
Season: 420 by Clyde Lee, 1964-65
Career: 1,223 by Clyde Lee, 1964-66

AVERAGE POINTS PER GAME

Season: 23.4 by Tom Hagan, 1968-69 (26 Games)
Career: 21.4 by Clyde Lee, 1964-66 (79 Games)

AVERAGE REBOUNDS PER GAME

Season: 15.8 by Clyde Lee, 1965-66 (26 Games)
Career: 15.5 by Clyde Lee, 1964-66 (79 Games)

ASSISTS

Game: 12 by Jan van Breda Kolff (vs Auburn) 2-24-73 at Nashville; (vs Georgia) 2-16-74 at Nashville; (vs Kentucky) 3-2-74 at Nashville
Season: 147 by Jan van Breda Kolff 1972-73
Career: 430 by Jan van Breda Kolff 1971-74

Leading Scorers

NAME	G	FGM	FGA	PCT.	FTM	FTA	PCT	REB	AVG.	PF	PTS	AVG.
CLYDE LEE												
1963-64	25	176	410	.429	119	176	.676	391	15.6	58	471	18.8
1964-65	28	239	516	.463	153	228	.671	420	15.0	74	631	22.5
1965-66	26	218	457	.455	153	206	.742	412	15.8	63	589	22.6
Totals	79	633	1383	.457	425	610	.697	1223	15.5	195	1691	21.4
TOM HAGAN												
1966-67	26	170	331	.514	103	132	.780	127	4.0	71	443	17.0
1967-68	24	161	333	.483	141	167	.844	106	4.4	72	463	19.2
1968-69	26	246	480	.513	116	133	.872	146	5.6	75	608	23.4
Totals	76	577	1144	.504	360	432	.833	379	5.0	218	1514	19.9
BOBBY THYM												
1953-54	22	110	276	.399	76	123	.618	199	9.0	80	296	13.5
1954-55	22	112	356	.315	128	177	.723	226	10.3	58	352	16.0
1955-56	23	118	298	.362	143	204	.701	242	10.5	62	379	16.5
1956-57	22	135	318	.425	106	171	.620	205	9.3	50	376	17.1
Totals	89	475	1248	.381	453	675	.671	872	9.8	250	1403	15.8
TERRY COMPTON												
1971-72	26	173	319	.542	109	153	.712	119	4.6	74	455	17.3
1972-73	26	191	388	.492	79	104	.760	137	5.3	88	461	17.7
1973-74	28	163	358	.455	89	102	.873	114	4.1	69	415	14.8
Totals	80	527	1065	.495	277	359	.772	370	4.6	231	1331	16.6
THORPE WEBER												
1968-69	26	138	282	.489	86	116	.741	213	8.2	100	362	13.9
1969-70	26	161	377	.427	86	131	.656	209	8.0	100	408	15.7
1970-71	26	174	390	.446	91	131	.695	251	9.7	94	439	16.9
Totals	78	473	1049	.451	263	378	.696	673	8.6	294	1209	15.5
AL ROCHELLE												
1953-54	8	10	36	.278	29	41	.707	25	3.1	11	49	6.1
1954-55	22	119	309	.385	117	157	.745	149	6.8	56	355	16.1
1955-56	23	134	345	.388	153	204	.750	151	6.6	33	421	18.3
1956-57	22	153	376	.407	75	96	.781	130	5.9	33	381	17.3
Totals	75	416	1066	.390	374	498	.751	455	6.1	133	1206	16.1
JIM HENRY												
1956-57	22	95	212	.448	101	151	.670	55	2.5	69	291	13.2
1957-58	24	182	393	.463	129	187	.790	81	3.4	88	493	20.5
1958-59	22	148	310	.477	118	150	.787	74	3.4	67	414	18.8
Totals	68	425	915	.464	348	488	.713	210	3.1	224	1198	17.6
BILLY JOE ADCOCK												
1946-47	14	67			26	47	.553			36	160	11.4
1947-48	22	144			88	129	.682			77	376	17.1
1948-49	22	130			79	125	.632			65	339	15.4
1949-50	25	112			91	141	.645			74	315	12.6
Totals	83	453			284	442	.643			252	1190	14.3

BABE TAYLOR

1952-53	19	95	276	.344	17	23	.739	41	2.2	54	207	10.9
1953-54	22	105	318	.330	62	74	.838	51	2.3	64	272	12.4
1954-55	20	137	384	.357	67	93	.720	71	3.5	58	341	17.0
1955-56	23	141	391	.361	42	57	.737	81	3.9	61	324	14.1
Totals	84	478	1371	.349	188	247	.761	244	2.9	237	1144	13.6

JEFF FOSNES

1972-73	21	69	129	.535	30	43	.698	72	3.4	26	168	8.0
1973-74	28	148	306	.484	58	79	.734	208	8.2	55	384	12.6
1974-75	26	238	432	.551	99	132	.750	234	9.0	65	575	22.1
Totals	75	445	867	.513	187	254	.736	514	6.8	146	1,097	14.5

BO WYENANDT

1965-66	26	127	271	.469	75	101	.743	177	6.8	69	329	12.7
1966-67	26	160	313	.514	75	101	.743	157	6.5	51	395	16.5
1967-68	26	124	289	.429	106	127	.835	173	6.7	78	354	13.6
Totals	78m	411	873	.471	256	329	.778	507	6.5	198	1078	13.8

DAN FINCH

1951-52	25	67	191	.351	58	96	.604	137	6.9	59	192	7.7
1952-53	18	124	351	.353	124	183	.678	247	13.7	58	372	20.7
1953-54	22	165	427	.386	151	211	.716	234	10.6	75	481	21.9
Totals	65	356	969	.367	333	490	.680	618	9.5	192	1045	16.1

PERRY WALLACE

1967-68	26	111	260	.426	30	60	.500	270	10.4	55	252	9.7
1968-69	26	135	308	.438	27	53	.509	274	10.5	39	297	11.4
1969-70	26	197	400	.493	67	87	.770	350	13.5	36	461	17.7
Totals	78	443	968	.458	124	200	.620	894	11.5	130	1010	12.9

Some statistics before 1950 not available

Civitan Club Sportsmanship Award

Year	Name	Hometown
1960—	Jim Henry	New Albany, Ind.
	Ben Rowan	Nashville, Tenn.
1961—	Larry Banks	Edwardsport, Ind.
1962—	Bobby Bland	Leitchfield, Ky.
1963—	Jerry Hall	Calvert City, Ky.
1964—	Clyde Lee	Nashville, Tenn.
1965—	Clyde Lee	Nashville, Tenn.
1966—	Keith Thomas	Louisville, Ky.
1967—	Bob Warren	Hardin, Ky.
1968—	Bob Warren	Hardin, Ky.
1969—	Tom Hagan	Louisville, Ky.
1970—	Perry Wallace	Nashville, Tenn.
1972—	Tom Arnhold	Columbus, Ind.
1973—	Terry Compton	Horse Cave, Ky.
1974—	Lee Fowler	Columbia, Tenn.
1975—	Bob Chess	New Concord, Ohio

Individual Honors

All-American Team

Year	Name	Hgt.	Pos.	Hometown
1965-66	Clyde Lee	6-9	Center	Nashville, Tenn.
1949-50	Billy Joe Adcock	6-2	Forward	Nashville, Tenn.

All-NCAA Tournament

Year	Name	Hgt.	Pos.	Hometown
1965	Clyde Lee	6-9	Center	Nashville, Tenn.
1965	Keith Thomas	6-3	Guard	Louisville, Ky.
1974	Jeff Fosnes	6-6	Forward	Lakewood, Colo.

SEC All-Tournament Team

FIRST TEAM

Year	Name	Hgt.	Pos.	Hometown
1939	Pinky Lipscomb	6-2	Forward	Nashville, Tenn.
	(High Scorer for entire Tournament with 42 points)			
1941	Pinky Lipscomb	6-2	Forward	Nashville, Tenn.
1951	Dave Kardokus	6-2	Forward	Evansville, Ind.

SECOND TEAM

Year	Name	Hgt.	Pos.	Hometown
1934	Willie Geny	6-4	Forward	Nashville, Tenn.
1936	Dick Plasman	6-5	Center	Nashville, Tenn.
1940	Ross Hanna	6-2	Forward	Nashville, Tenn.
1948	Billy Joe Adcock	6-2	Forward	Nashville, Tenn.
1949	Billy Joe Adcock	6-2	Forward	Nashville, Tenn.
1950	Billy Joe Adcock	6-2	Forward	Nashville, Tenn.
1951	Bob Smith	6-3	Guard	Nashville, Tenn.
	Al Weiss	6-4	Center	Chicago, Ill.
1952	Dave Kardokus	6-2	Forward	Evansville, Ind.

All-Southeastern Conference

PLAYER OF THE YEAR

Year	Name	Hgt.	Pos.	Hometown
1974	Jan van Breda Kolff	6-8	Center	Palos Verdes, Calif.

FIRST TEAM

Year	Name	Hgt.	Pos.	Hometown
1954	Dan Finch	6-3	Guard	Kirkwood, Mo.

1955	Al Rochelle	6-0	Guard	Guthrie, Ky.
1958	Jim Henry	6-0	Guard	New Albany, Ind.
1959	Jim Henry	6-0	Guard	New Albany, Ind.
1960	Bill Depp	6-7	Center	Edinburg, Ind.
1961	Bill Depp	6-7	Center	Edinburg, Ind.
1965	Bob Grace	6-7	Forward	Hopkinsville, Ky.
1966	Clyde Lee	6-9	Center	Nashville, Tenn.
1967	Tom Hagan	6-3	Guard	Louisville, Ky.
1968	Tom Hagan	6-3	Guard	Louisville, Ky.
1969	Tom Hagan	6-3	Guard	Louisville, Ky.
1973	Terry Compton	6-5	Forward	Horse Cave, Ky.
1974	Jan Van Breda Kolff	6-8	Center	Palos Verdes, Calif.
	Terry Compton	6-5	Forward	Horse Cave, Ky.

SECOND TEAM

Year	Name	Hgt.	Pos.	Hometown
1953	Dan Finch	6-3	Guard	Kirkwood, Mo.
1956	Clarence Taylor	6-1	Guard	Frankfort, Ky.
1957	Bobby Thym	6-1	Forward	St. Louis, Mo.
1957	Al Rochelle	6-0	Guard	Guthrie, Ky.
1960	Ben Rowan	6-4	Forward	Nashville, Tenn.
1960	Bill Johnson	6-1	Guard	Jeffersonville, Ind.
1962	John Russell	6-0	Guard	Webster Groves, Mo.
1962	Bobby Bland	5-10	Guard	Leitchfield, Ky.
1963	John Russell	6-0	Guard	Webster Groves, Mo.
1964	John Ed Miller	6-1	Guard	Union City, Tenn.
1964	Clyde Lee	6-9	Center	Nashville, Tenn.
1965	John Ed Miller	6-1	Guard	Union City, Tenn.
1965	Clyde Lee	6-9	Center	Nashville, Tenn.
1966	Keith Thomas	6-3	Guard	Louisville, Ky.
1967	Jerry Southwood	6-2	Guard	Evansville, Ind.
1967	Bo Wyenandt	6-4	Forward	Cincinnati, Ohio
1968	Bo Wyenandt	6-4	Forward	Cincinnati, Ohio
1968	Bob Warren	6-5	Forward	Cincinnati, Ohio
1970	Perry Wallace	6-5	Forward	Nashville, Tenn.
1971	Thorpe Weber	6-5	Forward	Joplin, Mo.
1972	Terry Compton	6-4	Guard	Horse Cave, Ky.
1973	Jan van Breda Kolff	6-7	Guard	Palos Verdes, Calif.
1974	Jeff Fosnes	6-6	Forward	Lakewood, Colo.
1975	Jeff Fosnes	6-6	Forward	Lakewood, Colo.

Vanderbilt Trophy

(For Best Free Throw Shooter)

Year	Name	Pos.	FTM		FTA	Pct.
1962	Bobby Bland	G	52	of	64	81.3%
1963	Roger Schurig	G	87	of	109	79.9%
1964	John Ed Miller	G	119	of	148	80.4%
1965	Keith Thomas	G	56	of	65	86.2%
1966	Keith Thomas	G	78	of	98	79.6%
1967	Jerry Southwood	G	61	of	77	79.2%
1968	Tom Hagan	G	141	of	167	84.4%
1969	Rudy Thacker	G	64	of	72	89.9%
1970	Ralph Mayes	G	48	of	59	81.4%
1971	Rudy Thacker	G	56	of	61	91.8%
1972	Tom Arnholt	G	81	of	91	89.0%
1973	Lee Fowler	F	51	of	67	76.1%
1974	Terry Compton	F	89	of	102	87.3%
1975	Joe Ford	G	94	of	112	83.9%

(For Best Rebounder)

Year	Name	Pos.	RB	Avg.
1962	Ron Griffiths	C	248	10.3
1963	Bob Grace	C	308	13.4
1964	Clyde Lee	C	391	15.6
1965	Clyde Lee	C	420	15.0
1966	Clyde Lee	C	412	15.8
1967	Bob Warren	F	219	8.4
1968	Perry Wallace	C	270	10.4
1969	Perry Wallace	C	274	10.5
1970	Perry Wallace	C	350	13.5
1971	Thorpe Weber	F	251	9.7
1972	Ray Maddux	C	278	10.7
1973	Steve Turner	C	203	7.8
1974	Jan van Breda Kolff	C	271	9.7
1975	Jeff Fosnes	F	234	9.0

SEC Sportsmanship Award

(Presented by the Tennessee Club
Based on Vote by League Players)

1965	John Ed Miller	....	Vanderbilt
1966	Clyde Lee	....	Vanderbilt
1968	Bob Warren	....	Vanderbilt
1970	Perry Wallace	....	Vanderbilt

Tournament Participation

NCAA (Won 1, Lost 3)

1965—Mideast Regional
Vanderbilt 83, DePaul 78 (ot)
Michigan 87, Vanderbilt 85

1974—Mideast Regional
Marquette 69, Vanderbilt 61
Notre Dame 118, Vanderbilt 88

SOUTHEASTERN CONFERENCE (Won 12, Lost 16)

1933
Vanderbilt 28, Tulane 25
Miss. State 48, Vanderbilt 36

1934
Vanderbilt 46, Georgia 29
Florida 24, Vanderbilt 23

1936
Georgia 42, Vanderbilt 37

1938
Vanderbilt 50, Alabama 26
Georgia Tech 50, Vanderbilt 18

1939
Vanderbilt 73, Miss. State 40
Vanderbilt 41, Alabama 33
Tennessee 34, Vanderbilt 31 (semifinals)

1940
Vanderbilt 46, Miss. State 36
Kentucky 44, Vanderbilt 34

1941
Vanderbilt 63, L.S.U. 49
Florida 47, Vanderbilt 41

1942
Auburn 36, Vanderbilt 34

1943
Tennessee 41, Vanderbilt 31

1944
Georgia Tech 63, Vanderbilt 51

1946
Tennessee 46, Vanderbilt 32

1947
Kentucky 98, Vanderbilt 29

1948
Tulane 67, Vanderbilt 53

1949
L.S.U. 60, Vanderbilt 56

1950
Tennessee 50, Vanderbilt 44

1951
Vanderbilt 88, Tennessee 52
Vanderbilt 70, Georgia 60
Vanderbilt 75, L.S.U. 63
Vanderbilt 61, Kentucky 57 (championship)

1952
Vanderbilt 61, Georgia 49
Florida 66, Vanderbilt 63 (ot)

CORN BOWL (Won 0, Lost 2) (Des Moines, Iowa)

1948
Drake 47, Vanderbilt 46
Dartmouth 64, Vanderbilt 52

SUGAR BOWL (Won 6, Lost 2) (New Orleans, La.)

1957
Maryland 71, Vanderbilt 56
Loyola (N.O.) 84, Vanderbilt 80

1964
Vanderbilt 83, Texas Tech 73
Vanderbilt 80, Louisville 47 (championship)

1967

Vanderbilt 73, Michigan State 63
Vanderbilt 80, Davidson 67 (championship)

1970

Vanderbilt 86, Cincinnati 83
Vanderbilt 92, Toledo 76 (championship)

ALL COLLEGE (Won 3, Lost 3)
(Oklahoma City, Okla.)

1949

Oklahoma A&M 62, Vanderbilt 61
Baylor 61, Vanderbilt 53
Vanderbilt 53, Alabama 44

1950

Texas 55, Vanderbilt 49
Vanderbilt 54, Baylor 53
Vanderbilt 56, Tulsa 49

SOUTHWEST CONFERENCE
(Won 1, Lost 2)
(Dallas, Texas)

1951

Vanderbilt 60, Baylor 53
Texas Christian 51, Vanderbilt 49 (semi-finals)
Texas 65, Vanderbilt 49

GATOR BOWL (Won 1, Lost 1)
(Jacksonville, Fla.)

1961

Virginia Tech 79, Vanderbilt 78
Vanderbilt 77, Navy 74 (3rd)

POINSETTIA (Won 2, Lost 0)
(Greenville, S.C.)

1962

Vanderbilt 60, Clemson 58
Vanderbilt 69, Furman 68 (championship)

LOS ANGELES CLASSIC
(Won 2, Lost 1)
(Los Angeles, Calif.)

1965

Vanderbilt 113, Syracuse 98
Southern California 74, Vanderbilt 72 (semi-finals)
Vanderbilt 94, Purdue 72 (3rd place)

TROJAN BASKETBALL
CLASSIC
(Won 0, Lost 2)
(Los Angeles, Calif.)

1974

Southern Cal 98, Vanderbilt 93
Jacksonville 107, Vanderbilt 104 (2 ot) (3rd)

VIT History

1963	First Round:	So. Carolina 75, West. Kentucky 60
		Vanderbilt 85, Memphis St. 79
	Consolation Game:	Memphis St. 88, West. Kentucky 83
	Championship Game:	Vanderbilt 106, So. Caroline 78
1964	First Round:	Oklahoma St. 60, Florida St. 56
		Vanderbilt 97, Baylor 78
	Consolation Game:	Florida St. 82, Baylor 64
	Championship Game:	Vanderbilt 60, Oklahoma St. 58

1965	First Round:	West. Kentucky 82, SMU 68
		Vanderbilt 71, Army 68
	Consolation Game:	Army 64, SMU 51
	Championship Game:	Vanderbilt 72, West. Kentucky 69

1966	First Round:	LaSalle 99, Nebraska 76
		Vanderbilt 98, Portland 63
	Consolation Game:	Nebraska 71, Portland 69
	Championship Game:	Vanderbilt 100, LaSalle 95

1967	First Round:	Oregon 76, Wake Forest 58
		Vanderbilt 85, Seton Hall 67
	Consolation Game:	Seton Hall 71, Wake Forest 70
	Championship Game:	Vanderbilt 70, Oregon 59

1968	First Round:	Kansas St. 66, No. Carolina St. 54
		Vanderbilt 85, Rice 77
	Consolation Game:	No. Carolina St. 69, Rice 58
	Championship Game:	Vanderbilt 90, Kansas St. 80

1969	First Round:	Auburn 70, St. Louis 66
		Dartmouth 83, Vanderbilt 82
	Consolation Game:	Vanderbilt 76, St. Louis 66
	Championship Game:	Auburn 85, Dartmouth 76

1970	First Round:	St. John's 95, Southern Methodist 80
		Vanderbilt 75, Clemson 61
	Consolation Game:	Clemson 67, Southern Methodist 51
	Championship Game:	St. John's 85, Vanderbilt 81

1971	First Round:	Memphis State 74, Ole Miss 71
		Vanderbilt 82, Bradley 80
	Consolation Game:	Bradley 72, Ole Miss 71
	Championship Game:	Vanderbilt 83, Memphis State 82

1972	First Round:	Western Ky. 71, Kent State 70
		Vanderbilt 70, Columbia 61
	Consolation Game:	Kent State 64, Columbia 53
	Championship Game:	Vanderbilt 103, Western Ky. 88

1973	First Round:	Tenn. State 63, Middle Tenn. 59
		Vanderbilt 82, Nebraska 58
	Consolation Game:	Middle Tenn. 76, Nebraska 65
	Championship Game:	Vanderbilt 67, Tenn. State 66

1974	First Round:	Southern Illinois 79, Austin Peay 70
		Vanderbilt 75, Va. Tech 72
	Consolation Game:	Va. Tech 73, Austin Peay 66
	Championship Game:	Vanderbilt 79, Southern Illinois 72

Record With Opponents
1900-1975
Won 838   Lost 564

	Won	Lost		Won	Lost
Alabama	37	35	Cornell	1	0
Albany Y.M.C.A.	1	0	Creighton	0	3
Alumni	2	1	Crescent (Brooklyn) A.C.	0	1
Arizona	1	0	Cumberland	25	3
Arkansas	1	0	Dartmouth	1	2
Arkansas State	2	0	Davidson	2	1
Army	2	0	DePaul	1	0
Atlanta A.C.	3	5	DePauw	0	1
Atwater Kent	1	0	Drake	0	1
Auburn	44	26	Drury College	1	0
Austin Peay	3	1	Duke	3	5
Baylor	6	1	Evansville	1	3
Bemis Y.M.C.A.	1	1	Florida	27	18
Bessemer	1	0	Florida State	1	0
Birmingham A.C.	7	10	Franklin College	0	1
Birmingham Y.M.C.A.	2	0	Furman	1	0
Boston College	2	0	Georgetown	1	0
Bowling Green	1	0	Georgia	42	14
Boys Club	2	0	Georgia Tech	37	29
Bradley	2	0	Hardin Simmons	1	0
Brigham Young	1	0	Hendrix	1	0
Buffalo All Stars	0	1	Holy Cross	0	1
Butler	0	3	Howard College	2	1
California	1	0	Hubbard Hardware	1	0
Calumet	2	1	Illinois	1	1
Camp Forest	1	0	Indiana	0	2
Carson Newman	1	0	Iowa State	0	2
Camp Benning	0	1	Jackson Y.M.C.A.	2	1
C.C.N.Y.	0	1	Jacksonville	0	1
Central (Ky.)	1	2	Jonesboro (Ark.) YMCA	2	1
Central (Mo.)	1	0	Kansas	2	0
Centre	1	2	Kansas City A.C.	0	2
Chattanooga	9	3	Kansas State	1	2
Chattanooga Ramblers	2	0	Kentucky	26	76
Chattanooga Tigers	3	1	LaSalle	1	0
Chattanooga Y.M.C.A.	5	0	Lipscomb	19	4
Chicago	1	0	Louisiana State	33	15
Chicago Y.M.C.A.	1	1	Louisville	5	3
Christ Church Cincinnati	0	1	Louisville Y.M.C.A.	3	2
Cincinnati	1	3	Louisville U.M.H.A.	3	0
Cincinnati Guaranty	0	1	Loyola (Chicago)	0	3
Clarksville	1	0	Loyola (New Orleans)	0	1
Clemson	5	3	Macon Y.M.C.A.	1	1
Columbia	1	1	Marquette	1	3
Columbia Military Acad.	1	0	Maryland	0	1
Columbus (Ga.) Y.M.C.A.	0	5	Maryville	1	0
Convair	1	1	Memphis	0	1

	Won	Lost		Won	Lost
Memphis State	3	1	Southern California	1	3
Memphis Y.M.C.A.	6	9	Southern Illinois	1	0
Mercer	7	5	Southern (Ky.) College	1	0
Miami (Ohio)	3	1	Southern Methodist	10	5
Michigan	1	2	Southwestern	6	1
Michigan State	1	0	Southwestern, La.	1	0
Middle Tennessee	20	3	Southwestern Presbyterian	6	1
Milligan	1	0	Stanford	0	1
Minnesota	0	4	St. John's (N.Y.)	1	3
Mississippi	39	14	St. Louis	2	2
Mississippi State	41	14	St. Louis A.C.	1	0
Missouri	1	1	St. Thomas (Louisville) AC	1	0
Mobile Y.M.C.A.	2	6	Syracuse	1	0
Montgomery Y.M.C.A.	3	2	Temple	1	1
Murfreesboro Normal	1	0	Tennessee	39	64
Murray	2	1	Tennessee State	1	0
Nashville A.C.	9	4	Tennessee Tech	4	4
Nashville Burk Terrors	1	2	Texas	3	2
Nashville Y.M.C.A. Peps	8	6	Texas A&M	1	0
Nashville Ramblers	27	21	Texas Christian	2	1
Navy	1	1	Texas Tech	6	1
Navy A.A.C.	1	1	Thayer Hospital	2	1
Nebraska	3	1	The Citadel	3	0
New Mexico	2	0	Toledo	1	0
New Mexico A&M	2	0	Tulane	22	10
New York Professionals	2	0	Transylvania	1	0
New York University	1	1	Tulsa	1	0
North Carolina	2	4	Univ. of Nashville	2	0
North Carolina State	1	1	Union	2	0
Northwestern	2	0	Vanderbilt A.S.T.P.	1	0
Notre Dame	0	1	Vermont	1	0
Ohio State	2	2	Virginia	2	0
Oklahoma	1	0	V.M.I.	2	0
Oklahoma A&M	1	1	V.P.I.	2	3
Oregon	1	0	Wabash	0	3
Owensboro Y.M.C.A.	1	0	Wake Forest	2	0
Park Field Aviation	1	0	Washington (St. Louis)	1	1
Pennsylvania	0	1	Washington & Lee	1	0
Penn Dixies	0	1	Washington State	2	1
Pittsburg, Kan.	0	1	Western Kentucky	9	10
Pittsburgh	0	1	Wetumpka, Ala.	3	0
Portland	2	0	Wichita Henrys	0	1
Princeton	1	0	William & Mary	3	0
Purdue	1	1	Wittenberg	1	2
Rome (Ga.) A.C.	1	0	Wyoming	1	0
Rice	9	2	Xavier (Ohio)	0	3
Samford	1	0	Yale	3	1
Seton Hall	1	0	20th Ferrying Cm.	1	0
Sewanee	46	4	20th Armored	2	0
Smyrna Bombers	0	2	508th Air Base	1	0
South Carolina	4	0			

Southeastern Conference Champions

Year	School	Record Conf.—Final		Coach
1933	Kentucky	8-0	20-3	Adolph Rupp
1934	Alabama	13-2	17-2	Henry Crisp
1935	L.S.U.	12-0	14-1	Harry Rabenhorst
	Kentucky	11-0	19-2	Adolph Rupp
1936	Tennessee	8-4	15-6	Blair Guillion
1937	Kentucky	5-3	17-5	Adolph Rupp
1938	Georgia Tech	9-2	18-2	Roy Mundorff
1939	Kentucky	5-2	16-4	Adolph Rupp
1940	Kentucky	4-4	15-6	Adolph Rupp
1941	Tennessee	8-3	17-5	John Mauer
1942	Kentucky	6-2	19-6	Adolph Rupp
1943	Tennessee	6-3	14-5	John Mauer
1944	Kentucky	0-0	19-2	Adolph Rupp
1945	Kentucky	4-1	22-4	Adolph Rupp
1946	Kentucky	6-0	28-2	Adolph Rupp
1947	Kentucky	11-0	34-2	Adolph Rupp
1948	Kentucky	9-0	36-3	Adolph Rupp
1949	Kentucky	13-0	32-2	Adolph Rupp
1950	Kentucky	11-2	25-5	Adolph Rupp
1951	Kentucky	14-0	32-2	Adolph Rupp
1952	Kentucky	14-0	29-3	Adolph Rupp
1953	L.S.U.	13-0	25-2	Harry Rabenhorst
1954	Kentucky	14-0	25-0	Adolph Rupp
	L.S.U.	14-0	21-5	Harry Rabenhorst
1955	Kentucky	12-2	23-3	Adolph Rupp
1956	Alabama	14-0	21-3	Johnny Dee
1957	Kentucky	12-2	23-5	Adolph Rupp
1958	Kentucky	12-2	23-6	Adolph Rupp
1959	Miss. State	13-1	24-1	Babe McCarthy
1960	Auburn	12-2	19-3	Joel Eaves
1961	Miss. State	11-3	19-6	Babe McCarthy
1962	Miss. State	13-1	24-1	Babe McCarthy
	Kentucky	13-1	23-3	Adolph Rupp
1963	Miss. State	12-2	22-6	Babe McCarthy
1964	Kentucky	11-3	21-6	Adolph Rupp
1965	Vanderbilt	15-1	24-4	Roy Skinner
1966	Kentucky	15-1	32-2	Adolph Rupp
1967	Tennessee	15-3	21-7	Ray Mears
1968	Kentucky	15-3	22-5	Adolph Rupp
1969	Kentucky	16-2	23-5	Adolph Rupp
1970	Kentucky	17-1	26-2	Adolph Rupp
1971	Kentucky	16-2	22-4	Adolph Rupp
1972	Kentucky	14-4	21-7	Adolph Rupp
	Tennessee	14-4	19-6	Ray Mears
1973	Kentucky	14-4	20-8	Joe Hall
1974	Vanderbilt	15-3	23-5	Roy Skinner
	Alabama	15-3	22-4	C. M. Newton
1975	Kentucky	15-3	22-4	Joe Hall
	Alabama	15-3	22-4	C. M. Newton

Head Coaching Records

Years	Coach	Seasons	Won	Lost	Pct.
1901-02	W. D. Weatherford	2	7	4	.636
1903	Grinnell Jones	1	6	0	1.000
1904, 1909	E. J. Hamilton	2	17	5	.773
1907	J. N. Stone	1	6	1	.857
1908	W. L. Troop	1	6	10	.375
1910	R. B. McGehee	1	10	3	.769
1911-12	C. T. (Zeke) Martin	2	17	11	.607
1913	Oscar G. Nelson	1	3	4	.429
1914-17	G. T. Denton	4	26	20	.565
1918	Ralph Palmer	1	6	3	.667
1919-20	Ray Morrison	2	22	6	.786
1921	Tom Zerfoss	1	8	14	.364
1922-23	Wallace Wade	2	24	16	.600
1924-27, 1932-36	Josh Cody	9	98	100	.495
1928-29	John (Red) Floyd	2	9	19	.321
1930-31, 1945-46	Gus Morrow	4	31	40	.443
1937-41	Jim Buford	5	48	49	.495
1942-43, 1947	Norm Cooper	3	24	25	.490
1944	Smoky Harper	1	11	4	.733
1948-58, 1960-61	Bob Polk	13	197	106	.650
1959, 1962-75	Roy Skinner	15	262	124	.679
	Totals	73	838	564	.598

SKINNER'S CAREER RECORD
(14 Collegiate Seasons, All at Vanderbilt)

	Overall			SEC		
	Won	Lost		Won	Lost	Finish
1958-59	14	10		8	6	5th T
1961-62	12	12		6	8	6th T
1962-63	16	7		9	5	4th
1963-64	19	6		8	6	4th
1964-65	24	4		15	1	1st
1965-66	22	4		13	3	2nd
1966-67	21	5		14	4	2nd T
1967-68	20	6		12	6	3rd
1968-69	15	11		9	9	7th T
1969-70	12	14		8	10	6th
1970-71	13	13		9	9	4th T
1971-72	16	10		10	8	4th
1972-73	20	6		13	3	2nd T
1973-74	23	5		15	3	1st T
1974-75	15	11		10	8	5th
TOTALS	262	124		129	92	

Season Records

1900-01—Won 2, Lost 2
COACH: W. D. Weatherford
CAPTAIN: Earnest Reese

Nashville YMCA Ramblers	19	22
Nashville YMCA Ramblers	24	9
Nashville YMCA Ramblers	14	12
Nashville A.C.	11	13
	68	56

1901-02—Won 5, Lost 2
COACH: W. D. Weatherford
CAPTAIN: H. W. Davis

Nashville YMCA Ramblers	27	14
Nashville YMCA Ramblers	25	4
Nashville A.C.	16	9
Nashville A.C.	17	12
Howard College	23	33
Howard College	29	19
Birmingham College	21	34
	158	125

1902-03—Won 6, Lost 0
COACH: Grinnell Jones
CAPTAIN: Ben L. Clary

Cumberland	44	14
Nashville A.C.	26	6
Nashville A.C.	24	11
Howard	25	11
Cumberland	44	14
Cumberland	24	21
	187	77

1903-04—Won 6, Lost 1
COACH: J. Hamilton
CAPTAIN: John J. Tigert

U. of Nashville	32	6
Nashville A.C.	34	9
Nashville YMCA Ramblers	12	5
U. of Nashville	36	4
Nashville A.C.	36	3
Nashville YMCA Ramblers	32	4
Cumberland	5	18
	187	49

1904-05
No Team Fielded

1905-06
No Scores Recorded

1906-07—Won 6, Lost 1
COACH: J. N. (Stein) Stone
CAPTAIN: J. N. (Stein) Stone

Nashville A.C.	14	23
N.Y. Professionals	30	18
N.Y. Professionals	38	23
Cumberland	21	17
Southwestern Presbyterian	27	15
Nashville A.C.	32	21
Nashville A.C.	38	25
	200	142

1907-08—Won 6, Lost 10
COACH: W. L. Throop
CAPTAIN: W. L. Throop

Columbia	16	34
Yale	23	27
Montgomery YMCA	15	34
Mobile YMCA	12	43
Birmingham A.C.	12	30
Birmingham YMCA	30	26
Nashville YMCA Ramblers	28	18
Southern Kentucky College	28	15
Cumberland	20	22
Nashville YMCA Ramblers	27	20
Southwestern Presbyterian	10	20
Central (Ky.)	28	14
Nashville A.C.	8	14
Birmingham A.C.	25	15
Cumberland	14	20
Wabash	7	27
	303	379

1908-09—Won 11, Lost 4
COACH: E. J. Hamilton
CAPTAIN: W. D. Neely

Nashville YMCA Ramblers	38	20
Chattanooga Ramblers	32	17
Atlanta A.C.	33	26
Columbus YMCA	18	19
Cumberland	25	19
Birmingham A.C.	33	30
Mobile YMCA	26	33
Montgomery YMCA	28	32
Birmingham YMCA	30	12
Chattanooga Ramblers	52	23
Sewanee	28	19
Southwestern Presbyterian	56	19
Cumberland	38	21
Nashville A.C.	43	33
Nashville A.C.	24	25
	504	348

1909-10—Won 10, Lost 3
COACH: R. B. McGehee
CAPTAIN: R. B. McGehee

Atlanta A.C.	53	30
Columbus YMCA	29	34
Montgomery YMCA	57	24
Mobile YMCA	25	24
Birmingham A.C.	50	30
Alumni	41	21
Cumberland	57	13
Sewanee	61	10
Central (Ky.)	28	52
George Town	45	34
Central (Ky.)	21	70
Louisville YMCA	54	39
Nashville YMCA	53	39
	574	420

1910-11—Won 8, Lost 2
COACH: Carl (Zeke) Martin
CAPTAIN: Carl (Zeke) Martin

Cumberland	45	20
Nashville YMCA Ramblers	74	13
Birmingham A.C.	26	39
Birmingham YMCA	53	25
Atlanta A.C.	42	34
Mercer	26	25

Wetumpka (Ala.) 60   7
Mobile YMCA 29   61
Sewanee 54   5
Cumberland 24   20
                              433   249

1911-12—Won 9, Lost 9

COACH: Carl (Zeke) Martin
CAPTAIN: Carl (Zeke) Martin

Central (Mo.)	30	23
Mobile YMCA	15	48
Wetumpka (Ala.)	62	11
Columbus (Ga.) YMCA	21	44
Rome (Ga.) A.C.	34	11
Atlanta A.C.	31	43
Birmingham A.C.	23	48
St. Louis A.C.	37	32
Cumberland	78	10
Union (Tenn.)	95	24
Memphis YMCA	19	21
Jackson YMCA	81	13
Cumberland	47	19
Louisville YMCA	27	29
Kentucky	17	28
Kentucky	18	22
Christ Church (Cincinnati)	27	47
Alumni	53	32
	712	504

1912-13—Won 3, Lost 4

COACH: Oscar G. Nelson
CAPTAIN: Oscar G. Nelson

Sewanee	41	13
Mobile YMCA	31	43
Wetumpka (Ala.)	41	9
Bessemer (Ala.)	31	23
Birmingham A.C.	20	43
Columbus (Ga.) A.C.	32	70
Atlanta A.C.	34	52
	230	253

1913-14—Won 6, Lost 3

COACH: G. T. Denton
CAPTAIN: Tome Brown

Murphreesboro Normal	53	5
Chattanooga Tigers	31	17
Cumberland	41	36
Georgia	32	41
Georgia Tech	55	41
Nashville YMCA Ramblers	31	32
Memphis YMCA	36	23
Union	54	20
Nashville YMCA Ramblers	23	41
	356	256

1914-15—Won 6, Lost 6

COACH: G. T. Denton
CAPTAIN: Robert M. Davidson

Cumberland	40	28
Atlanta A.C.	32	36
Chattanooga Tigers	21	41
Georgia	35	48
Louisville YMCA	18	32
Kentucky	39	34
Kentucky	24	36
Jackson YMCA	27	37
Memphis YMCA	33	20
Nashville YMCA Ramblers	44	38

Nashville YMCA Ramblers 39   33
Southwestern Presbyterian 85   20
                              437   403

1915-16—Won 11, Lost 3

COACH: G. T. Denton
CAPTAIN: Josh Cody

Cumberland	40	8
Mobile YMCA	41	37
Montgomery YMCA	53	29
Birmingham A.C.	54	32
*Columbus (Ga.) YMCA	39	41
Cumberland	81	13
Columbia Mil. Academy	36	8
Louisville, YMHC	35	16
Kentucky	39	25
Kentucky	23	20
Chattanooga Tigers	52	26
Nashville YMCA Ramblers	19	21
Memphis YMCA	32	19
Nashville YMCA Ramblers	23	25
	567	320

*Overtime

1916-17—Won 3, Lost 8

COACH: G. T. Denton
CAPTAIN: Frank Blair

Atlanta A.C.	15	32
Birmingham A.C.	24	26
Chattanooga Tigers	42	9
Nashville YMCA Ramblers	21	16
Washington & Lee	8	26
Louisville YMHA	29	13
Georgia	11	31
Nashville YMCA Ramblers	18	22
Memphis YMCA	19	26
Jonesboro (Ark.) YMCA	19	25
Nashville YMCA Ramblers	19	23
	225	249

1917-18—Won 6, Lost 3

COACH: Ralph Palmer
CAPTAIN: Alf Adams

Birmingham A.C.	32	24
Birmingham A.C.	32	29
Southwestern Presbyterian U.	79	16
Nashville YMCA Ramblers	23	36
Calumet	36	26
Transylvania	21	12
Louisville YMHA	39	17
Nashville YMCA Ramblers	17	26
Nashville YMCA Ramblers	35	30
	314	236

1918-19—Won 8, Lost 2

COACH: Ray Morrison
CAPTAIN: L. M. Groves

Birmingham A.C.	21	16
*Nashville YMCA Ramblers	34	27
Calumet	40	23
Kentucky	36	26
Centre	23	28
Jackson YMCA	44	18
Park Field Aviation	14	13
Memphis YMCA	14	23
Nashville YMCA Ramblers	36	25
Memphis YMCA	26	22
	316	221

*Overtime

1919-20—Won 14, Lost 4

COACH: Ray Morrison
CAPTAIN: Tom Zerfoss

Birmingham A.C.	30	24
Mobile YMCA	33	35
Montgomery YMCA	56	28
Chicago YMCA	26	14
Boys Club	36	6
Memphis YMCA	42	25
Georgia	40	18
Nashville YMCA Ramblers	27	29
Georgia Tech	39	21
Macon YMCA	41	35
Boys Club	21	14
Chattanooga YMCA	45	39
Chattanooga YMCA	41	20
Centre	29	18
Memphis YMCA	25	31
Maryville	22	10
Georgia Tech	32	3
Nashville YMCA Ramblers	13	24
	601	394

S.I.A.A. Champions

1920-21—Won 8, Lost 14

COACH: Ray Morrison
CAPTAIN: Garland (Gus) Morrow

Memphis YMCA	13	37
Birmingham A.C.	17	23
Birmingham A.C.	19	27
Middle Tennessee	14	9
Michigan	7	21
Southwestern Presby. U.	40	27
Marquette	6	29
Chattanooga YMCA	27	20
Memphis YMCA	12	26
Auburn	7	27
Georgia	17	33
Macon YMCA	21	30
Mercer	13	21
Tulane	32	13
Nashville YMCA Ramblers	17	12
Mercer	20	9
Centre	13	44
Kentucky	18	33
Louisville YMCA	16	11
Chicago YMCA	9	13
Nashville YMCA Ramblers	11	9
	349	474

1921-22—Won 8, Lost 8

COACH: Wallace Wade
CAPTAIN: Jule Thomas

Southwestern Presby. U.	36	24
Camp Benning	15	29
Jonesboro YMCA	23	13
Chattanooga	20	13
Kentucky	22	12
Mercer	18	17
Mississippi A&M	22	18
Nashville YMCA Ramblers	23	28
Nashville YMHA Peps	14	15
Chattanooga	24	29
Tennessee	5	20
Nashville YMCA Ramblers	13	14
Tennessee	15	16
**Citadel	37	22
**Georgia	26	27

Nashville YMHA Peps	28	22
	341	319

**—Southern Conference
Tournament

1922-23—Won 16, Lost 8

COACH: Wallace Wade
CAPTAIN: Oliver (Doc) Kuhn

Wabash	21	32
Cincinnati	22	41
Wittenburg	14	28
Ohio State	20	27
U. of Chicago	17	11
Clarksville	46	23
Jonesboro YMCA	19	7
Memphis YMCA	14	15
Nashville YMHA Peps	25	21
Chattanooga	28	27
Milligan	41	20
Bemis YMCA	43	16
Mississippi A&M	34	27
Nashville YMCA Ramblers	23	19
Hendrix	26	14
Georgia	25	16
Mercer	29	32
Mercer	37	35
Nashville YMHA Peps	22	15
Nashville YMCA Ramblers	30	34
Tennessee	28	25
**LSU	36	10
**VPI	23	26
Nashville YMCA Ramblers	36	24
	659	545

**—Southern Conference
Tournament

1923-24—Won 7, Lost 15

COACH: Josh Cody
CAPTAIN: Alvin (Pep) Bell

Kansas City A.C.	4	23
Louisville YMCA	31	25
Pittsburg (Kan.)	32	33
Crescent A.C. (Brooklyn)	14	42
CCNY	19	25
Buffalo All-Stars	23	46
Kentucky	13	23
Calumet (New Albany, Ind.)	25	28
St. Thomas A.C. (Louisville)	17	12
Mississippi A&M	24	23
Nashville YMCA Ramblers	19	25
Atlanta A.C.	21	36
Mercer	23	11
YMHA Peps	17	13
*Alabama	25	26
Nashville YMCA Ramblers	17	26
Nashville YMHA Peps	37	44
Chattanooga	34	22
Tennessee	21	32
Nashville YMHA Peps	22	30
**Clemson	42	14
**North Carolina	20	37
	500	596

*Overtime
**—Southern Conference
Tournament

1924-25—Won 12, Lost 13

COACH: Josh Cody
CAPTAIN: Gil Reese

Middle Tennessee	28	31
Memphis YMCA	21	23
Drury College	33	21
Kansas City A.C.	23	28
Butler	17	37
Franklin College	23	49
DePauw	21	28
Wabash	14	15
Owensboro YMCA	37	19
Mississippi	19	18
Nashville YMCA Ramblers	21	20
Memphis YMCA	33	19
Birmingham A.C.	22	34
Georgia	41	34
Mercer	30	31
Georgia Tech	37	26
Butler	13	33
Tennessee	27	18
Mississippi A&M	20	29
Alabama	22	29
Tulane	25	32
Nashville YMHA Peps	40	33
Nashville YMHA Peps	25	18
Nashville YMCA Ramblers	24	15
Middle Tennessee	30	29
	646	701

1925-26—Won 8, Lost 18

COACH: Josh Cody
CAPTAIN: John McCall

Evansville	22	39
St. Louis U.	22	35
Memphis	20	37
Bemis YMCA	28	31
Nashville Burk Terrors	9	19
Middle Tennessee	51	19
Mercer	22	18
Marquette	16	19
Georgia Tech	27	24
Mississippi A&M	27	36
Mississippi	18	32
LSU	23	24
Tulane	20	21
Nashville YMHA Peps	26	33
Alabama	19	23
Nashville YMCA Ramblers	21	12
Mississippi A&M	21	20
*Tennessee	32	36
Middle Tennessee	25	24
Nashville YMHA Peps	27	22
Nashville Burk Terrors	41	21
Cincinnati Guaranty	18	24
Western Kentucky	29	34
Kentucky	20	30
Nashville YMCA Ramblers	8	25
Nashville YMCA Ramblers	12	27
	604	687

*Overtime

1926-27—Won 20, Lost 4

COACH: Josh Cody
CAPTAIN: Malcolm Moss

Evansville	22	37
Marquette	22	15
Loyola (Chicago)	7	31
St. Louis U.	40	21
Western Kentucky	40	20
Middle Tennessee	59	19
Kentucky	48	32
Western Kentucky	25	26
Georgia Tech	29	36
Mercer	36	33
Sewanee	53	18
Mississippi A&M	35	34
Nashville YMCA Ramblers	50	28
Middle Tennessee	52	20
Sewanee	31	18
Mississippi	33	32
Nashville YMHA Peps	42	52
Auburn	39	35
*Evansville	46	44
Tennessee	35	25
**Washington & Lee	44	32
**Mississippi	32	20
**South Carolina	31	25
**Georgia	46	44
	897	677

*—Overtime
**—Southern Conference
Tournament

1927-28—Won 5, Lost 7

COACH: Johnny (Red) Floyd
CAPTAIN: Frank Bridges

Cumberland	41	30
Mercer	31	38
Kentucky	23	43
Middle Tennessee	35	29
Mississippi A&M	38	44
Sewanee	33	26
Auburn	28	62
Penn Dixies	24	34
Kentucky	29	54
Georgia Tech	31	41
Carson-Newman	66	40
Tennessee	28	26
	407	467

1928-29—Won 4, Lost 12

COACH: Johnny (Red) Floyd
CAPTAIN: Bertram (Triney)
Chaltant

Alumni	31	48
Cumberland	50	33
Sewanee	45	31
Nashville YMHA Peps	36	39
Georgia Tech	28	40
Nashville Burk Terrors	41	46
Memphis YMCA Triangles	30	36
Sewanee	29	23
Georgia Tech	15	40
Nashville YMCA Ramblers	19	45
Mercer	40	60
Nashville YMCA Ramblers	29	36
Nashville YMHA Peps	31	36
*Mississippi	46	48
Tennessee	24	26
Middle Tennessee	42	41
	536	628

*—Overtime

1929-30—Won 6, Lost 16

COACH: Garland (Gus) Morrow
CAPTAIN: Donald Cram

Louisville	22	24

Butler	14	39
Loyola (Chicago)	16	33
Purdue	22	43
St. Louis U.	16	46
Middle Tennessee	31	45
Cumberland	39	12
Western Kentucky	32	18
**Clemson	42	48
Sewanee	15	36
Alabama	18	36
Auburn	29	27
Clemson	27	32
Georgia Tech	25	46
Georgia Tech	37	41
Tennessee	21	23
Tennessee Tech	37	42
Nashville YMCA Ramblers	44	20
Sewanee	35	40
Middle Tennessee	34	33
*Tennessee	33	38
Nashville YMCA Ramblers	49	43
	638	765

*—Overtime
**—Double Overtime

1930-31—Won 16, Lost 8

COACH: Garland (Gus) Morrow
CAPTAIN: Shelby Coffey

Albany YMCA	39	22
Atwater Kent	40	21
Hubbard Hardware	41	32
Chattanooga YMCA	31	24
Middle Tennessee	42	20
Murray	48	29
Cumberland	50	26
Georgia Tech	35	44
Florida	42	25
Florida	43	35
Kentucky	37	42
Sewanee	35	17
Tennessee	41	40
Auburn	36	26
Sewanee	52	32
Louisville	32	23
Georgia Tech	45	32
*Duke	44	48
Alabama	29	36
Auburn	25	42
Chattanooga YMCA	48	23
Kentucky	23	43
Tennessee	34	37
*North Carolina	21	23
	913	742

*—Overtime

1931-32—Won 8, Lost 11

COACH: Josh Cody
CAPTAIN: William R. Schwartz

Ohio State	28	27
Wittenburg	24	39
Miami (Ohio)	28	22
Middle Tennessee	38	32
Auburn	23	36
Chattanooga	26	28
Georgia Tech	27	45
Florida	36	32
Florida	33	43
Sewanee	30	22
Tennessee	25	27

Auburn	23	38
Kentucky	37	61
Alabama	39	32
Sewanee	32	21
Middle Tennessee	35	40
Tennessee	22	27
Kentucky	32	31
*Duke	32	41
	570	644

*—Overtime

1932-33—Won 14, Lost 8

COACH: Josh Cody
CAPTAIN: Tom Henderson

Ohio State	26	45
Clemson	39	22
**South Carolina	31	29
*Tennessee	37	32
Tulane	35	21
Tulane	39	22
Georgia Tech	38	27
Auburn	25	24
Louisiana State	54	34
Louisiana State	52	26
Sewanee	25	19
Kentucky	29	40
Alabama	22	37
Wichita Henrys	38	40
Auburn	21	20
Florida	42	41
Florida	27	43
Sewanee	41	25
Tennessee	27	35
Kentucky	28	45
†Tulane	28	25
†Mississippi State	36	48
	740	700

Final SEC Standing: 2nd (11-5)
†—SEC Tourney at Atlanta
*Overtime
**Double Overtime

1933-34—Won 11, Lost 6

COACH: Josh Cody
CAPTAIN: Harold Huggins

Auburn	31	22
Georgia Tech	24	22
Clemson	27	25
Tulane	15	19
Tulane	23	21
Cumberland	34	21
Tennessee	31	26
Sewanee	60	28
Auburn	48	33
Kentucky	26	48
Alabama	32	38
Georgia Tech	38	30
Sewanee	40	27
Tennessee	34	45
Kentucky	27	47
†Georgia	46	29
†Florida	23	24
	559	505

Final SEC Standing: 5th (8-5)
†—SEC Tourney at Atlanta

1934-35—Won 9, Lost 11

COACH: Josh Cody

CAPTAIN: Jim Scoggins

Cincinnati	20	47
Clemson	22	32
Cincinnati	20	46
Auburn	37	27
Auburn	41	24
Tulane	50	34
Sewanee	47	20
*Georgia Tech	33	32
Alabama	34	33
Kentucky	22	58
*Indiana	30	39
Georgia Tech	53	25
Sewanee	62	32
Tennessee	29	39
Auburn	37	25
Louisiana State	41	56
Louisiana State	31	40
Creighton	28	53
*Tennessee	37	39
Kentucky	19	53
	693	754

Final SEC Standing: 4th (9-6)
No SEC Tourney Held
*Overtime

1935-36—Won 9, Lost 14

COACH: Josh Cody
CAPTAIN: Willie Geny

Miami (O.)	23	34
Indiana	18	56
Xavier	37	39
Pittsburgh	32	57
Evansville College	20	33
Chicago Loyola	22	25
Iowa State	28	38
Creighton	34	40
Creighton	30	46
Auburn	47	27
Sewanee	45	27
Tulane	44	31
Georgia Tech	43	22
Sewanee	40	16
Auburn	37	32
Kentucky	33	24
Alabama	30	32
Georgia Tech	42	40
Alabama	28	33
Tennessee	33	30
Tennessee	33	34
Kentucky	41	61
*Georgia Tech	37	42
	777	819

Final SEC Standing: 2nd (9-4)
†—SEC Tourney at Atlanta

1936-37—Won 6, Lost 10

COACH: Jim Buford
CAPTAIN: Ken Overly

Middle Tennessee	39	30
Middle Tennessee	39	12
Sewanee	46	26
Chattanooga	34	28
Georgia Tech	27	39
Alabama	23	19
Western Kentucky	27	40
Kentucky	26	41
Western Kentucky	15	35

Tennessee	30	50
Alabama	19	29
Georgia Tech	30	40
Tennessee	28	34
*Chattanooga	29	30
Kentucky	19	5
Sewanee	43	38
	474	542

Final SEC Standing: 11th (3-7)
Not invited to SEC Tourney
*Overtime

1937-38—Won 10, Lost 11

COACH: Jim Buford
CAPTAIN: Ed Hunter

n-Ole Miss	30	68
Austin Peay	43	42
Western Kentucky	25	39
Tennessee Tech	34	31
Austin Peay	49	31
Georgia Tech	25	59
Sewanee	28	32
Tennessee Tech	16	21
Alabama	39	36
Western Kentucky	18	38
Tennessee	30	37
Kentucky	19	42
Alabama	46	26
Georgia Tech	35	40
Florida	59	24
Chattanooga	44	30
Tennessee	26	38
Kentucky	24	48
Sewanee	41	35
†Alabama	50	26
†Georgia Tech	18	50
	699	793

Final SEC Standing: 10th (4-8)
n—Played at Memphis
†—SEC Tourney, Baton Rouge

1938-39—Won 14, Lost 7

COACH: Jim Buford, Princeton
CAPTAIN: Ed Hunter

Austin Peay	42	35
Cumberland	37	30
Lipscomb	42	31
Cumberland	48	36
Georgia Tech	24	30
Lipscomb	33	40
Sewanee	37	30
Tennessee	31	33
Kentucky	37	51
Alabama	36	34
Western Kentucky	31	51
Georgia Tech	49	42
Sewanee	70	42
Auburn	49	42
Western Kentucky	53	49
Tennessee	56	33
Chattanooga	61	24
Kentucky	27	52
†Mississippi State	73	40
†Alabama	41	33
†Tennessee	31	34
	908	792

Final SEC Standing: 6th (7-5)
†—SEC Tourney, Knoxville

1939-40—Won 10, Lost 12
COACH: Jim Buford
CAPTAIN: Ross Hanna

Austin Peay	28	40
Murray	46	37
Cumberland	51	39
Lipscomb	44	50
Auburn	51	45
Georgia Tech	43	49
Tennessee	23	29
Alabama	31	43
Auburn	50	46
Tennessee	31	34
Kentucky	40	32
Cumberland	56	49
Alabama	29	32
Georgia Tech	39	57
Sewanee	52	39
Lipscomb	41	44
Western Kentucky	25	36
Tennessee Tech	37	35
Sewanee	31	28
Kentucky	38	43
†Mississippi State	46	36
†Kentucky	34	44
	866	887

Final SEC Standing: 10th (5-7)
†—SEC Tourney, Knoxville

1940-41—Won 8, Lost 9
COACH: Jim Buford
CAPTAIN: "Pinky" Lipscomb

Sewanee	42	28
Georgia	50	44
Georgia Tech	48	55
Sewanee	46	24
Alabama	24	48
Auburn	44	45
Alabama	28	40
Kentucky	50	51
Lipscomb	57	42
Ole Miss	80	47
Auburn	47	39
Georgia Tech	54	41
Tennessee	36	37
Tennessee	25	46
Kentucky	31	58
†Louisiana State	63	49
†Florida	41	47
	766	741

Final SEC Standings: 11th (3-9)
†—SEC Tourney, Louisville

1941-42—Won 7, Lost 9
COACH: Norm Cooper
CAPTAIN: Harrison Rue

Sewanee	50	34
Auburn	33	35
Georgia Tech	39	32
Sewanee	50	20
Alabama	19	33
Auburn	45	50
*Alabama	33	37
Georgia	58	38
Mississippi State	41	38
Ole Miss	31	38
Lipscomb	59	29
Camp Forest	39	34
Georgia Tech	27	35
Tennessee	33	34
Tennessee	26	39
†Auburn	34	36
	617	562

Final SEC Standing: Tie for 9th (3-8)
†SEC Tourney, Louisville
*Overtime

1942-43—Won 10, Lost 8
COACH: Norm Cooper
CAPTAIN: Julian Olsen

Auburn	54	39
Georgia	39	35
Georgia Tech	29	43
Alabama	26	29
Alabama	31	27
Auburn	48	43
Kentucky	38	39
Mississippi State	40	45
Ole Miss	44	49
Kentucky	43	54
Ole Miss	55	30
Mississippi State	45	35
Georgia Tech	52	28
Tennessee	30	27
Lipscomb	41	28
Tennessee	22	44
Georgia	66	31
†Tennessee	31	41
	734	667

Final SEC Standing: 6th (9-7)
†—SEC Tourney, Louisville

1943-44—Won 11, Lost 4
COACH: Smokey Harper
Game Captains appointed

Thayer Hospital	42	22
Vandy ASTP	48	38
Lipscomb	50	45
Convair	60	68
20th Ferrying Cm	40	26
Convair	41	39
20th Armored	49	32
Tennessee Tech	59	42
20th Armored	49	32
Tennessee Tech	56	32
Lipscomb	40	35
508th Air Base	42	38
Navy A.A.C.	17	47
Navy A.A.C.	37	31
†Georgia Tech	51	63
	681	591

†—SEC Tourney
(Informal, No SEC Schedule)

1944-45—Won 6, Lost 6
COACH: Gus Morrow
CAPTAIN: Dave Scobey

Tennessee Tech	44	50
Lipscomb	65	35
Tennessee Tech	40	54
Smyrna Bombers	38	75
Sewanee	51	46
Thayer Hospital	38	44
Southwestern	59	40
Smyrna Bombers	53	74
Lipscomb	60	34
Sewanee	38	51

Thayer Hospital 50   38
Southwestern 66   48
                                          602   589
(Informal, No SEC Schedule)

1945-46—Won 3, Lost 10
COACH: Gus Morrow
CAPTAIN: Jay Ball

Louisville 27   60
Georgia 44   41
Southwestern 38   20
Ole Miss 39   31
Western Kentucky 32   45
Western Kentucky 29   42
Georgia 39   51
n-Kentucky 37   59
Kentucky 31   64
Murray 34   53
Tennessee 33   55
Tennessee 32   42
†Tennessee 32   46
                                          447   609

Final SEC Standing: 9th (2-5)
n—Played at Paducah, Ky.
†—SEC Tourney, Louisville

1946-47—Won 7, Lost 8
COACH: Norm Cooper
CAPTAIN: Tommy Owen

Sewanee 51   30
Sewanee 60   37
Alabama 36   49
Kentucky 30   80
Southwestern 64   39
Auburn 38   37
Alabama' 33   38
n-Louisiana State 52   62
Auburn 59   58
Mississippi State 64   44
Ole Miss 55   41
Tennessee 47   54
Kentucky 41   84
Tennessee 21   59
†Kentucky 29   98
                                          680   809

Final SEC Standing: 8th (4-7)
n—Played at Memphis
†—SEC Tourney, Louisville

1947-48—Won 8, Lost 14
COACH: Bob Polk
CAPTAIN: "Mike" Craig

Lipscomb 57   43
Mississippi State 46   51
Ole Miss 42   53
Ole Miss 71   49
Xavier (Cin.) 42   79
n-Tulane 56   64
Southwestern 64   40
Mississippi State 51   48
Tulane 44   63
Louisiana State 54   56
Xavier (Cin.) 42   62
Auburn 41   46
Alabama 31   60
Auburn 55   47
Lipscomb 57   37
Kentucky 51   82
Alabama 58   32

Tennessee 48   63
Kentucky 43   79
Tennessee 53   72
Southwestern 61   47
†Tulane 53   67
                                          1120 1240

Final SEC Standing: 12th (4-11)
n—Played at Memphis
†—SEC Tourney, Louisville

1948-49—Won 14, Lost 8
COACH: Bob Polk
CAPTAIN: "Mike" Craig

Lipscomb 65   41
Chattanooga 66   51
Cumberland 77   32
Lipscomb 57   37
cb-Drake 46   47
cb-Dartmouth 52   64
Washington (St. L.) 47   43
Tennessee 51   53
Ole Miss 62   49
Mississippi State 35   29
Auburn 46   48
Alabama 36   31
Tennessee 64   67
Kentucky 50   72
Auburn 52   42
Ole Miss 64   52
Alabama 68   42
Mississippi State 90   45
Louisiana State 61   51
Tulane 56   54
Kentucky 37   70
†Louisiana State 56   60
                                          1238 1080

Final SEC Standing: 4th (9-5)
cb—Corn Bowl Tourney, Des Moines
†—SEC Tourney, Louisville

1949-50—Won 17, Lost 8
COACH: Bob Polk
CAPTAIN: Billy Joe Adcock

Lipscomb 62   39
*New York Univ. 65   59
Temple 35   55
Chattanooga 75   40
Lipscomb 66   42
n-Temple 49   45
ac-Oklahoma A&M 61   62
ac-Baylor 53   61
ac-Alabama 53   44
Washington (St. L.) 53   55
Tennessee 67   52
Mississippi State 62   50
Ole Miss 44   37
Auburn 58   47
Alabama 44   47
Tennessee 50   44
Kentucky 54   58
Florida 54   34
Auburn 63   51
Alabama 47   38
Mississippi State 85   50
Ole Miss 80   47
Middle Tennessee 74   39
Kentucky 66   70
†Tennessee 44   50
                                          1464 1216

1950-51—Won 19, Lost 8

COACH: Bob Polk
CAPTAIN: George Kelley

Middle Tennessee	58	45
*Lipscomb	71	69
Florida	81	64
Holy Cross	62	64
New York Univ.	56	87
ac-Texas	49	55
ac-Baylor	54	53
ac-Tulsa	56	49
Lipscomb	57	59
Auburn	61	51
Alabama	49	35
Ole Miss	70	63
Mississippi State	63	60
Louisiana State	69	61
Tennessee	58	57
Kentucky	49	74
Tennessee	59	61
Georgia Tech	65	47
Sewanee	63	44
Tulane	55	90
Georgia Tech	69	67
Kentucky	57	89
Georgia	69	57
†Tennessee	88	52
†Georgia	70	60
†Louisiana State	75	63
†Kentucky	61	57
	1694	1633

Final SEC Standing: 2nd (10-4)
ac—All-Collegiate Tournament at
   Oklahoma City
†—SEC Tourney, Louisville
*Overtime

1951-52—Won 18, Lost 9

COACH: Bob Polk
GAME CAPTAINS

Bradley	55	5
Middle Tennessee	80	49
Lipscomb	78	63
Sewanee	86	63
Texas Tech	55	49
Rice	65	56
St. John's	54	69
Baylor	60	53
Texas Christian	49	51
Texas	49	65
Tennessee	80	60
Louisiana State	58	47
Auburn	73	61
Alabama	44	63
Florida	70	86
Tennessee	50	68
Kentucky	51	88
Lipscomb	80	69
Georgia Tech	92	67
Ole Miss	59	51
Mississippi State	86	61
Tulane	84	63
Georgia	73	51
Georgia Tech	83	58

Kentucky	45	75
†Georgia	61	49
Florida	63	66
	1781	1632

Final SC Standing: Tie for 2nd (9-5)
sw—SWC Tourney, Dallas, Texas
†SC Tourney, Louisville
*Overtime

1952-53—Won 10, Lost 9

COACH: Bob Polk
CAPTAIN: Bob White

Duke	88	94
Virginia	90	83
Lipscomb	92	66
Texas	84	66
Baylor	73	66
Tennessee	77	69
Yale	95	67
Tulane	53	76
Louisiana State	61	74
Georgia Tech	72	60
Florida	85	73
Georgia	97	66
Tennessee	79	83
Georgia Tech	79	85
Auburn	86	71
Mississippi State	75	82
Ole Miss	65	79
Alabama	80	88
Tennessee	85	64
	1496	1412

Final SEC Standing: Tie for 7th (5-8)

1953-54—Won 12, Lost 10

COACH: Bob Polk
CAPTAIN: Dan Finch

Sewanee	76	59
Texas Tech	75	71
Duke	71	66
Southern Methodist	72	65
Baylor	65	60
Rice	60	79
Auburn	96	48
Middle Tennessee	86	65
Tennessee	53	62
Georgia Tech	65	55
Mississippi State	79	69
Ole Miss	74	78
Georgia Tech	84	65
Kentucky	63	85
Auburn	73	76
Alabama	75	87
Tulane	63	71
Louisiana State	69	82
Kentucky	64	100
Florida	76	68
Georgia	83	67
Tennessee	76	80
	1598	1558

Final SEC Standing: Tie for 8th (5-9)

1954-55—Won 16, Lost 6

COACH: Bob Polk
GAME CAPTAINS

Sewanee	88	48

Wash. & Lee	104	88
Texas Christian	71	50
Texas	94	67
Stanford	64	72
Ole Miss	94	69
William & Mary	86	61
Tennessee	73	69
Georgia Tech	71	69
Miss. State	72	52
Ole Miss	63	77
Georgia Tech	83	63
Lipscomb	88	61
Kentucky	71	75
Auburn	79	74
Alabama	78	57
Tulane	58	62
Louisiana State	59	66
Tennessee	76	71
Kentucky	59	77
Florida	100	72
Georgia	78	57
	1709	1457

Final SEC Standing: Tie for 3rd
(9-5)

1955-56—Won 19, Lost 4
COACH: Bob Polk
GAME CAPTAINS

Sewanee	84	45
Texas A&M	79	69
Ohio State	76	67
Oklahoma	78	69
Georgia	85	61
Nebraska	66	48
Iowa State	76	87
New Mexico A&M	64	40
**William & Mary	89	80
Tennessee	84	57
Georgia Tech	72	59
Mississippi	88	73
Kentucky	81	73
Miss. State	69	49
Georgia	69	56
Alabama	61	88
L.S.U.	107	68
Tulane	74	67
Tennessee	96	68
Kentucky	55	76
Florida	80	75
Auburn	65	74
	1765	1513

Final SEC Standing: 3rd (11-3)
**—2 Overtimes

1956-57—Won 17, Lost 5
COACH: Bob Polk
GAME CAPTAINS

Minnesota	60	63
Sewanee	87	45
Ole Miss	90	61
Texas	94	67
New Mexico	81	59
Nebraska	78	54
Arizona	107	76
Wm. & Mary	80	65
Tennessee	71	68
Ga. Tech	81	73
Ole Miss	66	68
Miss. State	62	63

Ga. Tech	93	74
Kentucky	83	91
Auburn	83	78
Alabama	61	50
L.S.U.	78	66
Tulane	71	58
Tennessee	69	62
Kentucky	78	80
Florida	75	59
Georgia	75	51
	1723	1431

Final SEC Standing: 2nd (10-4)

1957-58—Won 14, Lost 11
COACH: Bob Polk
CAPTAIN: Jim Henry

Sewanee	91	53
Minnesota	85	89
V.M.I.	105	74
S.M.U.	58	72
Southwestern	98	48
The Citadel	90	61
Georgia	74	64
N. Mexico A&M	73	59
sbMaryland	56	71
sbLoyola (N.O.)	80	84
Brigham Young	89	56
Tennessee	55	67
Kentucky	81	86
Mississippi	68	59
Miss. State	74	62
Georgia Tech	60	81
Auburn	69	77
Alabama	60	65
L.S.U.	78	60
Tulane	80	65
Tennessee	83	70
Kentucky	61	65
Florida	53	73
Georgia	69	66
Georgia Tech	60	59
	1850	1686

Final SEC Standing: 7th (7-7)
sb—Sugar Bowl Tourney

1958-59—Won 14, Lost 10
ACTING COACH: Roy Skinner
CAPTAIN: Jim Henry

Sewanee	71	42
Minnesota	76	77
*Missouri	72	78
S.M.U.	72	80
Hardin-Simmons	80	52
Wyoming	70	65
Dartmouth	87	71
Virginia	75	64
Navy	61	67
Tennessee	60	65
Kentucky	75	66
Mississippi	79	74
Miss. State	65	83
Ga. Tech	61	80
Auburn	61	64
Alabama	81	59
L.S.U.	72	57
*Tulane	64	62
Tennessee	76	60
Kentucky	71	83
Florida	77	66

Georgia	78	50
Ga. Tech	67	71
Baylor	61	60
	1712	1596

Final SEC Standing: Tie for 5th
(8-6)
*—Overtime

1959-60—Won 14, Lost 9

COACH: Bob Polk
CAPTAIN: Ben Rowan

Sewanee	87	68
Minnesota	59	72
Arkansas St.	98	66
Rice	82	72
S.M.U.	67	86
Georgia	79	67
S. Carolina	85	73
Yale	76	65
Princeton	72	54
Tennessee	60	72
Kentucky	59	76
Ole Miss	66	58
Miss. St.	79	72
*Ga. Tech	66	74
Auburn	54	55
Alabama	54	61
L.S.U.	80	68
*Tulane	68	64
Tennessee	63	53
Kentucky	60	68
*Florida	75	81
Georgia	80	75
Ga. Tech	62	57
	1631	1557

Final SEC Standing: Tie for 6th
(7-7)
*—Overtime

1960-61—Won 19, Lost 5

COACH: Bob Polk
CAPTAIN: Bill Depp

Michigan	58	43
Fla. State	75	55
S.M.U.	76	64
Alabama	77	61
Rice	70	44
Texas Tech	80	78
New Mexico	66	59
Chattanooga	92	78
Sewanee	80	57
Tennessee	68	66
Kentucky	64	62
Miss. State	65	74
Ole Miss	72	74
Ga. Tech	69	56
Auburn	58	53
Alabama	73	70
Tulane	63	60
L.S.U.	61	65
Tennessee	76	60
Kentucky	59	60
Florida	77	60
Georgia	87	76
Ga. Tech	79	59
#Kentucky	67	88
	1712	1522

Final SEC Standing: Tie for 2nd
(10-4)
#NCAA Playoff at Knoxville

1961-62—Won 10, Lost 12

COACH: Roy Skinner
CAPTAIN: Bobby Bland

Sewanee	76	43
Texas Tech	64	71
*Alabama	65	63
Army	67	52
Rice	64	71
S.M.U.	73	91
Missouri	77	65
gbV.P.I.	78	79
gbNavy	77	74
Yale	79	69
Tennessee	83	85
Kentucky	68	77
Miss. State	100	86
Ole Miss	80	58
Ga. Tech	66	71
Auburn	69	89
Alabama	76	82
Tulane	77	65
L.S.U.	70	67
Tennessee	97	76
Kentucky	80	87
Florida	68	78
Georgia	69	71
Ga. Tech	88	74
	1810	1744

Final SEC Standing: Tie for 6th
(6-8)
gb—Gator Bowl Tournament
*—Overtime

1962-63—Won 16, Lost 7

COACH: Roy Skinner
CAPTAIN: John Russell

Rice	80	68
SMU	69	62
Duke	70	90
Pennsylvania	70	74
Louisville	95	72
VPI	80	72
pClemson	60	58
pFurman	69	68
Western Ky.	71	69
Tennessee	68	50
Kentucky	82	106
Miss. State	55	58
Ole Miss	79	72
Auburn	59	62
Alabama	74	73
LSU	56	63
Tulane	80	69
Georgia Tech	62	67
Tennessee	74	72
Kentucky	69	67
Florida	78	74
Georgia	82	64
Georgia Tech	75	74
	1657	1604

Final SEC Standing: 4th (9-5)
p—Poinsettia Tournament

1963-64—Won 19, Lost 6

COACH: Roy Skinner
GAME CAPTAINS

Rice	82	68
S.M.U.	79	60
Western Kentucky	82	60

*Duke	97	92
Arkansas	101	77
TCU	113	56
Louisville	91	82
vMemphis State	85	79
vSouth Carolina	106	78
V.M.I.	87	71
Tennessee	55	57
Kentucky	85	83
Mississippi State	90	56
Ole Miss	88	81
Arkansas State	108	73
Auburn	63	81
Alabama	111	73
Tulane	96	64
L.S.U.	66	64
*Georgia Tech	71	75
Tennessee	62	64
Kentucky	73	104
Florida	91	78
Georgia	69	81
Georgia Tech	103	89
	2154	1846

Final SEC Standing: 4th (8-6)
v—Vanderbilt Invitational
*Overtime

1964-65—Won 24, Lost 4

COACH: Roy Skinner
CAPTAIN: John Ed Miller

Rice	78	49
SMU	99	67
Western Ky.	94	79
VPI	64	69
North Carolina	78	84
vBaylor	97	98
vOklahoma State	60	58
Miami 'Ohio' Univ.	74	68
sTexas Tech	83	73
sUniv. of Louisville	80	47
Tennessee	77	72
Kentucky	97	79
Miss. State	94	70
Univ. of Miss.	84	70
Auburn	105	77
Tulane	85	67
LSU	96	85
Tennessee	66	79
Kentucky	91	90
Florida	80	78
Georgia	89	72
Alabama	75	54
Auburn	79	64
Tulane	85	62
LSU	106	69
nDePaul Univ.	83	78
nUniv. of Michigan	85	87
	2284	1945

Final SEC Standing: 1st (15-1)
v—Vanderbilt Invitational 1st
s—Sugar Bowl 1st
n—NCAA Mid-East Regionals 2nd

1965-66—Won 22, Lost 4

COACH: Roy Skinner
CAPTAIN: Clyde Lee

Wittenberg	87	59
Tennessee	53	50
North Carolina	81	72

Wake Forest	102	82
vArmy	71	62
vWestern Kentucky	72	69
University of California	91	64
Northwestern	59	58
laSyracuse	113	98
laUniv. of Southern Calif.	72	74
laPurdue	94	72
Tulane	91	69
Georgia	77	63
Mississippi	106	58
Tennessee	53	52
Kentucky	83	96
LSU	98	66
Auburn	68	63
Kentucky	90	105
Alabama	71	63
Auburn	91	76
Florida	89	86
Georgia	117	97
L.S.U.	102	84
Tulane	97	72
Mississippi State	90	92
	2218	1902

Final SEC Standing: 2nd (13-3)
la—L.A. Classic
v—Vanderbilt Classic

1966-67—Won 21, Lost 5

COACH: Roy Skinner
CAPTAIN: Jerry Southwood

Western Kentucky	76	70
SMU	89	76
Southwestern La.	101	68
Wake Forest	88	82
Duke	89	97
vPortland	98	63
vLaSalle	100	95
Florida	77	69
Northwestern	116	92
Auburn	51	64
*Alabama	84	81
*Kentucky	91	89
Tennessee	65	59
**Mississippi	78	70
Auburn	71	65
Mississippi State	79	64
LSU	79	77
Florida	75	83
**Georgia	51	41
Mississippi	72	67
Tennessee	53	70
Alabama	117	80
Georgia	71	61
Mississippi State	71	74
Kentucky	110	94
LSU	75	66
	2127	1917

Final SEC Standing: Tied for 2nd
(14-4)
v—Vanderbilt Invitational
*Overtime
**2 Overtimes

1967-68—Won 20, Lost 6

COACH: Roy Skinner
CO-CAPTAINS: Bob Warren
           Bo Wyendandt

*SMU	88	84

Auburn	78	65
North Carolina	89	76
*Davidson	81	79
Duke	76	75
Florida	72	74
vSeton Hall	85	67
vOregon	70	59
sbMichigan State	73	63
sbDavidson	80	67
Alabama	67	61
Kentucky	78	94
Tennessee	62	64
Mississippi	96	70
Auburn	74	65
Mississippi State	90	69
Louisiana State	99	91
Florida	85	91
Georgia	82	77
Mississippi	90	72
Tennessee	75	63
Alabama	89	74
Georgia	77	91
Mississippi State	84	73
Kentucky	80	85
LSU	115	86
	2135	1935

Final SEC Standing: 3rd (12-6)
sb—Sugar Bowl
v—Vanderbilt Invitational
*Overtime

1968-69—Won 15, Lost 11

COACH: Roy Skinner
CAPTAIN: Tom Hagan

SMU	97	94
Davidson	84	101
North Carolina	78	100
Mississippi State	108	87
Bowling Green	92	67
vRice	85	77
vKansas State	92	80
Southern California	85	75
North Carolina State	65	59
Georgia	80	102
Florida	62	55
LSU	94	92
Alabama	76	73
Mississippi	62	55
Auburn	79	92
Kentucky	89	103
Tennessee	61	65
Georgia	83	90
Florida	73	75
Mississippi	67	75
Alabama	89	74
LSU	85	83
Auburn	75	85
Kentucky	101	99
Tennessee	60	70
Mississippi State	120	83
	2142	2111

Final SEC Standing: Tie for 7th
(9-9)
v—Vanderbilt Invitational

1969-70—Won 12, Lost 14

COACH: Roy Skinner
CAPTAIN: Perry Wallace

The Citadel	89	58

Mississippi	87	75
Southern California	89	108
Sou. Methodist	104	99
L.S.U.	86	109
Mississippi State	93	79
Kansas State	78	91
vDartmouth	82	83
vSt. Louis	76	66
North Carolina State	70	76
Portland	124	73
Georgia	68	72
Florida	90	79
Alabama	88	85
Auburn	75	84
Kentucky	89	81
Tennessee	72	77
Georgia	90	94
Florida	79	81
Mississippi	80	83
L.S.U.	89	99
Alabama	101	79
Auburn	92	74
Kentucky	86	90
Tennessee	76	83
Mississippi State	78	72
	2231	2150

Final SEC Standing: 6th (8-10)
v—Vanderbilt Invitational

1970-71—Won 13, Lost 13

COACH: Roy Skinner
CAPTAINS: Ralph Mayes and
Thorpe Weber

Louisville	74	82
Miami, Ohio	74	67
Illinois	79	96
Mississippi State	86	73
Kansas State	74	81
vClemson	75	61
vSt. John's N.Y.	81	85
Ole Miss.	130	112
sbCincinnati	86	83
sbToledo	92	76
Georgia	76	69
#Florida	82	84
Alabama	93	76
Auburn	107	86
Kentucky	92	102
Tennessee	65	60
Georgia	74	60
Florida	92	81
Mississippi	88	94
L.S.U.	81	75
Alabama	74	75
Auburn	94	96
Kentucky	90	119
Tennessee	69	79
L.S.U.	85	87
Mississippi State	73	81
	2176	2140

#Three Overtimes
v—Vanderbilt Invitational
sb—Sugar Bowl
Final SEC Standing: Tie for 4th (9-9)

1971-72—Won 16, Lost 10

COACH: Roy Skinner
CAPTAIN: Tom Arnholt

S.M.U.	79	89

St. John's (N.Y.)	81	98
Boston College	82	75
vBradley	82	80
vMemphis State	83	82
Illinois	95	92
Rice	105	87
Mississippi State	69	76
L.S.U.	80	73
Georgia	80	76
Florida	104	87
Alabama	76	79
Cornell	101	80
Kentucky	80	106
Ole Miss	65	92
Auburn	85	77
Kentucky #	80	85
Tennessee	75	81
Georgia	91	98
Florida	90	74
Ole Miss	89	83
L.S.U.	104	83
Alabama	111	91
Auburn	93	87
Tennessee	74	87
Mississippi State	104	82
	2258	2200

Final SEC Standing: 4th (10-8)
v—Vanderbilt Invitational
#Overtime

1972-73—Won 20, Lost 6

COACH: Roy Skinner
CAPTAIN: Jan van Breda Kolff

Louisville	66	57
Kansas	72	64
S.M.U.	98	78
vColumbia	70	61
vWestern Ky.	103	88
Middle Tenn.	69	57
Ole Miss	59	57
Boston College	78	62
Memphis State	71	74
Louisiana St.	71	66
Georgia	89	86
Florida	72	80
Alabama	77	83
Ole Miss	59	49
Miss. State	75	69
Kentucky	76	75
Auburn	77	81
Kentucky	83	76
Tennessee	62	72
Georgia	87	52
Florida	78	71
Louisiana State	82	72
Alabama	78	87
Auburn	98	70
Tennessee	86	74
Miss. State	74	70
	2010	1831

Final SEC Standing 2nd (Tie)
v—Vanderbilt Invitational

1973-74—Won 23, Lost 5

COACH: Roy Skinner
CAPTAIN: Jan van Breda Kolff

Rice	89	80
Texas Tech	84	82
vNebraska	82	58
vTenn. State	67	66
Memphis State	75	71
Samford	69	65
Kansas	83	72
Vermont	91	56
* Alabama	73	72
* Miss. St.	75	69
* L.S.U.	81	84
* Georgia	91	71
* Auburn	96	51
* Tennessee	82	65
* Ole Miss	71	56
* Kentucky	82	65
* Florida	58	52
* Alabama	67	65
* Miss. State	60	59
* L.S.U.	91	88
* Georgia	83	78
* Auburn	89	79
* Tennessee	53	59
* Ole Miss	84	68
* Kentucky	71	69
* Florida	77	80
nMarquette	61	69
nNotre Dame	88	118
	2173	1967

*SEC Game
v—Vanderbilt Invitational
n—NCAA Mideast Regionals
SEC Standing: Tie for 1st

1974-75—Won 15, Lost 11

COACH: Roy Skinner
CAPTAINS: Jeff Fosnes, Butch Feher, Joe Ford

St. John's	73	53
Virginia Tech (VIT)	75	72
Sou. Illinois (VIT)	79	72
Texas Tech	95	86
Sou. California	93	98
Jacksonville (2 ot)	104	107
Nebraska	66	81
Middle Tennessee	81	68
Alabama	77	104
Mississippi State	96	85
Louisiana State	91	82
Georgia	102	80
Auburn	89	93
Tennessee	61	65
Ole Miss	80	66
Kentucky	90	91
Florida (ot)	90	101
Alabama	72	86
Mississippi State	76	72
Louisiana State	83	74
Georgia	81	78
Auburn	85	78
Tennessee	71	75
Ole Miss	86	80
Kentucky	84	109
Florida	102	83
	2182	2139